HUMAN TRAFFICKING
IN SOUTH AFRICA

Published by BestRed, an imprint of HSRC Press
Private Bag X9182, Cape Town, 8000, South Africa
www.bestred.co.za

First published 2023

ISBN (soft cover) 978-1-928246-58-9

© 2023 Human Sciences Research Council

Copy edited by Louis Botes
Typeset by Joan Baker
Cover design Joan Baker
Index by Michelle Colman
Printed by Creda Communication, Cape Town, South Africa

Distributed in Africa by Blue Weaver
Tel: +27 (021) 701 4477; Fax Local: (021) 701 7302; Fax International: 0927865242139
www.blueweaver.co.za

Distributed in Europe and the United Kingdom by Eurospan Distribution Services (EDS)
Tel: +44 (0) 17 6760 4972; Fax: +44 (0) 17 6760 1640
www.eurospanbookstore.com

Distributed in the US, its possessions, Canada, and Asia by Lynne Rienner Publishers, Inc.
Tel: +1 303-444-6684; Fax: +1 303-444-0824; Email: cservice@rienner.com
www.rienner.com

Suggested citation: Philip Frankel (2023) *Human Trafficking in South Africa*. Cape Town: BestRed

Table of Contents

List of Abbreviations

4P's + 1	Prevention, Prosecution, Protection + Partnerships
AHTC	Anti-Human Trafficking Committee (Botswana)
ANC	African National Congress
AMCU	Association of Mineworkers and Construction Union
ATIMC	Anti-Trafficking Inter-Ministerial Committee
BCEA	Basic Conditions of Employment Act No 75 of 1997
CEDAW	Committee on the Elimination of Discrimination Against Women
COSATU	Congress of South African Trade Unions
CGPU	Child and Gender Protection Unit (Lesotho)
CSE	Child sexual exploitation
CSO	Civil society organisation
CST	Child sex tourism
CTC	Counter-Trafficking Coalition
CTDC	Counter-Trafficking Data Collaborative
DEIC	Dutch East India Company
DHA	Department of Home Affairs.
DIRCO	Department of International Relations and Cooperation
DJCD	Department of Justice and Constitutional Development
DOA	Department of Agriculture, Land Reform and Rural Development
DOH	Department of Health
DOL	Department of Labour
DPP	The Directorate of Public Prosecution (Botswana and Eswathini)
DRC	Democratic Republic of the Congo
DSD	Department of Social Development
ECPACT	End Child Prostitution and Trafficking
ESA	Employment Services Act
FIFA	Féderation Internationale de Football Association
GBV	Gender-based violence
GLOTIP	Global Report on Trafficking in Persons (UNODC)
GSI	Global Slavery Index
HRC	Human Rights Commission

BEST
READ

1239 2139 0909

7329831-12

HUMAN TRAFFICKING
IN SOUTH AFRICA

Philip Frankel

HSRC	Human Sciences Research Council
ICC	International Criminal Court
IDP	Internally displaced person
ILO	International Labour Organisation
IOM	International Organisation for Migration
IMC	Inter-Sectoral Ministerial Committee
IMF	International Monetary Fund
ISC	Inter-Sectoral Committee
KGB	Committee for State Security (Russia)
KZN	KwaZulu-Natal
LRA	Labour Relations Act No. 66 of 1995
LGBTQ	Lesbian, Gay, Bisexual, Transgender and Queer
LSMP	Lesotho Mounted Police Service
MDJS	Ministry of Defence, Justice, and Security (Botswana)
MOU	Memorandum of Understanding
Mossad	Central Institute for Intelligence and Special Operations (Israel)
NC	National Anti-Trafficking Coordinator
NDP	National Development Plan
NIA	National Intelligence Agency
NICTIP	National Inter-Sectoral Committee on Trafficking in Persons
NFN	National Freedom Network
NGO	non-governmental organisation
NPA	National Prosecuting Authority
NPF	National Policy Framework
NUM	National Union of Mineworkers
OHS	Occupational Health and Safety.
PACOTIP	Prevention and Combating of Trafficking in Persons Act No. 7 of 2013
POCA	Prevention of Organised Crime Act No. 121 of 1998
PPE	personal protective equipment
PTSD	post-traumatic stress disorder
PTT	Provincial Task Team
RRT	Rapid Response Team
SACA	South African Central Authority
SADC	Southern African Development Community

SADOL	South African Department of Labour
SANDF	South African National Defence Force
SALRC	South African Law Reform Commission
SAPS	South African Police Services
SOA	Sexual Offences Act No 23 of 1957
SOP	standard operating procedure
STD	sexually transmitted disease
SWEAT	Sex Worker Education and Advocacy Task Force
TES	temporary employment services
TIP	Trafficking in Persons
UN	United Nations
UNGA	United Nations General Assembly
UV	ultraviolet
UNCTOC	United Nations Convention Against Transnational Organised Crime
UNHCR	United Nations High Commission for Refugees
UNICEF	United Nations Children's Fund
UNODC	United Nations Office on Drugs and Crime
VOT	victim of trafficking

Anti-Trafficking Coordination Structures in South Africa

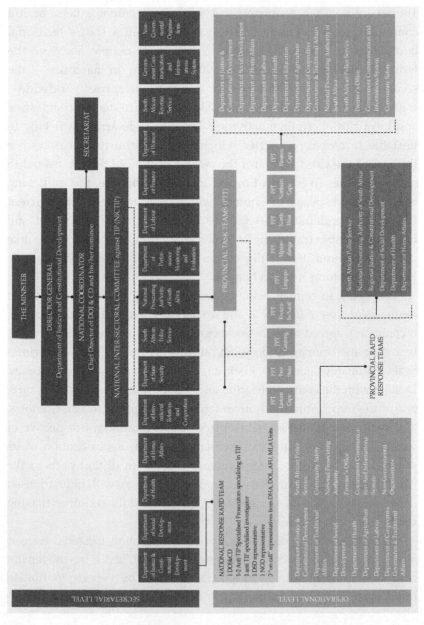

Preface

Trafficking involves acquiring and selling any valuable item, be it a commodity or substance. This can occur within a state's territorial boundaries or across its borders. While most people associate the term 'trafficking' with the international trade in narcotics – the second biggest source of profit for criminal enterprise worldwide – trafficking can encompass a much wider variety of deeply clandestine and intrinsically criminal activities. These include arms trafficking to unstable developing countries, which has precipitously increased since the end of the Cold War, and the selling of the old Soviet arsenal to many countries in Eastern Europe, including Ukraine; the trafficking of endangered species in Chinese 'wet markets' (to which the current COVID-19 pandemic is sometimes attributed); and minor but still hugely profitable trafficking in stolen cigarettes, alcohol or even 'fake designer' fashion items shipped under counterfeit labels by Chinese Mafias from Hong Kong to Naples.

Trafficking in human beings, involving men, women and children destined for sites of industrial and sexual exploitation around the globe, is commonly agreed to be the most egregious. In some legal circles, there is a view that human trade is an 'atrocity' crime on par with crimes against humanity, genocide, institutionalised rape and even war crimes. Dealing with the commodification and sale of human beings is, in turn, one of the most profound humanitarian challenges of the 21st century. This is because trafficking takes place in every country, irrespective of wealth, culture, constitutional guarantees, or the sophistication of its political system. Authoritarian military regimes in distant parts of the world, such as Myanmar, share a common experience with industrialised democracies such as the United States, Canada and the countries making up the European Union.

Trafficking is one consequence of mass migration triggered by war and persecution in the conflict zones of the world, hence the movement of hundreds of thousands of people, assisted by experts in human trade, from Syria, Afghanistan and Iraq via the Mediterranean to jump-off points in Turkey, Italy and, more recently, Belorussia. But human trafficking also takes place in the supply chains of some of the world's largest corporations and most prestigious multinational corporations involved in large-scale agricultural production, fisheries, industry, and, perhaps above all, medium- and large-scale mining. Trafficking is also rampant in the global hospitality industry, especially in countries offering opportunities for sex tourism.

In India at present, a buffalo costs US$350 while a child can be procured for around a tenth of that amount.[1] According to many anti-trafficking organisations at the national or global level, human trafficking, interchangeably called 'modern slavery', or simply TIP (trafficking in persons), is the most lucrative of all criminal businesses. TIP requires a low initial investment, has low 'running' costs and is a 'product' used repeatedly. Trafficking (taken to mean 'human trafficking) is also the fastest-growing crime with transnational syndicates earning a conservatively estimated profit of over US$150 billion per annum.[2]

The victims of human trade are often, but by no means always, young women, girls or even men forced into 'sex work' in its many manifestations or into involuntary prostitution in particular. Crimes of this character make up about a third of all trafficking. Alternatively, there is child trafficking for sex, cheap labour, or, more commonly, for sex and labour interchangeably. Even more chilling manifestations of human trafficking include the global trade in body parts driven by the worldwide shortage of kidneys and other organs for transplantation; 'baby-farming' where children are specially bred for prostitution, or illegal adoption and fostering, which is especially common in Africa. In all countries on the southern African continent, children are also periodically abducted or otherwise enticed into human sacrifice or 'muti-murder by deadly networks of unscrupulous traditional healers.

Although society conspires to make some people more vulnerable and at risk than others, anyone could be trafficked. This includes the young and impressionable who fall prey to the false promises of traffickers, undocumented migrants cast beyond the boundaries of legal existence, the mentally challenged, people marginalised by their LGBT (lesbian, gay, bisexual, and transgender) affiliations, and poor populations worldwide whose limited opportunities render them especially open to fraudulent enticement and, in some cases, outright abduction. Anyone can, in turn, be a trafficker. This includes friends, families and relatives who are often, inadvertently, or by choice, complicit with the actual perpetrators.

Much of this is misunderstood in many countries. This includes South Africa where our policies and priorities are almost exclusively focused on job-creation, housing, education, economic reconstruction, and recently, the spread of the COVID-19 disease. Apart from a handful of anti-trafficking activists and civil society organisations (CSOs) – many of whom belong to the National Freedom Network – very few of our political and governmental leaders have any real comprehension of the diversity and multifaceted nature of human trade, its prevalence, its dynamics and its inevitably destructive impact on individuals and communities.

Besides the occasional poster with references to a national 'hotline', virtually nothing is known about TIP among educators and learners in our schools. Most trafficking is simply associated with sex trafficking and there is limited understanding of the diversity of its manifestation. Even more concerning is that members of the criminal justice system, including members of the South African Police Service (SAPS), lawyers and magistrates, are often ignorant of the nature and consequences of trafficking. They seem relatively disinterested in it as an offence or are guided in their professional conduct by sensationalist and mainly inaccurate media reports. As we shall see further, for several years we have had a comprehensive, national anti-trafficking law on our statute books. However, at the SAPS station level, there is almost a complete lack of knowledge about its content and its execution in daily practice. Unfortunately, many police officers also avoid child trafficking cases because of their emotionally scarring consequences for the investigating officials.

More can be done to educate the public and key stakeholders in government, law enforcement and civil society in performing the cardinal '4Ps' of counter-trafficking. These involve the Prevention of TIP, its successful Prosecution by the criminal justice system, the Protection, rescue, and re-empowerment of victims, as well as the development of counter-trafficking Partnerships to assist policy implementation by civil society working alongside the government.

The chapters that follow use material from the past two decades when human trafficking appeared with full force on the South African landscape, with particular emphasis on post-2016 data contained in academic articles, unpublished postgraduate studies, monographs, conference papers, policy documents, a tiny handful of books that have been written on TIP (including my book of 2016), as well as some of the less sensationalised media reports over the past five or six years. This involves, in rough total, about 450 to 500 'items'.

This work also refers to the United Nations Office on Drugs and Organised Crime (UNODC) reports and publications of the International Organisation for Migration (IOM). Especially important at an international level are various barometers tracking TIP, which include the Global Slavery Index, the IOM's Global Counter-Trafficking Portal, the United States Department of State Audit (which monitors and evaluates world trafficking on an annual basis), and the new global Counter-Trafficking Data Collaborative.[3]

The secondary data used is supplemented by interviews with academic experts, victims, perpetrators, civil society and members of the various anti-trafficking provincial structures set up two years ago. The book includes interviews with key stakeholders including officials of the Department of Home Affairs (DHA), the Department of Justice and Constitutional Development (DJCD), the National Prosecuting Authority (NPA) and the SAPS. In the sections on commercial sex and labour trafficking, I have interacted over the years with, inter alia, commercial sex entrepreneurs, labour brokers and people in mine management with specialist knowledge about the procurement of labour and its exploitation in the illegal mining sector.

It is a measure of the clandestine and frequently unappetising nature of the crime that most interviewees insisted their identities remain confidential or heavily disguised. Those seeking anonymity included survivors of trafficking who are understandably fearful of attracting attention, participants in the often undercover counter-trafficking activity and, obviously, the perpetrators, a few of whom I met during my two-year period of research. Bearing this in mind, I would especially like to thank government officials who were cautiously receptive to academic intrusion, some entrepreneurs in the sex industries, a raft of social workers and psychologists dealing with child trafficking, legal brokers who explained the dynamics of their work, and civil society members of the provincial anti-trafficking task teams with whom I had a wealth of interaction in the earlier phases of my project.

So as not to mislead the reader, several points should be noted. First, there is no exact or even a near-exact figure as to the prevalence of trafficking in South Africa or on the wider global landscape. As will be indicated at various points, this reflects the underground nature of the crime, widely different understandings of its key components, as well as a host of methodological problems attached to its definition. Regardless of claims in the trafficking 'industry' to the contrary, statistical accuracy is still chimerical and likely to remain so for the indefinite future – despite several potentially fruitful and ongoing initiatives in tandem with my work. The data used by everyone engaged in trafficking research, including me, is thus overwhelmingly qualitative despite the odd flash of empirical analysis.

The book focuses, as did my previous work, on South Africa where we know more about trafficking than anywhere else in the immediate region.[4] I nonetheless include a section on countries bordering the Republic, or historically connected with it mainly because of mass migration across a variety of porous borders. The experiences of the wider subcontinent are also an important reference point for loosely comparing what has been achieved in the management of trafficking in South Africa against that of other nearby countries.

Most research in South and southern Africa has also focused on commercial sex trafficking, child trafficking and the legal responses to trafficking by various governmental stakeholders. At least two-thirds to three-quarters of what is generated annually excludes forced labour, which is possibly the most common type of trafficking at present. I have tried to restore the balance with a chapter on this subject.

Moreover, I have consciously tried to include what might be termed the 'outlier' aspects of trafficking, the so-called themes less considered. This is not especially difficult to do because there are gaping chasms in the South African trafficking literature which is, for the most part, repetitive and redundant. Most writings on sex trafficking add little to nothing to the extant body of research and we are fortunate that the prospect of legalising prostitution has at least opened up new lines of inquiry. It is still being debated whether child trafficking occurs as the rest of the world moves on. There is nothing at all on illegal child adoption or the role of fostering as triggers of TIP, nor has anything substantive been written about the impact of Covid two years since the onset of the pandemic. Most writings on counter-trafficking are historical or legalistic in their focus on the origins and nature of South Africa's only counter-trafficking law rather than the critical sociology around its implementation. The term 'counter-trafficking coalition' appears to have escaped the attention of most South African writers despite its extensive use for many years in the global literature. Other than a few general works and a handful of complaints about the operational insignificance of the Southern African Development Community (SADC), very little has been written about trafficking in the southern African region.

I have, in the circumstances, had to make several journeys into new conceptual territory and this has sometimes required seeking inspiration in the greater continental experience of trafficking north of Limpopo and, in some cases, beyond the African continent. In places where I have sought to globalise the debate beyond purely local material, I have also had to reach across the social sciences to incorporate material unfamiliar to most writings on trafficking, including concepts rooted in anthropology. Muti murders and trafficking in the body parts of children make no discernible sense without the intersection between crime and culture. The organisational theory is critical to understanding what works – or more frequently does not – in the network of counter-trafficking institutions set up by the government over the last three years.

Since the book is not meant to be an academic treatise I have kept the number of footnotes to a bare minimum. I have, instead, begun some chapters with an inclusive footnote covering the main subject matter. These sources are reflected in the material that follows. Important sub-themes and conceptual material critical for further investigation are treated in much the same manner.

The choice of title is also not incidental. It implies that trafficking takes place not only within countries in southern Africa but also across subcontinental frontiers. There is also a high level of interchangeability in the relationships between perpetrators and victims as well as between the different manifestations of trafficking such as sex, child and labour trafficking, and the 'harvesting' and sale of human organs. In this mainly subterranean world, today's perpetrators can become tomorrow's victims. Commercial sex work and trafficked labour involve adults over 18 years of age as well as children. Child trafficking can, in the worst-case scenarios, transform into organ trafficking. Organ trafficking, in turn, can sometimes morph into trafficking for sex and labour. Division for heuristic purposes is nonetheless necessary.

The book consists of seven chapters followed by a section of notes and a select bibliography focused, for the most part, on research accumulated since my previous book in 2016. The bibliography is also divided between research in South Africa and items that originate more widely afield.

Chapter 1, the introduction, is purposely designed to say a minimum about South or southern Africa in favour of the international an/or abstract aspects of TIP with which many readers may be unfamiliar. It begins with the definition of human trafficking as distinct from both classical slavery and contemporary forms of people or human smuggling which we encounter in daily reports of refugees moving transnationally. The chapter also examines, inter alia, the nature of the social vulnerability, which renders certain groups especially susceptible to trafficking; and the complex trafficking process from victim recruitment to their 'rescue' and, in an unfortunately minimum number of cases, their rehabilitation. The last segment of this discusses the dyad of victims and perpetrators as well as the ongoing debate over the prevalence of trafficking in South Africa.

The second chapter deals with commercial sex trafficking in the Republic, where a high proportion of TIP involves commercial sex work by adult women and, more particularly, involuntary prostitution. I examine the forces which impel women into involuntarily selling sex in different sociological locations, the process of recruitment, the nature of perpetration and the frequently horrendous side effects of trafficking-type sexploitation. The chapter also gives some attention to the current movement to legalise prostitution in the Republic as well as the possible consequences in the trafficking arena.

Child trafficking for sex or labour purposes is regarded in all legal systems, including our own, as the most severe form of TIP. Chapter 3 examines why children are especially at risk of being trafficked in the South African context, the cynical use of children for sex and labour, policies to reduce child susceptibility to traffickers and the requirements of an inclusive strategy to address this particularly pernicious form of crime. The chapter also discusses 'babyfarming', illegal adoption and fostering, which go essentially unexplored in the local child trafficking literature. There is a sub-section on traditional norms where culture becomes crime through channels such as forced child marriage, organ trafficking and muti murders.

Chapter 4 examines the various manifestations of labour trafficking dating back to the foundation of a refreshment station by the Dutch East India Company (DEIC) at the Cape in 1652. It analyses key indicators of forced labour, such as fraudulent and misrepresented recruitment, document confiscation, debt bondage, brokerage and wage crime. These issues impact supply chains in various sectors of the modern South African economy, such as agriculture, commercial fishing and both mainstream and illegal mining.

In line with the recommendations of the so-called Palermo Protocol at the turn of the millennium, South Africa has moved to align its trafficking laws with those embedded in international law. Chapter 5 deals with counter-trafficking in South Africa and analyses the often convoluted process of developing anti-trafficking institutions since the first recommendations of the South African Law Reform Commission (SALRC) around the turn of the millennium. This culminated in our one-and-only comprehensive anti-trafficking law: The Prevention and Combating of Trafficking in Persons Act of 2013, widely labelled PACOTIP.[5]

The chapter also deals with the main tool for the implementation of PACOTIP, namely the 2019 National Policy Framework (NPF) – later referred to as 'the policy framework'.[6] It analyses both the strengths and weaknesses of the institutional arrangements emplaced to give operational reality to the 2013 law, as well as the work of the provincial subcommittees established to execute the law at the grassroots. Official corruption and complicity with trafficking networks are highlighted and there is a detailed examination of the inadequacy of the referral process, from 'frontline' encounters with trafficking victims by the rapid response teams activated by the provinces, through their shelters, counselling, and the provision of other assistance to address then horrendous emotional and physical injury of trafficking survivors.

South Africa is the epicentre of a regional system of trafficking induced by a mixture of porous borders, poor police practices on the border, mixed migration flows and, in certain cases, corruption in political, bureaucratic and law enforcement circles. Chapter 6 examines this dynamic in eight countries either directly bordering or proximate to the Republic, namely, Lesotho, Eswatini, Botswana, Namibia, Zimbabwe, Mozambique, Malawi and Zambia. The focus is on trafficking that spills over from South Africa or trafficking syndicates working in or across South Africa, to as far afield as Europe, the Middle East, and South Asia. The section also analyses the extent to which southern African states have translated international norms and laws against trafficking into domestic law. There is also a sub-section on the role of the SADC as an instrument for counter-trafficking in the subcontinent and beyond.

The concluding chapter reverts to South Africa in the form of a 'what-is-to-be-done' exercise based on data gathered in our second year of Covid – 2021. In alignment with the '4P' concept, it examines the impact of the pandemic on the prevention of trafficking through various campaigns run by the government, the provincial anti-trafficking task teams, and civil society. The prosecution of offenders has been seriously compromised by obstructions in the criminal justice system and by complications in law enforcement associated with the pandemic. The functionality of public–private sector partnerships against TIP has been inhibited by lock-down regulations and curfews as have protection systems for people who have survived the trafficking experience. This provides a backdrop for what might occur in the following years.

This final chapter includes several key recommendations for action in the intermediate future on the part of private, public, and nongovernmental sectors acting jointly or separately. These recommendations supplement similar material elsewhere in the work.

CHAPTER 1

Human trafficking: An overview

The International Labour Organization (ILO) estimates that approximately 40 million people are victims of trafficking in persons (or TIP) of whom approximately two-thirds originate in the flesh markets of south and southern Asia, which consists of countries including Thailand and India. However, since the factors driving drive trafficking are both universal and global, no country or region today is immune from the processes whereby people at risk because of poverty, inequality or governmental corruption are sold, commodified and ruthlessly exploited. This includes advanced democracies such as the United States where so-called 'coyotes' are active in capturing and enslaving Central American migrants along the Mexican border, and rapidly urbanising countries in other parts of Latin America, in Europe (most notably Central and Eastern Europe) and the Middle East. Some of this is assisted by innovative digital communications that decrease the spatial distance between victim and perpetrator or by political crises like the Russian–Ukrainian war which is currently displacing added millions of people. As of 2016, there were an estimated 9 million persons in Africa, who are victims of so-called modern slavery. According to some conservative estimates, this figure accounts for over 20% of total global trafficking. This includes hundreds of thousands of 'boat people' originating in West Africa and the conflict zones of the Middle East assisted and then exploited by human smugglers working across the Mediterranean. At the other end of the continent, southern

Africa is believed to have recently entered the world's top-ten routes for human trade largely but not entirely because of undocumented cross-border migration from neighbouring states of the Republic which is intercepted for trafficking purposes.

There is no consensus among experts as to what trafficking involves. Since its recent 'discovery' as both a specific crime and an area of academic interest in the latter part of the 20th century, there has been confusion as to the delineation of trafficking from slavery and human smuggling. Considerable energy has gone into the relationships between trafficking and its cousin concepts. Although the boundaries are still unclear in many respects, the accepted view is that trafficking is not concomitant with human smuggling, which involves assisted movement across frontiers, because trafficking can take place domestically within states in addition to across their borders. What we are seeing in Europe, for example, may be human smuggling or trafficking depending on the point where traffickers-cum-smugglers give agency to those they are 'assisting'

'Modern slavery', which is s a term preferred in some accounts, is also not tantamount to so-called 'classical' slavery with its connotations of ancient empires and the dreadful Middle Passage of African slaves to the Americas from the 15th to 17th centuries. Some but not all trafficking today results in slavery. In either case, slavery of the modern variety also involves an array of technologies, from the phone to the Internet, unavailable to the classical perpetrator. This is because we live in an unprecedented inter-connected world – a global village as described by some analysts. It is now easier for traffickers to access a greater supply of potential victims, to buy them at a cheaper price, to sell them on and to meet replacement costs which arise in the 'business model' of the contemporary perpetrator.[1]

What we currently understand as 'trafficking' dates back about twenty years to the Convention on Organised Crime adopted by the United Nations in 2001 with three associated protocols.[2] These were the Protocol Against the Smuggling of Migrants by Land, Sea and Air, which can be used to bring traffickers to account; the Protocol against the Illicit Manufacture and Trade in Firearms, their Components and Ammunition; and, what concerns us most, the Protocol to Prevent, Suppress and Punish

Trafficking in Persons Especially Women and Children, supplementing the United Nations Convention against Transnational Organized Crime, (United Nations, General Assembly Resolution 22.25).

In this third instrument, widely deemed the 'Palermo Convention', human trafficking, or as some prefer, modern slavery, involves:

[T]he recruitment, transportation, harbouring or receipt of persons, by means of threat or use of force or others forms of coercion of abduction, of fraud, deception, of the abuse of power or of a position of vulnerability, or of the giving or receiving of payments or benefits to achieve the consent of a person having control over another person for the purpose of exploitation. (United Nations Protocol to Prevent, Suppress and Punish Trafficking of Persons, Especially Women and children, 12 December 2000)

Seen in these terms, trafficking is not a single crime but a collection of crimes whose common aim is to reduce people to sexual or other types of labour units that can be sold, exploited and abused as would a medieval chattel.[3] Trafficking, in turn, is an umbrella term covering a variety of criminal practices, including forced labour, sexual exploitation, organ trafficking, child labour, child soldiering and forced child marriage. Despite the different interpretations of Palermo that have emerged in its twenty-year existence, most analysts take it to embody three distinct yet interconnected elements in the trafficking process. These are the recruitment and then possible movement of victims across a town, region or, international border; their subsequent socialisation in which the victim is inducted into the norms, values, purposes and punishments of the trafficking regime; and, finally, following sufficient compliance their exploitation as cheap labour, for economic and/or sexual purposes.

In line with the intention of Palermo to put forward as a prototype for inclusion into domestic law, South Africa has also developed its own, systematic anti-trafficking instrument, the Prevention and Combating of Trafficking in Persons Act (No. 7 of 2013), commonly referred to by the acronym PACOTIP. In accordance with its provisions a person is guilty of trafficking when he or she:

delivers, recruits, transports, harbours, sells, exchanges, leases or receives another person within or across the boundaries of the Republic using the threat of harm, the threat or use of force or any other form of coercion, the abuse of vulnerability, fraud, deception, abduction, kidnapping, the abuse of power; the giving of payments or benefits to obtain the consent of a person or authority over another person; the direct or indirect giving or receiving of payments, compensation, regards or benefits or any other activities aimed at either the person or an immediate family member of that person, or any other person in close relationship to that person, for exploitation.[4]

Much of this echoes Palermo even though there is still no one-size-fits-all consensus twenty years later. All trafficking, nevertheless, is socially embedded in the sense that there exists an overall predisposing factor that 'guarantees' that trafficking takes place. There are, therefore, many theories of how trafficking happens.

At the macro level, trafficking has been indirectly attributed to just about anything, from poverty and inequality arising from neo-liberal policies of the IMF (International Monetary Fund) and World Bank to governments who perpetuate legal, political and economic systems that underwrite trafficking through corruption. In these cases, corrupt leaders of government and law enforcement have a stake in TIP which serves their financial and political interests. According to other analysts, trafficking is a 'natural' by-product of the dense transnational flow of goods, ideas and people quintessential to the post-industrial age. Global supply chains consisting of layers of sub-contracting are also often blamed for creating an enabling environment for TIP, especially where production is outsourced to developing nations paying lower wages, with fewer regulations, and minimum protection for workers and 'forced labour on the fringes of supply chains'. According to a further school of thought, trafficking occurs because of human movement in the post-industrial age and the demand for cheap labour at a time when it is estimated that 258 million people live in countries other than their place of origin. Global tourism is also a driver of development and trafficking, particularly in countries that specialise in transnational sex tourism.

Trafficking rings are increasingly caught up with political extremism. Since the September 2001 attack on the World Trade Center, the traffickers and the terrorists are often conceived as two sides of the same coin, sharing ideas, networks and, above all, money. War is also a conduit for trafficking, as we see daily in Africa or, more recently, in Ukraine where the displacement of millions of people works to the advantage of trafficking networks seeking sexual victims and exploited labour. 'Peacekeeping' is also, ironically, a source of trafficking important for us in this country – South African troops on missions to Africa north of the Limpopo have a history of allegedly committing sexual crimes and other related offences, including TIP.[5] Likewise, natural disasters, including the severe drought that has impacted parts of southern Africa since the millennium, open up opportunities for human trade. During 2007, for example, many parents in Eswatini were alleged to be selling their children to virtually anyone with money to access water and food for starving households.

While most analysts of trafficking employ largely immeasurable macro-theories to explain TIP, some explanations focus on more granular factors in the immediate environment where trafficking occurs. Innumerable theories see the origins of trafficking to lie among marginalised individuals or groups vulnerable and more susceptible to traffickers. This is because of the coincidence between poverty and inherited psychologies open to manipulation by perpetrators working along a spectrum from organised crime and transnational syndicates with a major stake in child sexual exploitation (CSE) to small groups and individuals who become traffickers on an incremental or opportunistic basis. Typical of the latter are trafficking crimes bounded by time and space which arise out of the 'opportunity' structures linking perpetrators to victims.[6]

Human trafficking, thus, has many forms and modalities and, as we shall show in succeeding chapters, many, if not all, of these manifestations are present in South and southern Africa. This includes commercial sex trafficking (which may involve individuals from the age of 10 upwards), child trafficking (normally defined as pertaining to young adults under 16 or 18), and labour trafficking, which is tantamount to forced labour and is largely understudied in preference to other two major counterparts.[7] More 'specialised' forms of TIP are also present in the subcontinent as well as on the global stage. These include organ trafficking or 'organ harvesting' driven by cultural practices, trafficking for child marriage, illegal adoption, baby-farming and the shortage of transplantable body parts in the modern medical economy. It also includes some relatively new types of TIP recently designated by Interpol, such as sex tourism and the trafficking of both adults and children for criminal purposes leading to assault, housebreaking and organised child begging, which is prevalent in numerous developing countries.

As we have already hinted, there are no exact figures as to the extent of TIP, either worldwide, in Africa, in South Africa or the southern African subcontinent. Nor do we know the exact proportion of men to women and children who are trafficked for various exploitative purposes. However, it appears that worldwide about half of all trafficking victims are women or children primarily procured for involuntary sexual activity in brothels or sexual entertainment facilities, or as prostitutes on the streets of the major cities of the world. Prostituted women are especially valuable for traffickers because they can be 'consumed' repeatedly, unlike drugs, which once used, require renewal. Of the remainder of the victims, some are males who are used for sex purposes and cheap labour in various exploitative settings. Alternatively, they are adolescents, sometimes as young as six or seven, who are traded for paedophile purposes or sexual or commercial labour. Many of the victims are undocumented migrants who cross borders unaccompanied in the process of seeking work, or members of families who have previously travelled trans-frontier.[8]

On the global market, trafficked people are normally cheap. These unfortunate people are bought and sold and, in many cases, resold, in accordance with the economic laws governing commodities. Prices, however, vary according to the laws of supply and demand in local markets so that women and young girls are generally cheaper when procured for sex in developing as opposed to highly industrialised countries. The demand for women in prostitution and other forms of sex work is also ongoing and difficult to regulate. Women with potential in the sex industries are ultimately about three times more valuable than forced labour in construction, mining and industry, and ten times more valuable than women in domestic servitude. In some cases, women are trafficked for sex and service work interchangeably. Since trafficked people are also low maintenance except in special cases, adept traffickers in South Africa can expect an average return in the range from 20 to 800% on their initial investment.

South Africa has, moreover, all the prerequisites for a successful trafficking state as identified by global analysts.[9] Some of this has to do with global developments that characterise wider relationships between developed and underdeveloped countries in the procurement and international transport of sex workers. However, some of the problems are indigenous. This includes our lengthy, porous, and poorly patrolled landward and maritime borders; an advanced and relatively unmoderated banking system which is attractive to both local and international traffickers concerned with laundering their profits; and huge inequalities, which encourage push-and-pull urbanisation that can be favourably worked to the advantage of traffickers en route. There are many opportunities for trafficking activity along the trajectory from the poverty nodes to the small towns in the first instance and eventually to the big cities. The relative failure of the ruling ANC to deliver on many of its electoral promises since 1994 has also fuelled expectations, especially among urban populations. Many of these individuals are unemployed, under-employed and consequently susceptible to the overtures of trafficking perpetrators who offer innocent men, women and children access to money, jobs and social opportunity. Counter-trafficking is also impeded by residues of apartheid, which discourage a large proportion of the population from approaching the police to report trafficking offences. This is especially the case where it involves undocumented migrants competing with locals in the job market and women in prostitution. Both locals and especially migrants are normally victims of corruption at all levels of government undermining effective law enforcement.

In this enabling environment, it would be surprising if there was no human trafficking in South Africa. This has been recognised in the first major research report on TIP by the Human Science Research Council (HSRC) in the decade after the millennium. The report identified South Africa as a source of trafficking, as a destination point for victims sent especially from southern Asia and as a transit or holding point for trafficked men and women destined for export into African, European and Middle Eastern markets. Much of this was confirmed in the IOM 'triplet' of studies conducted around the same period and in repeated annual surveys sent out on a country-by-country basis by the United States' State Department since the second decade of the 21st century.[10] All comment on the three primary routes along which the majority of trafficking takes place, namely the northern border over the Limpopo to points north, the north-eastern border dividing South Africa and Mozambique, and trafficking via Lesotho where many people from all parts of Africa congregate. Landward trafficking is supplemented by victims arriving by air in South Africa at its three international airports where border officials are often in the pay of international syndicates. As we speak, maritime trafficking is also on the increase along South Africa's lengthy seaboard.

Trans-frontier trafficking is supplemented by domestic TIP within the territorial boundaries of South Africa.[11] This tends to occur mainly, but not entirely, across historic migration routes from poverty nodes, such as the rural areas of Kwa-Zulu-Natal and Eastern Cape, to medium-sized towns and major cities. Some local trafficking is, like its Latin American counterpart, 'stepwise'. This is in the sense that victims are first brought to towns for a protracted 'testing' period and are then sent on to the major metropolitical areas such as Johannesburg, Durban or Cape Town. There are also several internal dispersal points from which trans-frontier migrants trafficked from the north or northeast are distributed to sites of exploitation. Rustenburg is one such site servicing the requirement for mining labour along the North-West platinum belt. Needless to say, the big cities are the main attraction points for both traffickers and their victims, especially for victims brought from South and South-East Asia destined to be re-exported into the European market.

All of this involves a process which is complex, nuanced and heterogenous. Trafficking activity is ultimately situation dependent. This means that trafficking patterns may differ according to the personalities and social circumstances of both victims and perpetrators, the culture of the situation in which trafficking takes place, the age of the victims, their patterns of behaviour, membership of social networks or the experience of the traffickers themselves. Having said this, the recruitment process where victims are 'introduced' to the trafficking experience largely conforms to definitions made explicit in the 2013 PACOTIP legislation. This means that victims can be abducted, kidnapped or otherwise coerced into slave-like conditions.In reality, however, most recruitment, the first phase of the trafficking process worldwide is based on fraud and deception meant to manipulate the expectations of victims. In South Africa and elsewhere this includes false promises of employment, marriage, future work and other benefits. Many women trafficked from the rural areas into the metropole are also groomed ostensibly for modelling work in the cities, but ultimately end up in metropolitan brothels. Child trafficking is sometimes based on outright purchases from desperate families or adults posing as legal guardians.[12] There are also cases where human smuggling or romantic attachments in the first instance turn into straight trafficking thereafter. Many undocumented migrants are lured into trafficking situations by unrealistic expectations of work across borders.

Recruitment can take place anywhere, from an open piece of veld near the borders to relatively upmarket bars, restaurants, and other recreational locations in the cities. In many cases recruitment is assisted by friends or family who help, sometimes unknowingly, to connect perpetrator and victim. Recruitment worldwide is normally followed by the transportation of victims to the sites for their exploitation. This can involve trans-frontier movement, movement from a rural to an urban community, intra-community transportation or even taking the victim from one house to another.

The 'socialisation' of victims into the trafficking culture may or may not involve the outright use of physical violence to induce victim compliance. Women trafficked into involuntary sex work and prostitution are alternatively force-fed with alcohol or narcotics to engender dependence. In many cases, however, more insidious techniques include the confiscation of identity documents, physical isolation and threats against the family of the victim. Labour trafficking, for example, often involves victims signing vague 'contracts' which lead to a forced form of labour and wage debt. The subsequent exploitation of victims in harsh labour or sex work is sometimes assisted by victims lacking knowledge of their rights and where to seek assistance. This is especially problematic for undocumented migrants who still face arrest and deportation by the South African Police Service (SAPS), notwithstanding the provisions of PACOTIP.

As already inferred, women, including adolescent girls make up about half of all trafficking victims both worldwide and in South and southern Africa. Most, but by no means all, are trafficked for purposes of sexual exploitation along a range of activities which work in strip clubs, massage parlours or in brothels where the majority of activity involves prostitution. Roughly 14% of women victims are also now being trafficked worldwide for 'lighter' types of forced labour than men and this is, from what we know, currently on the rise. Men, in turn, may make up about 40% of victims worldwide, and are mainly used in labour trafficking for demanding work on farms, in mines, industry, fisheries, transport and most other sectors of economies.[13] We also know that a percentage of men is trafficked for sex work, but this is relatively under-researched because most of this type of labour predominantly involves children or adolescent females.

According to some estimates, adolescents of either gender under eighteen make up about 30% of victims. Much as is the case with their adult counterparts – girls are mainly used for commercial sex and the majority of the boys for cheap labour. The labour trafficking of children is especially pronounced in sub-Saharan Africa relative to Europe where exploitative work by adults is more common.

Overall, about half of all trafficking victims are used for sexual exploitation, about 38% for forced labour and 12% for 'other' forms of trafficking, which include organ trafficking, criminal activity ranging from pickpocketing to drug cultivation, baby selling, forced marriage or forced begging. Most of the latter involve children or adolescents. The forced labour component as well as trafficking for the removal of organs is becoming more prevalent. Some countries have also reported illegal adoption, sometimes involving, pregnant women.

Trafficking victims come from a diversity of sociological and demographic backgrounds. Most are nonetheless the members of groups-at-risk or otherwise vulnerable populations abused by perpetrators. Many in this category are 'on the move' as a result of urbanisation, mainly due to political displacement and a lack of economic opportunity, and, in a few cases, along the pathways to upward mobility. The prototype victim by global standards is an at-risk person who is normally under 35 years of age. This is much the case in South Africa. Here, as is the case elsewhere, these victims are often individuals whose personality lends them to seduction by traffickers or who are members of a disadvantaged group with few resources, social support, employment opportunities or prospects for upward social mobility. These individuals may include disaffected young men, poor women, innocent children, child runaways, undocumented migrants, members of the LGBT+ communities, and the disabled or populations challenged by emotional and physical circumstances. Some of the victims live in a nether world between slavery and legality, with migrant farmworkers in the United States being a case in point. Others are the victims of cultural or ethnic exclusion whose negative impacts are crystallised in the process of internal or cross-frontier migration. Many victims suffer serial or secondary victimisation at the hands of brutal and corrupt law enforcement or state bureaucrats ironically involved in rehabilitation work designed to re-integrate the victim into society after 'rescue'.

In South Africa, from what we know, about half of the total victims are young or adult women trafficked mainly for commercial sex purposes with a substantially smaller group trafficked for labour. Men make up the overwhelming majority of labour trafficking victims, except for some young men who are trafficked into the sex market. As elsewhere in the world, both male groups tend to be under-reported. As we shall see in a later chapter there is also huge controversy among analysts regarding child trafficking. While some researchers detect substantial numbers, others have found that most children on the move across borders are a result of human smugglers rather than trafficking perpetrators. This excludes children moving internally who may be more susceptible to traffickers than their cross-border counterparts. In any event, children are primarily trafficked for sex, labour or for both in many instances.

Victims, it must be emphasised, do not necessarily fit the highly gendered tropes in much trafficking literature where men perpetrate crimes against women. Nor are they necessarily one-dimensional pawns or defiled playthings without any agency as described in stereotypical trafficking narratives. Albeit their options are constrained in the trafficking process, victims sometimes have choices which range along a continuum, from passivity to victims having a relative capacity to manipulate the situations in which they find themselves. Notwithstanding caricatures of children widely portrayed as blindly innocent, this occurs even among children on the move who are smuggled or trafficked across South Africa's borders.

Many children in the streets of big cities, such as Johannesburg or Cape Town, are streetwise and, like their counterparts elsewhere, have complex pre-existing vulnerabilities before being trafficked. These pathways to being trafficked frequently include youth offenders, missing children and previous sex abuse or victimisation. Children trafficked for sex exploitation are often introduced to their abusers by other children who share common social networks, which sometimes include perpetrators. Some women, with the initial appearance of being trafficked into prostitution, are working consensually and on a professional basis.

Traffickers can be anybody, irrespective of gender, age or socioeconomic circumstance. Overall, however, men make up approximately 60% of perpetrators whereas women make up about around 36%. In certain regions, such as Central America and east Asia, there are equal numbers of female and male perpetrators.[14] The remainders are boys and girls who recruit younger learners into sexual exploitation in exchange for narcotics. Women are especially involved in the recruitment phase of trafficking processes. To realise higher levels of life opportunity, teachers and parents may even surrender their offspring or learners to strangers who promise the earth but then turn out to be members of trafficking gangs. They can be schoolmates who recruit younger learners into sexual exploitation in exchange for narcotics, or parents who exploit their children for begging, house-breaking or other criminal purposes. In some poor rural communities, parents or teachers pass on children to trafficking gangs anticipating that their offspring will find improved life opportunities in the cities. Urban gangs often traffic in their repertoire of criminal activities, which may include drug dealing and sales of light-calibre weapons. There are trafficking gangs of the 'governance' type. These are transnational organised criminal groups controlling communities and territories and are involved in an array of illicit markets. These gangs have contacts in the deep state and the potential capacity to overthrow state institutions and undermine government institutions. Other perpetrators are brokers negotiating child labour in rural villages, as well as licensed multinational recruitment agencies supplying men to mines, farms and other labour-intensive enterprises and legally using trafficking labour inadvertently in their supply chains. Each of these demands different responses from the criminal justice system and a specialised organised crime unit may be required where there is a large, structured trafficking group. Where trafficking involves a more intimate relationship between perpetrator and victim, approaches similar to those dealing with domestic violence may be more appropriate.

As already noted, some trafficking involves organised criminal groups who have control of communities or territories and may be involved in multiple illicit markets. These so-called 'governance-type' traffickers are different from 'business-type' perpetrators involved in a range of criminalities but composed of two or three traffickers for whom slavery is a core activity on their agenda. In a recent study of 489 cases conducted by UNODC for its 2018 report, 30 were of the governance type, 141 were of the business prototype, and a further 101 were individual criminals. As a generalisation, organised groups in the 'governance' sector traffic more victims, over a longer time and with greater violence.[15]

Ultimately, the situation in South Africa reflects global perpetrator patterns with a spectrum from highly articulated criminal organisations dealing inter-dependably in drugs, arms, and humans via small local operations, to incremental traffickers – mainly composed of individuals engaged in trafficking on a spontaneous basis. Perpetrators can, in other words, be individual or small groups acting opportunistically as circumstances dictate to global syndicates of corporate proportions led by criminal masterminds with business and management models. This contrasts with the opposite end of the spectrum where TIP offenders are overwhelmingly ordinary people, low-skilled and unemployed, They conform, according to one theorist, with the 'banality of evil'

The perpetrators in South Africa are as complex and sociologically varied as their victims. These perpetrators include Chinese Triad gangs simultaneously involved in smuggling abalone, ivory, endangered species, and trafficking labour via Lesotho into the mainstream and illegal mining industry. In the case of sex trafficking, perpetrators include domestically based South Africans at work for medium to large-scale international operators, South Africans abroad who ship victims to the Republic on an agency or order basis, Eastern European criminal networks and Nigerian gangs working at the interface between drugs, small arms smuggling and human trade. Some perpetrators working with women in prostitution are members of international 'kingpin' syndicates involved in TIP through layers of local sub-contractors, but others are, at ground-level, merely opportunistic and small-time predators.

Frontline perpetrators, particularly big criminal syndicates who ply their trade with relative impunity despite an international regime that identifies modern slavery as an especially depraved activity, are also backed up by a range of less visible service providers working behind the scenes to make perpetration possible. These include transporters, such as taxi and bus operators, bringing victims to the cities from the borders; manufacturers of fraudulent documents, such as passports, used to illegally cross borders; owners of hotels, houses, apartments, and boarding houses where brothels and drug dens are situated; and 'bottom bitches' at the top of the brothel hierarchy acting on a supervisory basis.

Perpetrators often have networks that provide access to fellow perpetrators, potential victims and, as importantly, law enforcement officers and other members of the criminal justice system in many countries. This is especially significant in South Africa where there is a bulk of evidence pointing to corruption, collusion and positive or negative complicity in the face of trafficking crimes.

Modern perpetrator networks also include gatherers of intelligence and data. In an age of digital technology, social media and the internet are of paramount importance in linking perpetrators, victims and customers. This is no less important in South Africa where perpetrators increasingly scan the internet for victims to be groomed, as well as potential customers. In some cases, 'johns' are provided with pins that allow access to sites on the underground or 'dark internet' where young women, ostensibly virgins, are auctioned. Trafficked women in prostitution as well as prostitution professionals have a long history of advertising openly in the print media and are today increasingly at work on a multi-media basis aimed at the market. Children for sexual exploitation are also available on various sites on the underground internet, which is trawled by a mixture of 'businessmen' and sexual deviants.

All trafficking contains acts, means and purposes. The nature of the act may change depending on the point along the spectrum of the perpetrators. Thus, the front line of perpetration may involve recruitment and transportation of the victim, while the end of the spectrum involves control over the victim for one or another form of exploitation. The means may involve various levels of violence, but, as we have already inferred, most frequently involves fraud, deception or abuse of power where the victim is vulnerable. The purpose of a trafficking act may be the sexual exploitation of the victim, his or her subjection to forced labour, servitude and slavery, or even his or her dissection for organ removal or sale of body parts.

These are the rudiments of all human trafficking that are in one form or another embedded in all anti-trafficking laws, reaching back to Palermo. The sociology of perpetration is, with all things being equal, far more complex. Traffickers, for example, may be male or female (albeit that conventional wisdom believes that trafficking is a gender crime involving mainly males exacting control over women). There is also no universal profile for the age of offenders although perpetrators tend to be younger in the case of sex and child trafficking. Perpetrators can, in turn, be of any age or nationality despite the stereotype in South Africa that a disproportionate number of traffickers originate in West Africa, especially Nigeria, and come to South Africa to perpetrate a variety of criminal acts among which trafficking is, in some respects the most violent.

If the crimes committed by traffickers under South African law are analysed and convictions secured, several offender patterns emerge. Firstly, all turn on misrepresentation to the victim, which then turns into outright entrapment. In the case of *State versus Nanthumbi*, for example, the child victim was lured with promises of work before exploitation. This is similar to the case of *State versus Amaku and Another* where a young girl was imported from a rural area and then transported into a Johannesburg brothel.[16]

In almost all cases, victims are subjected to terrible abuse aimed at inducing compliance with the wishes of the perpetrator (or perpetrators). The case against Ovekachi Okechuwe, where young women were forced to take narcotics following abduction and transport into brothel work, is disturbingly characteristic. There is also the Springs brothel case of 2019 when a woman and two teenagers were similarly forced into brothel work, drugged and then raped by their Nigerian perpetrators. Rape is, in fact fairly common along with force-feeding of narcotics. In addition, young men are forced to watch and perform in pornographic moves which are then placed on the internet as a perverse form of marketing to sex-buying clients. In almost all cases of sex trafficking, the victims are very young (sometimes in their teens), originate in impoverished areas, and in some cases are intellectually challenged. Some are relatives of the perpetrators who have used the internet or social media to attract clients to various locations that move geographically in order not to attract local attention.

There are instances of children being drug addicted, raised for prostitution and then circulated on a multi-use basis by associated networks. There are other cases where these mobile brothels are used by eminent members of the public or even South African Police officials who return escapees from brothels to their perpetrators. This necessarily demoralises victims who lose all respect and confidence in the law. Needless to say, living conditions in most brothels are indescribably horrific. Food is often denied to workers who are imprisoned other than times when they are 'servicing' clients. There is at least one known instance of a young girl being forced to witness the murder and dismemberment of a fellow sex worker.

Among the earlier cases that have appeared before the courts a number stand out as especially horrific. These include the most-often quoted case of *State vs Amien Andrews*, which is distinctive in many ways. Firstly, it was prosecuted preceding South Africa's ratification of Palermo using legislative instruments available at the time. In this case, the accused took advantage of two destitute young women who were gang-raped and, in one case, denied urgent medical attention. Some 46 young victims were alleged to have been trafficked by Andrews over the years before being prosecuted. In the case of *State vs Aldina Santos*, three Mozambican children were confined in a Pretoria brothel where they were sexually exploited in various ways. In April 2022, Dos Santos was sentenced to life imprisonment for sex trafficking in a facility that was allegedly patronised by prominent businessmen and high government officials. In the case of *State versus Matini and Another*, the accused was charged with sexual exploitation of mentally disabled victims.[17]

Trafficking may be incidental in the sense that it comes from an incremental act with little premeditation. In many cases, it may also be the work of a network of criminal people coming together to reap the profits of sexual exploitation or forced labour. While most trafficking is not specifically organised in the sense of two or more people coming together to commit a criminal act, human trafficking is almost always bound up in the conventional wisdom with transnational networks that span the boundaries between drugs and human trafficking and who work to exploit the often enormous opportunities available for corruption. This is especially the case where the government has been successfully penetrated and where corruption is, as in South Africa, structurally embedded in the political system. Many of the failures in anti-trafficking policy since the promulgation of PACOTIP in 2013 stem from a lack of political will on the part of state officials. In many cases, these failures may be attributed to connivance and division of the spoils between criminal elements, senior politicians and highly placed bureaucrats.

In South Africa, as elsewhere in the world, it is an invariably difficult task to extricate victims from trafficking networks. Many victims lack the psychological resilience to break free from their perpetrators following long periods of physical and emotional abuse. In some cases of sexual exploitation, women refuse to be rescued by police or well-meaning civil society organisations because they identify with their perpetrators and have become dependent on them as lines of narcotics supply, or because they distrust the police. In many cases, traffickers and police act in mutual self-interest and collusion. A later chapter addresses the enormous problems confronting victim re-empowerment and integration into the social mainstream in the post-rescue period.

How much trafficking takes place in South Africa and its connection with the global economy in the wider world? How does this compare with other states at a similar developmental level? Is trafficking an 'epidemic' as some observers suggest, or does trafficking occur on an incremental basis, namely, case by case by case towards some minimal magnitude? Where does South Africa fit in a global constellation where the incidence of humans is inexorably on the incline?[18]

Much of this is smoke-and-mirrors in analytical circles because trafficking is so clandestine. Here in the Republic, in the surrounding subcontinent and worldwide, it is virtually impossible to accurately identify the figures, except at the top of the iceberg when perpetrators are brought to courts. Even then, many traffickers escape conviction or sentence in a manner commensurate with the seriousness of their crimes. This is partially because the greater number of victims do not report being trafficked for a variety of reasons, which include being at risk from their perpetrators or profound stigmatisation in the community where they originate. Survivors of trafficking experience are also deeply traumatised and in many cases, it is difficult if not impossible for law enforcement to put together a coherent case, make arrests or feed an investigation through the courts to the point of conviction. Sentencing for trafficking in the Republic is notoriously inconsistent and is hidden behind lesser offences, either because members of the criminal justice system fear retribution from trafficking gangs or because of involvement in the crimes committed.

Because human smuggling can become trafficking recruitment along the way, there is no distinct delineation between one and the other. Many erstwhile migrants coming across the Limpopo assisted by guides find that they are entrapped by their bus or taxi- drivers and arrive in unfamiliar places in Johannesburg populated by traffickers on the make. Trafficking at the national level is also far more difficult to measure at a crowded community bus stop. Therefore, this cannot be generalised to an aggregate figure for a province or nationally. As a result, most trafficking figures are estimations based on weak research design, unclear methodologies and poor-quality data, which effectively precludes evidence-based assessments. Most studies worldwide are, in fact, overwhelmingly anecdotal, lack empirical evidence and involve what one analyst has deemed 'the uncritical repetition of dubious statistics'. This includes many ostensibly new-generation micro-studies of the granular 'lived realities' of trafficking, as well as calculations made by the major barometers such as the Global Slavery Index (GSI), the annual reports of the US State Department and the Counter-Trafficking Data Collaborative (CTDC).

In South Africa, as elsewhere, the social reproduction of information is also skewed by invasive factors that sometimes make it difficult to distinguish between fact and fiction. Media reports on the extent of trafficking are almost inevitably sensationalist and in South Africa as well as in other countries there is almost always a conflation between sex work and sex trafficking used in arguments over the legalisation of prostitution. Access to good supportive data in terms of the prevalence is normally difficult to locate in many cases where law enforcement and the state bureaucracy is corrupt and at times attempts to mystify trafficking events as far as possible. Both the South African National Defence Force (SANDF) and the SAPS have vested interests in manufacturing high trafficking statistics as this legitimates their role in militarising and securing the borders. Even where police forces and members of the governmental bureaucracy are honestly concerned with prosecuting perpetrators, police and case data may be inaccurate because of a lack of rigour in its collection and management. Potential statistics on sex trafficking are mainly precluded by sex workers and other victims who sometimes exist in complex relationships with their perpetrators. More commonly, victims fear the police as being hand-in-glove with the traffickers. Even the toughest policemen steer clear of the horror of child trafficking and most prefer to make arrests for other crimes where cases are less complex and easier on the road to promotion.

In addition, the Department of Home Affairs (DHA) often conflates trafficking with 'illegal immigration' to boost its activity against undocumented migrants. There are allegations in a recent report that this results in practices that violate the rights of undocumented migrant children. In an infamous and insupportable allegation aimed at tightening immigration laws and travel regulations, the DHA has estimated that there are '30 000' trafficked children. Statistics from certain organisations, such as the network of NGOs dealing with victims, also need to be viewed with circumspection, given that some counter-trafficking organisations inflate the numbers to raise money and satisfy donors. Some practitioners and analysts also engage in turgid and impenetrable debates over trafficking frequency as a means to quote figures with double agendas.

Moral panics, such as fear about mass prostitution at the time of the 2010 World Cup, lead to commentators inflating trafficking statistics.[20] Sampling techniques and variations in operational definitions of trafficking under more normal circumstances may be inconsistent from one analyst to another and could lead to an exaggerated or diminished number of both victims and perpetrators. The conceptual linkages between the various manifestations of trafficking also overlap so that clear-cut cases of child or sex trafficking frequently fuse. Child trafficking, for example, may be either smuggling or trafficking according to one's initial expectations.

There have been numerous attempts over the years to assess the prevalence of trafficking in South Africa with mixed results. These include the Molo Songololo study just after the millennium where the Cape-based NGO identified 28 000 child prostitutes in South Africa; the three studies of the IOM, around the same time, which eschew statistics but deem trafficking to be 'substantial'; an analysis of sex workers in Cape Town that found minimal involuntary prostitution; and the Tsiriledzani/HSRC study that identified trafficking to be of 'crisis proportions'.[21]

The IOM victim help service in Pretoria estimates dealing with 51 cases between 2005 and 2010 but these refer only to those victims who had drifted into its network looking for assistance. The Pretoria database is, in many cases, largely inaccessible because of fear of perpetrators. Meanwhile, the GSI estimated in 2016 that 248 700 people were living in conditions of modern slavery in the Republic.

According to the SAPS, some 3 957 children and 23 803 adults are 'missing' and unaccounted for over the 15 years from 2000–2015. The

SAPS has also released figures which show that between 2007 and 2017 at least 188 sex trafficking cases were reported under the interim TIP provisions in the Sexual Offences Amendment Act of 2007. In addition, 2 132 cases were reported to SAPS under the PACOTIP Act in 28 months from 9 August 2015 to 12 December 2017.[22] This forms part of the roughly 625 000 contact crimes per annum with the SAPS making 62 649 arrests for sexual offences. Although this is not evidence of trafficking per se, there is also a relatively high incidence of kidnapping, some of which is consistent with the provisions of the Palermo Protocol or South African counter-trafficking legislation.

The greater majority of offences inevitably go undetected because of constraints on victim reporting and on the SAPS posed by large-scale alternative crime. Much of what is visible currently represents the tip of the proverbial TIP iceberg. On the other hand, if one bears in mind that there are (a) multiple victims and perpetrators in each complex trafficking case; (b) that perpetration always involves a group or network of criminals lending support to perpetrators in commissioning a trafficking crime and land in court, and (c) that one offender in five is arraigned before the courts – then the SAPS figures rise very substantially. Considering the likelihood that police conservatively encounter one-in-ten in trafficking crimes because of ignorance about anti-trafficking law, overwork or laziness, the sheer total of participants in local trafficking victims, perpetrators and their service organisations then rises conservatively to the roughly 250 000 put forward by GSI figures.

This is a demonstrative figure meant to illuminate the extent of the trafficking problem in the Republic. It takes no account of the possible hundreds of thousands of victims who elude the SAPS through personal cunning, acts best located in the private realm or victims with perpetrators who have sufficient guile, money or networks to effectively escape detection. It also presumes that law enforcement has the capacity to arrest traffickers they encounter and that these arrests will lead to prosecution and conviction. In operational reality, however, many trafficking crimes are simply bypassed by police with other agendas.

Trafficking may be on the increase for a variety of reasons including improved methods adopted by perpetrators in groups or syndicated criminal arrangements because of alterations in the law or because of the availability of new vulnerable victims. The onset of Covid, as we shall see in a later chapter, is especially pertinent in this regard. There is no doubt that we need vastly improved quantitative methodologies aligned with these developments. Later chapters address the different forms of trafficking, in particular, those dealing with sex and child and labour trafficking respectively.

The disputes over the arithmetic of trafficking in South Africa and the wider world will in all probability continue ceaselessly. In the meantime, there is no debate over the gruesome human and social costs of modern slavery, human trafficking, TIP, modern slavery or what you will. These have been extensively catalogued before but the chamber of horrors involves, for the record, physical, spiritual, sexual and emotional degradation of the victims, in many cases, far beyond life-long recovery. At a more macro level, human trafficking also has many economic and political implications for the state.

With this in mind, the book now turns to commercial sex trafficking, child trafficking and forced labour.

CHAPTER 2

Sex trafficking

Prostitution and sex work have existed since time immemorial and are, as the saying goes, 'the world's oldest profession'. Issues at the interface of sexual exchange, trafficking and human rights have, in turn, motivated some of the most important conventions and treaties in modern international law. In retrospect, some of these instruments are somewhat redundant, for example, the International Agreement for the Suppression of White Slave Trafficking (1904) designed specifically to protect 'white' women from being trafficked, or the UN Convention on the Suppression of Trafficking in Persons and the Exploitation of Prostitution for Others, notorious for globally illegalising prostitution 'even with the consent of that person'. But others are more positive, including the Rome Statute leading to the creation of the International Criminal Court in 1998. This was a watershed in that it defined enslavement, rape, sexual slavery, enforced prostitution, forced pregnancy, enforced sterilisation and 'any other form of sexual violence' on the back of the Rwandan and Yugoslavian genocides as crimes against humanity.

The turn of the millennium was also significant in the history of international law concerning sex trafficking. In 1999, for example, the UN General Assembly (UNGA) passed the Optional Protocol on the Elimination of Violence Against Women. This was followed a year later by the Palermo Protocol, which we have already noted to be arguably the most important piece of international legislation in the historical trajectory of human trafficking. Although Palermo conflates all sex trafficking with prostitution, it nevertheless positions sex trafficking as more heinous than its labour counterpart.

Issues of sexual exchange have figured in the South African trafficking landscape since the arrival of Dutch settlers at the Cape in 1652. Two 'Abyssinian' prostitutes accompanied Jan van Riebeeck whose sailors were quick to establish relations with indigenous Hottentot women. There is also a long association between mine labour and sex trafficking going back to the emergence of 'native' mining communities following the discovery of gold on the Witwatersrand towards the end of the 19th century. This includes the activities of the Nongoloza Mathebula gang, which was notorious for kidnapping women and boys for the supply chains into the Rand mining compounds, as well as the 'jackrollers' who established a ring of brothels staffed by trafficked young women in the black townships in the 1980s and 1990s. As recently as the Marikana massacre (2012), Basotho men were known to be transporting young women for the use of 'home-boys' in the mines of the western platinum limb around Rustenburg, as well as in near-mine communities.[2]

What is sex work?[3] There are many interpretations including that of the WHO which defines it as the relatively simple 'provision of sexual services for money'. This can involve anything from prostitution – taken by some as concomitant with sex work – to activities such as stripping, massage, 'adult' sex shows and the manufacture of pornography. Its' first 'serious' analysis in the context of trafficking took place by the Cape Town-based NGO, Molo Songololo, which published two studies on the trafficking of women and children in 2001. These report various types of trafficking, most of which still pertain today. Substantial qualitative evidence of sex trafficking also occurs in the HSRC study of trafficking, which concludes that South Africa imports sex workers, exports women into African, Middle East and European markets and serves as a transit point for prostitutes entering and then leaving the country on an export basis. This pattern is subsequently reaffirmed by several later studies by individuals and international organisations that have examined sex trafficking over the last fifteen years.[4]

Having said this, we know relatively little about the details of prostitution and sex trafficking when measured against the accumulated information in places like the United States, Canada or Europe. Because of some of the methodological problems inherent to the study of trafficking, which we have already mentioned, we have no definite figures on prevalence. South African studies have consequently ranged from sex trafficking of crisis proportions involving millions of girls and women to a mere handful in major cities like Cape Town. We also have no idea – and probably never will – of the proportion of women engaging in sex work voluntarily and as a matter of choice, as opposed to others who work under compulsion, without agency, at the behest of traffickers who come in various forms from the individual to transnational syndicates dealing in the import and export of both South African women as well as those of other nationalities, under compulsion and without agency.

As with trafficking in general, the clandestine nature of sex work, especially if criminal, precludes exact supply-side calculations, especially when sex workers are teenagers or pre-adolescents attracting the attention of law enforcement authorities. Autonomous-type sex workers are, in many cases, highly mobile, moving into and out of the market as economics and professional considerations dictate. There are fortunate cases where the distinction between trafficked and non-trafficked sex work largely disappears when short-term working relations are established with entrepreneurs and then terminated. Generally speaking, the SAPS are not especially helpful in working out the arithmetic of sex trafficking, either because arrests for prostitution without aggravating circumstances fail to take place as a consequence of police concerns with a more serious crime, or because many police are involved in brothel-type enterprises.

Several other factors are mediating the relationship between sex and trafficking which complicate its analysis. Many South African families are, as elsewhere, reluctant to report missing females, especially after they become participants in the sex industries. This implies under-reporting by victims who are often fearful or shamed in a culture of violence and gender discrimination inevitably ingrained in the trafficking regime who ultimately fail to register the existence of trafficking. Non-disclosure agreements between social welfare and health providers based on confidentiality agreements with emotionally traumatised survivors of the trafficking experience are also problematic when it comes to disclosing trafficking offences with a reasonable degree of accuracy. There are also many instances where the police have refused to release sex trafficking information since the SAPS first recorded these offences in their list of crimes in 2008. This is because of fear of compromising ongoing prosecutions which may or may not have anything to do with trafficking crimes, or because publicly available data on police behaviour might embarrass law enforcement.

This is not to say that we know absolutely nothing about the dynamics of human trade based on sex. As elsewhere, trafficked or non-trafficked prostitution in South Africa involves a differentiated and multi-modular situation, each with its own but interconnected patterns for entry, operational coda, power relations and precipitating circumstances. There are victim accounts that in many cases constitute primary research information regarding the experiential pathways of women who have been trafficked, their origins and background before being recruited for trafficking purposes, the methods used by traffickers, the roles and activities of women initiated and then moved around while in the sex industry, their initiation into these roles, how sex workers are controlled, resistance to the conditions under which women in prostitution in SA are forced to live, and the health consequences of working under compulsion. Court records of prosecutions of perpetrators, video clips in the public media as well as unpublished post-doctoral theses that have recently surfaced all help put together a more coherent picture of the world of sex trafficking.

There is also some documentation on the perpetrators, their agents, their pimps, and the men on the internet with the proclivity to write about their experiences of buying women and their behaviour inside sex work establishments.[5]

We know, for example, that young women can be bought for ongoing sexual purposes for as little as R8 000 to R12 000, and that when supply is saturated one-off sex encounters can be procured for R50. This is often the case in the poorest communities of near-mine settlements where local women compete with 'foreign' prostitutes trucked in by labour brokers dealing with a mixture of sex and mine labour.

Sex work and prostitution of a trafficking character are also highly differentiated according to class criteria. The option of working independently, which is available to prostitutes at the upper end of the market, is generally not available lower down the hierarchy where women become entrapped by their reliance on pimps and traffickers of various persuasion to provide premises for sexual activity and other essential services demanded by clients. These include alcohol and drugs, which are freely shared among all. At the bottom of the ladder, as in other countries, there is street or curb-side prostitution, which is carefully supervised by pimps or the agents of trafficking organisations. In many of these cases of 'survivalist sex', women face double jeopardy because of police harassment and blackmail that often results in the exchange of sexual favours.

Within our territorial borders, women under the guidance of their pimps work the migration routes from the rural areas to the cities, as well as many residential sites in the metropoles themselves. Johannesburg and Cape Town include the inner city areas where trafficking extends out from dilapidated high-rise buildings into the wider community.[6] Limpopo and North West Province have been identified as critical hubs for sex trafficking. As the CTDC and other reports indicate, trafficked sex is also international with women being imported from various areas in Europe and southern Asia for temporary service in South Africa. According to an HSRC report, the South African market has a high demand for Thai and other South East Asian women. According to the CTDC, this continues today although there is a supplementary inflow from Eastern and Central Europe. Some recent reports focusing on Ukraine note the possibility of an increase in women from these areas in the wake of the current refugee crisis because neighbouring territories, such as Moldova or Transdniestria, have a long history of exporting sex workers into the markets of Europe and further afield on a trans-continental basis. T

The great majority of foreign women coming to South Africa for prostitution appear to do so voluntarily and do not necessarily foresee long-term residence in the country. They only become victims of traffickers who approach them and 'contract' them for work and subsequently confiscate their passports. Many women in this foreign category begin on a strictly business basis which then becomes adversarial. This is the point when local pimps begin to use strong-arm methods to victimise, disempower and generally safeguard their human investments. There is also sex trafficking of men inside and outside the Republic but this is still largely unexplored given the tendency of trafficking studies to concentrate on the female side of the sex trade.[7]

There are laws against sex trafficking some of which predate the PACOTIP. These include the Sexual Offences Act (No. 23 of 1957) as amended (known as the SOA) as used in the case of Elizabeth Maswangaye who was accused of soliciting young women into brothel work with false promises of conventional employment. In this case, the accused was sentenced to five years imprisonment.[8] Since the SOA can only be used to prosecute sex exploitation and not TIP, prosecutors have also deployed the provisions of POCA, (the Prevention of Organised Crime Act No. 21 of 1998), mainly against transnational syndicates, such as Thai traffickers, with a record of inveigling young women into debt bondage and then exporting them as prostitutes to South Africa. The Immigration Act (No. 13 of 2002) is also frequently invoked against undocumented men and women destined for the sex industries crossing South Africa's frontiers.

The situation has somewhat improved since the advent of PACOTIP which is a systematic, national instrument transcending all other laws against sex and other types of TIP. The victims, for example, no longer face the possibility of prosecution alongside their traffickers. Sentencing, however, remains erratic and there are far too many cases where offenders are given a slap on the wrist for a serious, complex crime, triggered by a mix of structural and contingent factors in which victim vulnerability, or 'openness' to victimisation, is central. Document mismanagement, pressure on judges, weak testimony on the part of traumatised victims and many other recurrent problems in the criminal justice system means that the outcome of the relatively few sex trafficking cases coming to court has also been inconsistent. This was especially so in the period before PACOTIP when a potpourri of laws with different sentencing consequences was mobilised to prosecute various 'milestone' sex traffickers cases. In the case of the notorious predator and previously mentioned sex trafficker, Amien Andrews, the accused was charged with assault to do grievous bodily harm, kidnapping, and rape and subsequently sentenced to 17 years imprisonment.[9] Other prosecutions for sex trafficking have taken place under a diversity of laws with different sentencing consequences.

Multiple systemic-type conditions create an enabling environment for sex traffickers, both within South Africa and across its borders.[10] These 'entry-points' or 'gateways' for both independent and trafficked prostitution include economic desperation and disadvantages experienced by some young girls and women, poverty in the communities where they subsist; lack of a sustainable income, housing and food; and high levels of gender-violence – all of which are preyed on by recruiters, traffickers and their agents.

Socio-cultural stimuli associated with sex trafficking in South Africa and elsewhere, include expectations woven around consumerism, materialism and the demand for instantaneous gratification. There is substantial literature on the complex interface between sex trafficking and the demand of adolescents, including teenage girls, for designer-brand clothes, cellphones, tablets and other facets of post-industrial technology.[11] Gender bias and paternalism also assist sex trafficking to become an entrenched, inherent and unreported facet of daily existence.

Various cultural practices can also deteriorate into the abuse associated with sex trafficking under survivalist conditions. In many communities, prostitution as an acceptable mode of work can be easily converted into outright trafficking. It is common in some rural families for girls to be sent away at times of economic stress with many invariably ending up being exploited by uncles or older men, some of whom sell their young relatives to predatory gangs searching for victims. In some cases, rural families on the economic margins sell directly to traffickers from the urban areas, sometimes in the hope that their young women will improve their life chances in the cities. Moreover, human traffickers or their agents may be people that victims trust, such as a close associate, a family member, an employment agent, or a neighbour

Some traditional practices, such as *'lobolo'* – a system of bride pricing – when abused, can result in sex trafficking, but this is more commonly associated with *ukuthwala* – an altogether more lethal process of child-bride purchasing that occurs mainly in the eastern and north-eastern Cape. Originally a form of negotiated marriage arrangement designed to ensure reproduction on the part of chieftains and tribal authorities, *ukuthwala* is frequently shaped by Nigerian gangs seeking to procure women for sex trafficking.

Proximity to traffickers in densely populated high-crime areas increases the exposure of women to sex predators offering fraudulent opportunities for upward mobility. This was emphasised in one of the earliest studies on the sex trafficking of women in South Africa. Other contingent factors that inform the context of sex trafficking include the displacement and dislocation of young women in the face of inter-parental violence, sibling violence and parental use of intoxicating substances. Family breakdown concurrent with socioeconomic shortages represents a powerful concoction for bringing young women into trafficking circles.

Lifestyles that induce many young women to experiment with drugs and alcohol, frequent bars and shebeens, commit petty criminal acts and practise risky sex behaviour can also lead to entrapment by predators. Vulnerability is further increased when young women are left at home for long periods by parents consumed with job-related, financial or recreational issues external to the household environment.

Frequent interaction between victim and offender or even the personality of the victim can also be decisive in turning otherwise 'normal' social relationships into sex trafficking. While some girls do not accept offers from strangers, others become embroiled in trafficking networks as a result of promiscuity, immaturity, inadequate social skills, and confrontational responses to problematic situations. Before entering the sex trade, many victims fail to understand the nature of TIP, sometimes because of stereotypes woven around prostitution.

Migrant women, particularly when undocumented, are especially susceptible to situational-type sex trafficking because of the anxiety accompanying their journey. In 2009, the IOM cited family breakdown and religious and ethnic persecution as the main enablers of trans-border migration and sex trafficking. Ten years later, oppressive political and economic conditions in countries around sub-Saharan Africa remain enablers for TIP leading to exploitative sex work.[12] In some families in the region, girls are seen as burdens and liabilities, which often leads to direct family pressure or even coercion and precipitates entrance into the sex industry. This can occur at home before girls or women cross the borders, at the frontiers themselves, or once migrant women have difficulty obtaining sustainable work upon arriving at their places of destination. In some circumstances, migrant women are disinclined to assimilate. Xenophobia in the job or housing market precipitates these women into survival sex work in urban areas south of the Limpopo.

Refugee women, especially war rape survivors, experience victimisation while developing coping mechanisms against trauma in their countries of exile or at destination points across regional borders. Some are forced into exploitative marital unions with older men as an accepted means of economic survival, while others turn to prostitution when rejected by their families. There is also some evidence that migrant women recruit fellow nationals into sex work as well as alleged cases of foreign nationals forcing their female relatives into prostitution following arrival in South Africa.

Contemporary sex trafficking is either 'foreign' (trans-border) or domestic (internal). The former characteristically involves young Thai women, women from Eastern European states, such as Romania or Bulgaria, and others from ex-Soviet states, such as Ukraine or Belarus, who are attracted to South Africa by the prospects of making money. These women may have a history of prostitution and be specifically imported into the Republic as 'tourists' or otherwise enter with fraudulent papers. Some of this involves illegal (or legal) entry via the main international airports. On the African continent, the majority of women who find themselves exploited in sex work come into the country across its land borders by various means of transport or even on foot. South Africa is an important transit point for girls and young women originally from Thailand and who are then re-exported to a range of countries such as Saudi Arabia, Belgium, Macau or Mauritius. In some cases, women are sent to regional countries for grooming and then sent to their eventual destination.

Debt bondage, where sex trafficking intersects with labour trafficking, is commonplace and some women sex workers have been lured into South Africa under false pretences, forced into sex work and then murdered. One incident that made headlines in 1998 involved Asian women whose dead bodies were found on a railway track by the SAPS. These Asian women were brought into the country under false pretences and were told they would be working in high-end restaurants where they could mingle with and marry rich men. When they arrived in South Africa, they became entangled in debt bondage and their passports were taken from them

Even though trans-frontier trafficking is the focus of most research into commercial sex work and modern slavery, the numbers in this category are small in comparison with the substantial numbers of young to middle-aged women forcibly prostituted within South Africa itself. This mainly involves trafficking along internal migration routes from poverty nodes, such as those in KwaZulu-Natal and the Eastern Cape, to medium-sized towns and cities including places like Welkom, Nelspruit, Rustenburg and the main metropolitan areas. Some of this trafficking happens in stages from initial movement to a town or small city, for example, Port Elizabeth, then onwards to urban areas such as Johannesburg or Cape Town. Wealthy Gauteng is often the destination of choice but there are also alternative routes such as between the Northern and Western Cape where traffickers run lucrative operations involving the entrapment of teenage girls from the constricted economies of the northern region.

The internal routes from the northern and eastern borders into Africa are especially opportune for traffickers operating on or near the frontiers. Some migrant women and men may simply be undocumented but subsequently, fall into the arms of trafficking syndicates when job opportunities fail to materialise in the urban markets.[13] Part of this particular group may be kidnapped en route to Johannesburg, Durban or Cape Town by taxi operators in league with traffickers.

Women forced into involuntary prostitution from these sources, supplement other sex workers who are already in the metropoles. Some are sold by traffickers to brothels while others work the streets supervised by pimps at the lower end of the market. Needless to say, the trafficked population often functions alongside professional sex workers who have come onto the scene based on their recognisances. Many of the latter nevertheless turn to traffickers for protection, including protection against the SAPS.

In normal circumstances, there is a continuum between freelance women walking the streets in anticipation of passing customers to brothels where women are held against their will in a fixed location. Both types of prostitution occur across South Africa in suburban, urban and rural areas as well as within or near concentrations of both legal and undocumented migrants. Some sex enterprises using trafficked women work openly, particularly when and where corrupt police have a stake in operations. Others are deeply underground makeshift ventures, especially in the larger towns and cities where buildings have been repurposed or converted into brothels. Many sex entrepreneurs constantly change location and find other means of operating their businesses to both disorientate their workers and escape police detection.[14]

The demographic profile of female victims is highly complex, as are other facets of commercial sexual exploitation. Most of the women working in short-term prostitution or a state of bondage are under the age of 25 and, in some cases as young as 11.[15] This is often driven by the absence of a responsible guardian when traffickers with fraudulent purposes are encountered. Some traffickers target this age bracket because clients believe very young women to be especially docile and compliant in catering to their sexual demands. At a time of the ongoing HIV epidemic, clients sometimes believe that relationships with very young women, particularly virgins, are disease free and can provide a cure for HIV and other sexually transmitted diseases (STDs), including, more recently, COVID-19.

While there is a marked preference of urban customers for 'exotic' Thai or Chinese women arriving in South Africa through one of our three major airports, trafficking often reinforces social distinctions. Wealthier clients are invariably attracted to the better class of women in well-furnished premises, while the lower end of the market involves quick sex in any number of indoor or outdoor locations. There is a relatively higher concentration of so-called 'coloured' sex workers in the Western Cape, but otherwise, women may come from any of South Africa's diverse population groups and provinces. Cross-racial transactions involving black women with men from other racial groups are becoming more frequent, but the converse is highly irregular as some brothels work on a 'whites only' basis.

Despite most studies focusing on the most deprived women in the population, sex workers as a group are not homogenous. The classic division between sex workers acquiring their clients on the streets or in some sort of residential premises is not immutable given that many sex workers procure cross-sector work. Economic inequalities inevitably force poorer women into survivalist sex, and more than twenty-five years after apartheid, street workers are still overwhelmingly black. Some of them are considerably older than the norm and trade on their experience in brothel work, while others cater to specialist tastes of buyers going beyond the 'normal'. There are also class differences and, perhaps most importantly, debates over the agency, a minority of sex workers exists who are high-end professionals working independently of traffickers on a voluntary and commercial basis. Many have the financial means necessary to practise customer selection while the digitalisation of the industry provides a measure of personal protection by creating distance between the service provider and client among sex workers with access to electronic methods of advertising and client recruitment.[16]

Albeit that personality may make the critical difference between vulnerability and victimisation, it is difficult to develop specific profiles of victims. Many trafficked sex workers appear to feel materially deprived, helpless, valueless, with low esteem, and a history of sexual and emotional abuse. Personal dislocation and displacement create added opportunities for perpetuation.

Perpetrators in the sex industry are sometimes 'lone wolves' but are often parts of multi-layered hierarchies with frontline workers at the foundation. Organised crime is increasingly involved in South African sex trafficking and in these instances, the line of predators can be transnational. There are complex cases where Asian women are recruited by organised criminal networks working through South African Asian-based agents who connect with Nigerian gangs on site in SA. In one of these cases, multiple payments were ultimately made from a reputable bank in Rotterdam.[17]

The perpetrators in human trafficking are also involved in alternative criminal activity in the form of fraud; narcotics trafficking; trade in rhino horn, tusks, abalone and wildlife, illicit diamond dealing; car theft and truck hijacking; arms dealing, or anything else that makes money. These perpetrators also trade in pornography to compromise their victims, as well as 'snuff' videos, which are sold through the underground internet. Some are rumoured to be ex-members of intelligence agencies such as the KGB or Mossad.[18]

Nigerian traffickers are said to sell body parts of murdered prostitutes and also engage in baby farming. South African perpetrators are often equated with Nigerian gangs working among highly concentrated populations, in wealthy suburbs of major cities, in medium-sized towns and even in rural areas. Albeit a caricature, some of the 'kingpins' of the commercial sex world are of Nigerian extraction. Nigerians also appear as agents for bigger international gangs, providing money and logistics for local operations. Otherwise, perpetrators at all levels stem from a variety of origins. This includes individual South Africans working as representatives for various global networks or living in up-market residential areas in the main cities. People of Lebanese or Pakistani extraction have been identified as some of the key role-players in trafficking activities in Gauteng and some of the other provinces.

Controllers and operators of the sex industry vary. Some sex businesses are family owned and others may be owned or backed by prominent local community members, including judges, politicians, businessmen and lawyers. Many brothels or sites of abuse are open to the public, but some screen buyers to ensure a modicum of protection for their workers. Some up-market brothels have exclusion policies and the majority are disinclined to allow sex with children.

Various information suggests that the entry points into sex work and prostitution involve previous participation in some aspect of the sex industry. Stripping, for example, and working in massage parlours converts into prostitution, which can then convert into trafficking. In reality, however, there are an infinite number of connection points between innocent victims and their victimisers. Recruitment might take the form of entirely innocent but vulnerable victims-in-making, entering and socialising in networks alongside perpetrators, who become a source of gifts, including cell phones and narcotics. These victimisations can then blossom into regular communication, victim dependence and ultimately exploitation.

Victims outside the sex industries can also fall prey to sex traffickers in the process of seeking employment or some sort of reinforcement against their feelings of anomy in the context of consumer culture. This can involve any number of gifts from erstwhile traffickers, from cellphones through cocaine to opioids, heroin and other heavy-duty narcotics. There are cases of girls apprehended on their way to school or running errands for their parents, chloroformed to stifle resistance and then taken in a subdued state to brothels. There are even cases where sex trafficking is the culmination of initial romantic attachments between perpetrator and victim.

Recruiters and pimps use various techniques to seduce victims and adjust according to particular circumstances. These include extensive 'grooming', involving promises of money, drugs and food, to marginalised young women who are destitute, drug-addicted, in debt, or otherwise open to high-risk sexual behaviour. Substance addiction assists the overtures of traffickers to both adolescent and adult women: this often involves a self-reinforcing spiral where addicts procure narcotics from traffickers, are trafficked and ultimately made dependent on their perpetrators for lines of supply.

In an age of mass communication, victims and buyers are messaged by print advertising, and increasingly the internet and social media. Electronic media are also important in disseminating the view that prostitution is an acceptable form of employment in a way which blurs the thin distinction between voluntary and involuntary sex work. Spaces for recruitment for trafficked sex workers are multifaceted and include dark suburban streets, escort services, peep and fantasy shows, massage and beauty parlours, casinos and gambling premises, bars, shebeens, restaurants, warehouses, health and after-hour clubs, saunas, private apartments, brothels of all types, including the many in informal settlements.

The sites to which victims are transported for exploitation are also dwellings used for quick prostitution, hotels, rented houses, migrant hostels, near-mine housing, military bases, so-called 'lolly-lounges' and even legitimate front businesses. Johannesburg's Park Station is well-known as a holding area for trafficking women coming into the metropole from nearby Soweto as well as other points more distant. Premises where 'business' takes place rank from luxurious in the case of trafficked women engaged in attracting wealthy clients, to shacks in former township areas. Some places are barracks where women are housed nightly before being transferred to their site of work during daytime hours. In many cases, brothels with trafficked women trade brazenly, either because their owners collude with the SAPS or because they have sophisticated security systems designed to quickly detect any undesirable intruders. In the cities, it is common to see police vehicles parked near brothels, while on the frontiers, the border police are highly manipulable in examining passports.[19] Much like other trafficking offences, it is extremely difficult to investigate sex trafficking cases even when the perpetrators are (infrequently) arrested.

There are instances where the SAPS have helped traffickers to recapture escaped women victims. Meanwhile, in brothels and other places where women are trafficked and sexually exploited, control is maintained, often brutally. Here again, there is a continuum between 'soft' and 'hard' measures, ranging from persuasion from psychological manipulation designed to distort belief systems, to the use of cocaine, cheap heroin or other mind-bending drugs. Brute force involving gang rape, torture with hot irons, tooth pulling, beatings with bars and other forms of gross violence are also used.

Compliance is also induced through blackmail, confiscating money and documentation, threats to families and children and other forms of debt bondage. In some establishments, sex workers are forced to pay fines from their 'earnings' if they spend too much time with a single client, for sick time and during times of menstruation. Victims are often allegedly shackled and kept in isolation, forced to witness the punishment of other victims or forced into making pornography which is then distributed on the internet. Nigerian and sometimes local women are also threatened with 'juju' preceded by the shaving of pubic hair.

Buyers, the proverbial 'johns', come from all age groups and socioeconomic classes with the majority of men being married. Prominent men in the political or business world are often consumers of services. Women employees are expected to comply with all requests, no matter how perverse, including the expectation of sex without condoms. There are many cases where men become physically or verbally abusive in the absence of compliance.

There are many studies (including a number in SA) in the medical and social science literature on the health consequences of women forced into prostitution. All indicate that trafficked women suffer severe health problems related to injuries caused by violence. Many women sustain injuries, such as broken bones, bruises, and mouth and teeth injuries which require health interventions that are inaccessible. Most women also contract sexually transmitted infections, including HIV and AIDS. Most fear pregnancy or otherwise suffer emotionally from their experiences. Ongoing depression, hopelessness and anxiety mixed with anger and rage are common among survivor women. Many have suicidal thoughts and have tried to hurt or kill themselves. The extensive role of narcotics in the sex industries aggravates these circumstances.

Although there is evidence of some women developing intimate relationships with the men who pimp them – the so-called 'Stockholm Syndrome' – pimping almost always degenerates into victim-battering or some form of emotional or physical coercion designed to break down resistance on the entrance to the prostitution business. Given that lack of exit is one of the characteristics of trafficking, most women in the sex industry are not free to do so. Some refuse 'rescue' by the police for a variety of complex reasons, including financial reasons in cases where women are voluntary sex workers. Other victims under-report the abuse to which they have been subjected, at least partially, because of the shame and loss of identity which is central to disempowerment and victimhood.

Moreover, despite severe victimisation, many women are not simply victims. Like many who have experienced extreme subjugation (e.g., those unfortunates who have survived genocidal events), they still find extreme ways to cope, while resisting exploitation and violence. The vast majority use drugs and alcohol after entry into sex work to numb themselves to the trauma of unwanted sex. More positively, many women try, some multiple times, to leave the sex industry, despite economic barriers, drug dependency, and pimps who beat them and/or threaten the lives of their children.

The legal regime against trafficking, PACOTIP, the SOA and the Criminal Law (Sexual Offences and Related Matters) Amendment Act (No. 32 of 2007) is ineffective in dealing with the human trade for sex standing alone. One of the key criticisms of the SOA, prior to PACOTIP, is that it cannot prosecute for trafficking as opposed to sexual exploitation. There is also the view that sex trafficking has been over-emphasised in counter-trafficking circles to the disadvantage of other of its expressions, especially labour trafficking. Having said this, PACOTIP needs to be consistently and rigorously enforced, even in cases where it comes up against the interests of organised crime. This is likely to be difficult because of the power exercised by transnational criminals, the high degree of collusion on the part of the SAPS with TIP of a sexual nature, and because of passive collusion where the authorities, both the police and the state bureaucracy, turn a blind eye. The SAPS must nonetheless receive the resources to investigate and prosecute trafficking kingpins – the people at the top.

The central and provincial governments should work more consistently with a variety of community-based groups to design and implement victim services and support networks in various regions of the country under the policy framework. There should be a joint effort of government, women's and community groups to act quickly on behalf of trafficking victims and to provide long-term assistance. More funding and more public finance are required for research, education, training and services for trafficking victims. Local government should also be assisted to implement municipal ordinances that, inter alia, clamp down on local sex venues.

More resources and services are needed for women in the sex industry, especially those who have been trafficked. For example, we need more effective witness protection programmes, healthcare systems, housing/ shelter initiatives, counselling and legal services, English-language education, job training and financial assistance. Laws against buying women must be strengthened. Specific legal measures recommended the publication of buyers' names in the newspapers, and more 'johns schools' where first-offender buyers are 'educated' about the harm of prostitution to the women, the neighbourhood and themselves.

Community involvement is essential to prevention and protection. Education and public awareness campaigns about trafficking require extension across civil society, especially among key role-players such as learners, teachers, unions and organisations in the private sector. Media and social service providers must be sensitive to the complexities of community participation in anti-trafficking campaigns, especially within immigrant communities.

Programmes to divert the survivors of sex trafficking into meaningful work need to be expanded beyond those currently in existence. These include tailor-made initiatives that provide training and funds to assist in the reduction of vulnerability in the various segmentations of the sex market. At the micro level, this includes training and funds to empower survivors to overcome some of the socioeconomic challenges that induce women to enter sex work.

Finally, re-empowerment programmes for survivors need to be drastically improved. In the first instance, this includes places of shelter for women who are interdicted either by the SAPS or the DSD (Department of Social Development) and who require legal, psychological, medical or emotional support. Conditions in some cases are notoriously bad. A later chapter covers these issues in more detail.

Given the enormous difficulties confronting the effective prosecution of sex trafficking cases, there needs to be a considerable change in the criminal justice system. Evidentiary standards need to change because the current prosecution of traffickers depends mainly on testimony from victim witnesses. Sentencing guidelines should reflect the seriousness of the crime. The criminal justice system must be made more immigrant-friendly through the greater use of culturally appropriate procedures.

Many social service providers reported that the current system hampers victims from coming forward who fear deportation. Trafficked women should not be treated as criminal illegal immigrants but as victims of violence and human rights abuses. Women in the process of emigration should be made aware of their civil and legal rights when in this country under the Constitution, the Bill of Rights, the Victims Charter and the PACOTIP.

Many women in the sex industry, but not all, do not recommend this form of work as a career. When asked if women enter the sex industry voluntarily, most believe that women who are trafficked and prostituted had few other options. In one recent study, many spoke about prostitution as a final option. Many others also believe that prostitution should be decriminalised in modern South Africa so that buyers and service providers acting consensually in a commercial relationship are not subject to prosecution. Other stakeholders, both within and outside the sex industry, are in favour of broader legalisation involving decriminalisation, the licensing of workers and brothels, periodic health tests and overall greater protection for workers from abusive, clients, not excluding the police.

All this is controversial, not only because the countries who have gone the decriminalisation route have not succeeded in improving the conditions for the key stakeholders, but also because moral and ethical issues inevitably intrude on these types of social choices. In this regard, the way forward in the management of sex trafficking invariably begins with the questions of whether or not voluntary prostitution should be accepted and then regulated on the statute books

At this point, the future of prostitution in relation to trafficking remains unclear. This is because the South African Human Rights Commission (SAHRC) is currently examining the possibility of replacing the SOA with legislation to decriminalise sex work in its various manifestation. Public consultation was scheduled for late 2021 but it is already clear that use will be made of one or another of the various models that have been developed to 'normalise' sex work in several other countries. With adjustments being made for indigenous conditions this means that the future will possibly involve either the total or partial abolition of current present legal constraints. This would allow sex workers to compete in an open market much as other workers' laws allow. In all likelihood, it would lead to a situation where the sale of sexual services is legalised but where most other aspects of sex work more broadly remain under legal control.

Based on international experience this would involve the establishment of a system of regulation and licensing where brothels and sex workers are brought within a regulatory regime but where much else in the commercial sex industries remains much the same. This is the kernel of two options already on the table before Commission as of June this 2022.

Portended changes are driven by several factors. As it stands there is an inconsistency between the law and the reality of prostitution and other forms of sex work. Despite the statute books, hardly anyone has been arrested and then subsequently convicted for prostitution in recent years unless there are aggravated circumstances, such as the presence of child prostitution, or serious cases where prostitution coincides with large-scale narcotics trafficking. Given that law enforcement is structurally under-capacitated, at least partially, because policing is saturated with rape cases and gender violence, this is unlikely to change in the foreseeable future.

In current circumstances, sexual offences legislation is almost entirely irrelevant to prostitutes working in the relatively advantaged upper sections of the market, as well as their lower-end counterparts engaged in street work in dangerous and insalubrious conditions. In South Africa, as elsewhere, the latter have limited if any access to health and safety benefits afforded other workers through legislation. This has negative impacts on public health in a country with high levels of tuberculosis, HIV and AIDS, other sexually transmitted diseases and Covid.

Police-driven harassment and gender-based violence are also characteristic of the current prostitution landscape, especially in the case of undocumented migrant women engaging in high-risk survivalist sex work in the streets or, to a lesser extent, in various types of residential brothels. This is partially because of the intrinsic brutality in police ranks, and partially because the prosecution of sex workers depends mainly on 'sting' operations requiring an informer network. Either way, there are countless reports of police harassment and sexual assault from advocates of decriminalisation, organisations assisting sex workers as well as sex workers themselves.

Although sex work is still highly stigmatised in many circles, the moral climate has substantially changed with the advent of democracy and the reduced isolation of South Africa from global norms and practices. In many respects, the SOA is redolent of apartheid, however, South Africa now adheres to various international conventions that reflect the role of its own Constitution and Bill of Rights in the protection of women and children. The overall trend towards the modernisation of sex work within the wider context of sexual relations is also mirrored in various institutional developments within the country itself. These include heightened advocacy in favour of decriminalising women in labour in a network of organisations centred on SWEAT, the South African union on sex workers, as well as an ongoing string of reports, reviews and commissions ultimately converging in the recommendations of the SALRC. Since the end of apartheid, the network of concerned organisations includes the Human Rights Commission, the Commission for Gender Equality, the ANC Women's League and SWEAT (the Sex Education Task Force).[20]

Having said this, the narratives over sex work and decriminalisation in the South African context are multi-layered, complex and in some respects, incomplete.[21] While we have at our disposal a variety of global precedents and experiences on which to draw – from the Netherlands, Germany, Canada and parts of America and Australia-Asia – these are not necessarily directly transplantable into the dissimilar conditions of modern South Africa in where sex work is driven less by law than by poverty and gender violence. Apart from one or two notable exceptions, conversations in the Republic are also conducted within a statistical vacuum which becomes progressively empty in movement from such relatively understood phenomenon as prostitution into the more exotic expressions of sex work in general. Relative to the more industrialised countries that have experimented with various types of decriminalisation after the mining of extensive data banks with social information, we still actually know very little about the potential impact of decriminalisation on such key stakeholders as gays, male prostitutes and sex workers in far-rural areas.

In general, the jury is still out on the issue of whether non-implementation of the law, partial decriminalisation or some system of registration will best work to substantively improve the lives of sex workers and reduce trafficking incidence. Each approach has inherent risks. Regulation, for example, does not necessarily preclude a proportion of prostitutes from continuing to work outside the law because of the stigma attached to prostitution, licensed or otherwise. As the Netherlands case suggests, this means being subjected to the same battery of disadvantages, prejudice, and risk of TIP prior to decriminalisation. As the global experience of registration also indicates, it cannot be automatically assumed that brothel owners or even their workers will necessarily comply with the law in all its financial and public health implications, even if the SAPS were to have the interest and capacity to enforce a new system for legalised prostitution. Anything short of total legalisation is also unlikely to address police harassment of sex workers because there will still be a law to enforce, especially against outdoor workers.

Following the decision of the Netherlands to decriminalise sex work in 2001, most global commentators on legalisation agree that it must address both supply and demand. This refers to the number of workers coming into the 'erotic industries' as well as penalising the buyers of sexual services.[22] Yet the link between demand and supply is still unclear and highly variable despite decades of analysis and the experiences of numerous states going down the road to decriminalisation in the emulation of the Dutch model. Some Nordic models suggest that decriminalisation can best reduce the incidence of sex trafficking only when the consumers of sexual services are prosecuted. Some theories see the key factor to be obedience to laws in the political culture, while the third point of view believes that decriminalisation makes no difference to the rate of sex trafficking and that prostitution is driven by poverty and gender violence. In these cases, trafficking is so lucrative and it is probable that perpetrators will continue to traffic sex workers irrespective of what the law might say.

In the last analysis, it seems that decriminalisation only reduces sex trafficking when the government is effective and where law enforcement is accountable.[23] This requires a supportive culture where there is public acceptance, understanding and sympathy towards the polymorphous nature of prostitution. This infers that some immeasurable proportion of the general population does not believe that all sex workers are trafficked and that prostitution is inherently immoral.

In the last analysis, there is no empirical evidence on how South Africans view the legalisation of sex work as opposed to maintenance of the present system. Most, it seems, adhere to the conservative or 'oppressionist' paradigm where women in prostitution are seen as acting involuntarily as victims of trafficking experience.[24] Alternatively, sex work can be seen as vocational, leaving women (and men) an element of choice or agency. There is also little consensus on these points and even less on whether (or not) decriminalisation will work in the interests of sex workers, of law enforcement or the moral tone of the nation. Movement towards decriminalisation was nevertheless well under way during mid-2022. Parliament is expected to conduct vigorous debates on these issues in the early part of 2023.

CHAPTER 3

Child trafficking

There is unanimity among criminologists, trafficking practitioners, governments and even some perpetrators that child trafficking is the most heinous form of modern slavery, largely because trafficked children can be used on a multipurpose basis. This means a child who is initially trafficked for sexual purposes can become a source of forced labour. Alternatively, a child originally trafficked for forced labour can be induced into performing criminal activities or can be redesignated as a sex worker.

The possibility that children under eighteen may be among the most at-risk groups has, in turn, spawned an unprecedented raft of global conventions, protocols, memoranda, joint actions, recommendations and declarations whose common purpose is to define child trafficking, develop the means to act against its practice, and to accord as much, if not more, human rights to children under international law as those guaranteed by to adults. These instruments include the Universal Declaration of Human Rights; the CRC Optional Protocol on the Sale of Children, Child Prostitution and Child Pornography; the 1989 UN Convention on the Rights of the Child; and the Protocol to Suppress and Punish Trafficking in Persons, Especially Women and Children attached to the United Nations Convention against Transnational Organised crime. Article 3(a) of this protocol defines child trafficking as the 'recruitment, transportation, transfer, harbouring and/or receipt' of a child for exploitation, while

Articles 19 and 32-36 of the over-arching Convention prohibits the exploitation of children in any form and any context. By global standards, any child who is exposed to violence, exploitation or abuse can be considered a victim of crime and enjoys various entitlements including access to assistance, protection and support, services for recovery and rehabilitation as well as access to justice.

Child trafficking is documented in every region of the world and ostensibly involves millions of victims per annum. In South Africa, where the protective regime includes the provisions of international treaties to which South Africa adheres, such as the International Declaration on Human Rights, South Africa's own Constitution and Bill of Rights, the wide-ranging Children's Act of 1957 as well as the 2013 PACOTIP legislation where, in line with international practice, children are granted extra protection and regarded as an exception in law when it comes to proving the guilt of traffickers.[1] Child trafficking ranks second after adult sex trafficking as a focal point in the South African trafficking literature. Yet, across the globe, in the southern African region and in South Africa itself, the number of trafficked children is unknown and has been disputed over the years with conclusions ranging from very few victims to very many.[2]

This dispute regarding the number of children has to do with the fact that few countries publish national estimates. However, it is mainly due to the covert and criminal nature of this practice, the relative inarticulateness of the victims and the emotion attached to trading in babies, pre-adolescents and teenagers. Low levels of public reporting as well as poorly maintained police records on the harm done to children further aggravate a situation where it is frequently difficult to identify victims. This in turn reflects many children whose births go unregistered or are otherwise 'on-the-move' and who are hard to track. These mobile populations include transnational stateless children, unaccompanied minors coming across the borders in search of their undocumented parents, and children circulating internally for many reasons from family dysfunction to personality disorders. With an eye to its market, the mass media also sensationalises cases of child trafficking and this adds to the general disorder.

In the absence of reliable quantitative data aggregated according to age and gender, it is virtually impossible to track the various forms of sexual exploitation to which our children are exposed and to develop policy responses. Analysts agree that there is a need to substantiate child trafficking on an empirical basis. Analysts also agree that the estimated 19,7 million children in South Africa are faced with several acute social disabilities that render them highly susceptible to violence, trafficking and exploitation. Some 56% of this population lives beneath the national poverty threshold. Child mortality rates in South Africa are higher than in most countries, while South African children are exposed to sexual, physical and emotional assault in huge numbers. According to the 2016 report, many children report neglect and having witnessed violence. All this underwrites high levels of drug and narcotics use among people under eighteen, a very significant proportion of whom become runaways from familial breakdown or are abducted by family and non-family members on the migration routes running between the rural and urban areas. Many children have vanished and are listed as simply 'missing'.[3] It would be surprising if children were not trafficked in these circumstances.

This is the gist of a fairly large literature dating back to the two watershed Molo Songololo studies at the turn of the millennium. These studies, for example, suggest both boys and girls as young as four being trafficked for sexual purposes and then go on to identify how this takes place in multiple ways. The HSRC study almost a decade later is deeply rooted in the notion that child trafficking is intrinsic to the view that South imports, exports and transit trafficking victims. Child trafficking is further confirmed in two studies of South Africa by ECPAT (a network of civil society organisations that works to end the sexual exploitation of children)., two further studies conducted by the IOM, and in many academic studies at the post-doctoral level. Child sex exploitation also figures persistently in the annual United States State Department Reports on the state of trafficking in South Africa.[4]

In general, child trafficking takes place in three stages that mirror the TIP process in general: Firstly, recruitment occurs when a recruiter approaches a child, or in some cases, a child directly approaches a recruiter. Recruitment is initiated in many different ways: adolescents may be under pressure to contribute to their families, children may be kidnapped or abducted into trafficking, or families may be trafficked together. Then, movement will occur – locally, regionally, and/or internationally – through a variety of transportation types, including by car, train, boat, or foot. Ultimately, the final goal of child trafficking is exploitation, whereby traffickers use the services of children to garner illegal profit.

Much the same as adult sex work, child trafficking for sexual purposes is driven by poverty, as well as so-called 'poverty-plus' factors, identified by the United Nations Children's Fund (UNICEF) and the World Bank, where poverty does not in itself lead to a child being trafficked but where a 'plus', such as family illness, conflict or the appearance of perpetrators, combines with poverty to increase vulnerability. Additional factors in this category include family dysfunctions of various types, for example, experiences of neglect, abuse or violence within the family; the experience of violence in other institutional settings, such as foster homes; exploitative relationships; gender-based violence and discrimination; experiences of living or working on the streets; precarious and irregular migration situations; aspirations to work and to earn money; and limited opportunities to enter or remain in school or vocational training. Despite 'free' education for the poorest 60% of students for whom government waives tuition fees, many families are unable to support their offspring in school because of the costs of uniforms and other school-related expenses. The displacement of children at an early age into the market is also assisted by South African schools' legislation that allows school governing bodies to collect school fees if they deem so in any given year.

There are estimated to be around 120 million homeless children in the world, 30 million of whom are in Africa where they pose easy targets. An estimated 2,2 million of South Africa's children fall into this category due to HIV and AIDS, the migration of parents desperate for work, and various factors separating children from their mothers and fathers on a semi-permanent if not life-long basis.

Rural poverty is an especially important driver of child trafficking in South Africa and worldwide. This is not only because trafficking gangs scout these economically marginal areas from which most internal migration emanates but also because children, especially but not entirely young girls, face deadening life prospects in these areas. Girls, in particular, are susceptible to psychological manipulation and often submit easily to perpetrators whose overtures are peppered with the prospects of a fruitful life in the city. Many of these potential 'models' end up in urban brothels. Parents are often unable to provide for their families and consequentially exploit their children for financial reasons. These influencers lead to children being more inclined to take riskier jobs to sustain life for themselves and their families. In some cases, parental decisions that expose their children to traffickers are activated by the belief that migration to an urban setting will provide the education that will allow their children to escape their abject circumstances.

About an eighth of all migrants worldwide are youths in the 15–24 age group. However, not all young people moving to the cities do so involuntarily. In South Africa as elsewhere, this is an upwardly mobile group seeking education and employment in the urban areas. A large proportion are trans-frontier migrants and have difficulty accessing travel documents. These migrants also make use of contacts who may or may not be in the business of human smuggling. Either way, they run the danger that their 'guides' will hand them to traffickers either en route to or in the cities. As undocumented persons, these young people encounter exploitation from all manner of people who offer jobs, housing and employment. This includes the often-corrupt police who feed off the fears of deportation facing the undocumented.

Many children engage in high-risk behaviours. Largely due to limitations on cognitive development, children are overall less discerning than adults when confronted with the false promises, fraud and seduction used by traffickers to ensnare their victims. Authority figures, such as teachers, often play a facilitative role in the entry of children into the trafficking world. Children are much more easily socialised into a trafficking culture after recruitment and sometimes act as agents for others. Girls as young as twelve are extremely malleable and easily trained as prospective prostitutes. These young girls can command a premium because virginity is highly prized by certain consumers.

The sexual exploitation, of children, deemed CSE, is unsurprisingly widespread. In a survey of approximately 5 000 teenage children in 2016,

35,4% of school students reported being exposed to some form of sexual abuse, including girls at 14 years old and boys a bit later at 15. Given the widespread cellphone usage in SA, the susceptibility of children to grooming by perpetrators through social media and the internet is possibly equivalent to most other countries. Child sex workers in South Africa make up a portion of the 1,8 million children conservatively estimated by the ILO as being steered into sexual exploitation by traffickers worldwide. Typically, this goes beyond providing sexual services to 'clients' (child prostitution) to include a parallel involvement in the manufacture, production and distribution of child pornography, participation in sex tourism or performance in public or private sex shows.

In southern Africa, there are a growing number of children who move unaccompanied across frontiers to improve their life chances or to locate a sibling or parent who has already completed a transborder crossing. Some are not directly entrapped by traffickers but by human smugglers who hand them over to traffickers before, during or after a frontier crossing.[5] Criminal syndicates working across borders are suspected of being involved in many of these transactions which are frequently overlooked by law enforcement officials on or within South Africa's borders.

Children of either gender involved in sex work may be remunerated in cash, or more commonly, denied their earnings as part of the process of disempowerment. Child participation in the sex industries can take place in the streets or indoors, in such places as brothels, discotheques, massage parlours, bars, hotels and restaurants. From the existing data, it appears there may be several dozen brothels in Johannesburg alone with 5 000 girls, some as young as thirteen, being victims of sexual exploitation in one form or another with the intention to groom them for prostitution. The families of the victims are frequently threatened to maintain the girls in sex work.

Before the Covid epidemic, all the major cities were centres for international sex tourism involving girls between 10 and 14 in a manner that confirms some of the findings of the HSCR study a decade later. Children are used in the manufacture of pornography and there is some evidence suggesting that under-18s are used involuntarily for forms of sexual performance. Drug dependency and debt bondage are frequently used to maintain young people in prostitution in a network of clubs and dilapidated buildings in the inner city areas. Hillbrow in Johannesburg contains a significant population of child sex workers many of whom are smuggled in for involuntary prostitution from as far afield as Mozambique. In Cape Town, underage girls have been servicing the needs of passing sailors for at least the last twenty years, if not longer.[6]

The local network is supplemented by regional trafficking of child prostitutes; some coming from Mozambique are inveigled into sex work as 'waitresses'. Children as young as eight years old function as prostitutes working for money or food at truck stops dotting the subcontinent. There are cases where trafficking rings in the Northern Cape have recruited young girls who are then sold into sex slavery in Gauteng. There is also the typical case where a Nigerian gang promised work to a young rural girl who was then forced to take drugs and then sell sex on the streets of Cape Town.

There is evidence of Malawian girls being held as sex slaves in Johannesburg's flatland, as well as of street children abducted in Lesotho and then transported across the Free State border to work at the narrow interface between sex and labour exploitation on nearby farms.[7] This takes place with the connivance of border police on both sides of the Lesotho-South African border. There are also young girls trafficked into near-mine communities or sometimes into mine housing right across the industry but especially along the platinum belt in North-West Province. There are also numerous spine-chilling cases of sex trafficking that have appeared in the criminal justice system in recent years. Many of these crimes are associated with Nigerian gangs operating in South Africa. In the wake of PACOTIP very severe sentences have been imposed in most if not all cases.

It is an especially malignant component of South Africa's labour landscape that an estimated 577 000 children between the ages of seven and seventeen are also trafficked as cheap labour, including what would be classified as 'the worst forms of child labour' as described in global conventions. Some 81 000 children in this category are involved in work that violates South Africa's Basic Conditions of Employment Act and a further 349 000 are involved in work inappropriate for their age. This means work that deprives children of their potential and dignity, is mentally, physically socially or morally harmful, deprives children of education by obliging them to leave school prematurely, or requires them to combine school attendance with excessive periods of work.

Child labour possibly involves as many as 200 million child labourers across the globe with Africa being pre-eminent among other regions. One-in-five African children are estimated to be used as exploited labour. In South Africa, this involves an estimated 577 000 children, some as young as seven, toiling in circumstances that conform with the 'worst' forms of child labour as defined in Article 32 of the International Labour Organisation Convention on the Rights of the Child, the United Nations Convention on the Protection of the Rights of All Migrant Workers and Members of Their Families, 1990, the ILO Minimum Age Convention (1973) and the ILO Worst Forms of Child Labour Convention, 1999[12].

South Africa is an adherent to most international child's rights instruments. Several domestic instruments are also pertinent to protecting the rights of this third of the overall population. These include the Basic Conditions of Employment Act (No. 75 of 1997) (BCEA), which lays down the minimum age of work as 15 and the minimum age for hazardous work as 18. Article 13 of the Constitution also prohibits forced labour of anyone while Article 141 of the Children's Act (No. 38 of 2005) prohibits child trafficking and the use of children in illicit activities. There are also dedicated child labour instruments such as the dedicated child labour laws such as the Child Labour Programme of Action (which provides Child Support Grants in the form of monthly direct cash transfers to primary caregivers who have vulnerable children), and, more recently, the Child's Protection Act which prohibits persons convicted of child trafficking from working with children.

The government has also established institutional mechanisms for the enforcement of laws and regulations on child labour.[8] These include the South African Department of Labour (DOL), which enforces child labour laws, conducts inspections, refers victims to social workers and reports law violations to the SAPS for prosecution. The DOL also convenes the Provincial Child Labour Intersectoral Committee and coordinates child labour programmes The SAPS is responsible for enforcing the Children's

Act through the investigation of instances of the worst forms of child labour while the Department of Justice and Constitutional Development (DJCD), through its Children's Court, focuses on litigation involving children accused of or victimised by crimes, and cases involving child abuse, abandonment, and neglect The DSD provides child protection and social services to vulnerable children, including victims of human trafficking and manages shelters for children living and working on the streets. Children are protected under the general auspices of the policy framework against human trafficking while there are several important programmes specific to child labour.

Powerful drivers of child labour are similar to those driving CSE and, in many cases, child sex and labour trafficking go hand-in-hand. Child labour and trafficking are necessarily cumulative across generations so under-educated children give rise to more vulnerable child labour. Exposure to exploitative labour also rises with age so sixteen and seventeen-year-olds are the populations most at risk to the fraudulent.

While the proportion of children working as cheap labour in manufacturing is possibly not as pronounced as in some other countries of the world, sub-adults in South Africa appear in several guises. These include vulnerable and homeless children trafficked into 'piece' jobs as well as displaced young girls doing casual or domestic work, which often functions as high-risk entry points for commercial sex trafficking. Children are trafficked from poor rural areas or peripheral townships to urban centres, such as Cape Town, Durban and Johannesburg. Boys are forced to work in street vending and food service operations. Many are non-resident or refugee children denied access to education for failure to present identity documents such as birth certificates. Disabled children and orphans are especially vulnerable to trafficking as cheap labour.

As is the case in most other sub-Saharan countries, the early entry of children into labour and violations of children's rights are especially pronounced in the agricultural sector where children as young as five or six work under parental pressure as farm labour for exceptionally low wages or no wages at all. A comparative study between domestic child labour rates in urban and rural regions in sub-Saharan Africa reveals that 84,3% of child labourers work in the rural sector. Most (99,8%) of these children aged five to fourteen are engaged in child labour for some form of economic activity in these regions. Much of this is enshrined in traditional norms and values assigning children at an early age to become the proverbial 'hewers of wood and drawers of water'. South African children also labour in the agricultural sector where they are denied both food and shelter.

Most infringements of children's rights occur outside the towns and cities. Yet, young and vulnerable children are also found in the informal sectors of urban economies where they work in Dickensian conditions in small-scale businesses and light industries. Children are also known to be employed by illegal mining try. Children are also valuable because of their ability to complete jobs due to their size that adults cannot. This underwrites children working in illegal mining, either in artisanal mining or in navigating narrow underground passages. operations that have no apparent safety standards.

Violation of the labour laws governing children is widespread if occasionally punctuated by joint operations by the authorities. In November 2019 one such operation involving SADOL's Inspection and Enforcement Services branch in Gauteng and the South African Police Service (SAPS) arrested seven Chinese nationals after an anonymous tip that they were trafficking illegal immigrants for labour from Malawi (37 children). But at any one time, there are no more than 100 child labour cases before the courts, most involving trafficking from the region. The situation is so problematic that a 2019 report by the United States Department of Labour concluded that South Africa was making 'minimal advancement' to eliminate existing cases of worst labour.[9] Even while the government is making efforts to collect data and asserts that child labour is decreasing, both the scope and reach of social programmes are insufficient to address the problem, especially in agricultural and domestic sectors

Adequate enforcement of the child labour laws by the DOL profits from newly produced manuals to deal with counter-trafficking in general but officials lack the training to allow them to detect and act upon transgressions of the law. Labour inspectors are not authorised to assess penalties, and social programmes are not sufficient to address the scope of child labour. The number of labour inspectors is likely insufficient for the size of South Africa's workforce, which includes more than 22 million workers. Sources indicate that the inspectorate has limited resources to carry out its mandates. Although substantial amounts have been invested in improving the capacity of labour inspectors since 2019, the DOL acknowledges that this is still insufficient to skill specialised inspectors in specific sectors of the economy, for example, agriculture, mining, and industry. As a result, labour inspectors are undertrained to identify the perpetrators and victims of child labour trafficking with any reasonable degree of accuracy. Some labour inspectors encounter difficulties in accessing farms due to concerns for their safety or fear of entering private property.

Child sex tourism (CST) is a specific form of CSE (child sex exploitation), and South Africa is 'not immune from this disturbing phenomenon'.[10] Before Covid, South Africa was one of the 'well-established' and biggest African destinations for the burgeoning worldwide tourists-for-sex industry. This usually involves men from the world's richer countries travelling to developing societies to engage in sexual activity with vulnerable young women, adolescents and children. Often linked to global child pornography networks, these activities are a severe violation of children's rights and transgress both international and domestic instruments emplaced for child protection. Activities of this nature generally occur in African countries where mechanisms to protect children from CSE are ineffective, law enforcement is weak, there is structural corruption in the police and communities, and there are levels of vulnerability amongst children. Child sex tourism depends upon the existence of a tourist infrastructure that is relatively easily accessible from other parts of the world. It also relies on poor systems for immigration control, and what one commentator has deemed the existence of 'low-risk' places where 'activities go unnoticed' and 'motives unsuspected.

We do not know the extent of this mainly unexplored facet of child trafficking where tourism, essentially between developed and developing countries, is used as a mechanism for gaining access to children. Many sex tourists are paedophiles whose interaction with male or female children is super-clandestine and, from a policing or academic perspective, difficult to track in the face of the rising numbers of African tourists. While CST can be either domestic or international, the latter is especially difficult to research for prevalence because of the high level of transnational mobility spawned by mass consumerism and globalisation and the increased porousness of both official and non-official points between states. This is especially salient for South Africa with its long landward and maritime boundaries as well as its weak system for immigration control, which at times fails to discriminate between genuine tourists and those with a record of previous crimes against children in some other country.

There are numerous hotspots for CST in South Africa where 'disparities of wealth' bring together wealthy people from the north with poor children from the south. These places of 'silence and seclusion' include the Eastern and Western Cape, Gauteng, and Mpumalanga. Yet, it is difficult to take effective action against tourists who move from one location to another with a view to sexual encounters with children, especially in countries where, like South Africa, tourism is a major component of foreign investment, job creation, and economic development. Many of the problems that have arisen in addressing CST in South Africa reflect wider issues negatively impacting child protection such as the management of data, the capacity of the SAPS to deal with CSE cases and various problems around the Child Protection Register. Arrests for CST are rare, follow non-disclosure, and the perpetrators are almost always treated lightly by the law. Few people have stood accused of child rape, indecent assault or trafficking. The overwhelming majority of apprehended sex tourists are simply allowed to leave the country and return to their home base to commit similar offences

There is no shared understanding of CST and the legal situation governing sexual acts between foreigners and local children is complex and unclear. There are also perennial problems of translating international law into domestic norms. While South Africa has extradition treaties with many countries, many suspected sex tourists are not returned to face justice in their origin countries unless they have a record of child molestation or related crimes. It is also uncertain whether tourists on paedophile registers in their home countries may be excluded from entry into the Republic.

The mechanics of CST are similar to CSE in the form of children being seduced by lavish gifts, money or false promises to engage in offences which are then unreported. Members of the tourism industry are frequently involved in CST either directly or indirectly. These include taxi drivers, hotel staff or shuttle services with specialist knowledge as to where children can be procured for a nominal fee. In some cases, members of adult prostitution networks act as points of referral in identifying victims. Countering CST as a form of perverted recreation also requires the involvement of the tourism industry in public-private-sector partnerships that balance child rights with protecting the income derived from tourism in the national economy. Yet, leaders of the industry, typically fear negative repercussions that disclosures on sexual encounters between tourists and children might have on tourism development. This is especially true as we return to a post-Covid world of fluid travel. Some efforts have been made to control the entry and exit of foreigners travelling with children. Despite this, there is no accredited list of tourist companies, least of all any system to monitor performance, to domestically prohibit child trafficking.

Illegal adoption, sometimes termed 'child laundering', also occurs in South Africa, both within its borders and on an inter-country basis. Some of the country's 'missing' children to whom we have previously referred are possibly sold to bogus parents in violation of the Children's Act of 2005 which defines such activity as a distinct form of trafficking.[11]

Once again, as with other forms of child trafficking, we lack exact statistics as opposed to anecdotal evidence gathered by social workers and practitioners in the child protection system. Illegal adoption is invariably a clandestine crime. It is generally unreported and is difficult to verify after a transaction takes place. Nonetheless, South Africa has all the features of an 'enabling environment' which directly or indirectly encourages the sale of children for adoption in an underground market. These include structural factors such as large-scale child or baby abandonment driven by poverty; illiteracy and other social disabilities that discourage birth registration; complexity in the adoption process, which leads otherwise lawful people to turn to illicit adoption; a culture of judgementalism, which makes it difficult to place children with special needs, older children and as well as the offspring of rape survivors; and a poorly regulated adoption sector that mirrors wider deficiencies in the child protection systems.

Certain population groups are also excluded from the legal adoption regime. This includes undocumented migrants who face deportation should they attempt to adopt a child, children absorbed into communities by 'informal adoption' legitimated by traditional values but outside the child protection system, as well as mothers under the age of 18.) There are also too few adoption professionals and organisations to service adoption demands in far rural areas, and far too many institutionalised children who characteristically provide a recruitment ground for potential traffickers.

Legal or irregular adoptions are inherently open to abuse because they involve changing a child's identity. There are multiple opportunities for unscrupulous people to induce, exploit, sell and traffick children along the chain between a child and his or her ostensible 'parents' who may (or may not) be involved in child trafficking. Since the opportunities and risks rise inversely in relation to age, the adoption of infants, toddlers and babies who are vulnerable is especially pernicious. Adopted children in South Africa are, therefore, protected in various ways by a regime including a Register of Children and Parents, which is a key 'matchmaking'. The DSD is also empowered to accredit the over 150 adoption organisations and approximately five dozen social workers in private practice and to monitor adoption processes while making available state facilities for stray or abandoned children.

Relative to the domestic front, there are few inter-country adoptions from South Africa to the wider world and we have very limited knowledge about how many fit into the illegal realm. Despite the lack of research on transracial adoption in the internal arena, anecdotal evidence shows us that illegal adoption covers a wide range of possibilities. Much like human trafficking itself, these range from abduction with violence to more subtle means of persuasion by which children are 'laundered' from their natural parents. In many cases, intermediaries on the parent or adoptee sides are an important element of the dynamic, which frequently includes social workers as well as officials whose input is essential to doctoring various papers required in the procurement process.

Abducted children are an especially malignant aspect of illegal adoption but the motives behind these venal acts are often both mixed and, in some cases, obscure. According to professional social workers, there are outright revenge acts where a couple or one member of a couple simply steal a child, in some cases because of physical or mental disability on the part of their offspring. The SAPS seldom prosecutes, least of all investigates, these acts because of their frequency, the problems of negotiating parental responsibilities and because many otherwise stalwart police personnel have a caseload which includes relatively more serious acts such as murder, rape or gender violence.

Fraud as a facet of the illegal adoption environment takes many forms and again frequently involves complicity by intermediaries between the natural parent and the adoptee. In some cases, women who are unwilling or unable to take care of their offspring are assisted by family members to identify substitute parents. Transactions of this type can involve philanthropic motives or an exchange of money or gifts between the families of the 'new' and 'old' parents. Empathic social workers may assist these exchanges, often with the help of some sort of legal person who provides 'authentic' papers. Birth certificates can often be obtained from corrupt officials in government departments such as the DHA.

There are numerous unregistered cases of babies disappearing from clinics shortly after birth, especially in rural areas. In some cases, family members are reluctant to avoid the sometimes complex issues of birth registration and have adopted these children. However, in other more lethal cases babies are reported as officially dead and then appear on the public adoption registers. New parents can sometimes use devious means to have babies listed as 'abandoned' and there are outright cases of 'baby farming' where expectant mothers are leased out to erstwhile parents who may or may not have official evidence to support procurement.

'Available' children are sometimes extracted from reluctant natural parents through false promises that the child will be allowed to maintain links with its natural parents or will be returned on reaching adulthood. The identification of vulnerable mothers including the unwed, the poor or ethnically marginalised, is sometimes done in good faith by maternity workers, clinics, hospitals or in adoption agencies where mothers are lodged until birth. This is sometimes accompanied by false information about the costs or life chances of a child born to disadvantaged parents following 'prospecting'. This refers to parents visiting marginalised communities and suggesting that families surrender their offspring to better-placed parents. In many cases it appears that this goes in tandem with various techniques for bypassing the matching system, for example, making payments to place a child higher on the list for adoption held by clinics or adoption agencies. In these cases, the connivance of officials is necessary.

Given the narrow division between many of these transactions and outright child trafficking, the government has attempted some degree of regulation. Most recently this has involved three proposed amendments to the Children's Act aimed at. concentrating all adoptions in the DSD foster-care system. Most contentiously, these amendments make it illegal for anyone to 'give or receive, or agree to give or receive, any consideration, in cash or kind, for the adoption of a child,'. This will, according to its critics in the adoption community, terminate legal adoption at a time of rising baby abandonments.

Social workers are currently being trained to expand the DSD's capacity to meet its new responsibilities. However, an effective adoption system serving the interests of society, children and prospective parents as well as inhibiting child trafficking is unlikely in the immediate future for several reasons.

The anticipated hegemony of the DSD will slow down the rate of adoption to the advantage of the underground market. This is because already scarce adoption professionals – psychologists, social workers and attorneys – charging legitimate fees to cover the technical complexities of adoption will be forced out of practice by the constraint on financial restrictions. Accredited Child Protection Officers dependent on often irregular DSD subsidies are likely to be hardest hit. Some are likely to close and this will widen the space for the illegal sector. Increased workload on the DSD implied in the new framework will inevitably slow the pace of legal adoptions and some adoptees currently working within the law may turn to alternative channels. The quality of adoption screening will in all likelihood decrease given that newly trained social workers under the auspices of the DSD will be inexperienced relative to their counterparts in civil society. The bureaucratisation of adoption will also negatively impact inter-country adoptions by the roughly a dozen accredited organisations under the SACA (South African Central Authority) because they inevitably involve financial transactions of one sort or another. The new policies for the DSD also violate the so-called 'subsidiary principle' enshrined in the Hague Convention; they will lead to more children being institutionalised (environment-friendly location enticing for traffickers).[12]

Irrespective of changes in the adoption process, the cost of official adoption is already prohibitively expensive for the majority of South Africans. This is despite financial support in the form of DSD subsidies to child protection organisations and periodic but non-mandatory adjustments of fees charged to individuals by social workers. The estimated R12 000 to R15 000 required per adoption domestically is well beyond the means of the poor who also have to consider the costs of raising a child after adoption. Many people, especially at the lower end of the economic ladder are threatened by fly-by-night adoption agencies, (or even rogue elements in the DCPOs) using a mix of coercion and persuasion to surrender their children. This sometimes involves the financial exchange against which the DSD now claims to be acting or false promises of a better life for their offspring. Non-disclosure of these transactions is often preferred by parents under financial stress or otherwise enforced by, among others, influential and powerful Nigerian gangs working as 'baby mafias' alongside sex trafficking and the international trade in small arms and narcotics. Some children in the market are simply stolen, abducted or found by traffickers combing the streets of the urban areas looking for a profitable course of income.

Child desertion is a crime under South African law. Yet the pandemic has escalated the supply of displaced babies, toddlers and very young children, thus reducing their price for child traffickers intent on exploiting market opportunities. There are also high levels of structural corruption among officials in state departments. An example of this may be found among officials in the DHA who falsify documents such as birth certificates that obscure the origins of children or their parents in return for under-the-counter payments.

While the dividing line between fostering and adoption is often unclear, fostering, the impermanent equivalent of adoption, can also be an entry point for the violation of child rights, up to and including trafficking.[13] This has two manifestations. The first of which is children institutionalised in the state protective system. Both here and abroad many are characteristically vulnerable to violence by poorly trained staff or staff with linkages to outside trafficking networks. As a generalisation, South African orphanages and foster homes, many operated under the auspices of the DSD, suffer institutional deficits. This makes them easy picking places for displaced children waiting for a referral to foster parents, a proportion of whom may also turn out to be abusive.

Fostering is also a route to child trafficking because of the largely informal 'sharing' of children through the extended family system which is deeply entrenched in traditional African child-raising practices. This is not as prevalent in South Africa as it is in western African countries where fostering has been termed a 'template' of child trafficking and one of its major drivers. Nonetheless, the practice of transferring displaced children to other families is still problematic because, as with illegal adoption to which it is akin, trafficking can take place in the process of child movement.

From what we know, child fostering in South Africa shaped by informal cultural norms involves a multiplicity of role players working with a variety of intentions. Apart from the child itself, this includes parents at source (if they exist), foster parents in a recipient capacity, siblings, children from both stable and unstable families, married and single mothers, healthy and handicapped parents, and many others including family friends.

Fostering in Africa occurs for a variety of reasons, which include strengthening extended family ties, redistributing child labour and making life-cycle adjustments to household size. Some of these fosterlings are of the 'socialising' variety where transactions are customarily driven by the natural parent or parents who believe family transfer will be in the interests of the child. Much of this is driven by 'insurance' on the part of deprived families who believe that sending a child to another family or a relative temporarily will allow him or her to develop skills and moral qualities.

Most fostering arrangements in South Africa moving in and between families in the urban and rural areas are a consequence of 'parent incapacity'. These are, for the most part, cases where the parents and their offspring have little agency over the costs of child-rearing and child placement. While most of these placements are the result of structural poverty and socioeconomic deprivation, they are triggered by a multiplicity of circumstances. These include but are not necessarily related to the death of a parent or parents and the subsequent destitution of the child, the inability of parents to serve the developmental needs of the child, an unwanted pregnancy, or even, in some African cases, the onset of a social or natural disaster which precludes the natural family from meeting the basic needs of their children.

From what we can discern, fostering has a variable outcome. Some researchers attest to the positive aspects of fostering in providing the best care for children leading to adulthood, especially when their biological parents are unable to do this. As a generalisation in the South African experience, foster children appear to fare better when they are very young, placed in the care of grandparents, and the absence of other children.

In many instances, good fostering can assist children to bridge their circumstances and acquire educational and vocational skills, especially where the foster father is well-disposed to the reception of a child from another segment of the extended family. Children sent to relatives as a matter of tribal custom are sometimes well cared for by kin, clan or the community and provided the emotional support necessary for positive child development. There are many situations where fostered children who have moved on maintain good relationships with their foster parents.

On the other hand, there is substantial evidence from Africa and worldwide which suggests that kinship placement, especially if based on parental incapacity, can go seriously wrong in some cases. Findings in various West African studies draws attention to the abusive practices resulting from fostering. South African evidence also suggests that foster children receive an almost invariably poorer education relative to children in their natural environment. In the worst-case scenario, these children become trafficking victims. Either inside or outside traditional cultural networks, foster children may be neglected or abused in the household to which they are transferred as a result of a social or economic crisis in the fostering family Relatives or kinship contacts may not deliver on their fostering obligations as a matter of choice or pervasive poverty. There are numerous cases where foster children are taken away from their extended family as a consequence of neglect or maltreatment and then rerouted back into inadequate parenting or agency care. Fostering is often associated with migration processes in western and southern Africa where lack of documentation impacts the life chances of children.

Nurture, love and care can often turn to abuse and violence. In the absence of goodwill, relatives sometimes violate kinship norms and principles of reciprocity by forcing children of either gender from school into excessive household duties akin to domestic servitude and hard labour. Even when foster parents are close relatives, they are more likely to exploit foster children than their own offspring. This frequently occurs when mutual agreements between parents and fostering household break down, where the costs of fostering rise precipitously despite initial good intentions, or in cases of urban children being transferred from their urban homes to relatively depleted rural environments. Family friends who are increasingly being included in fostering systems are generally less dependable than relatives, especially where children originate in broken homes, are orphans or come from a background of economic setbacks.

Fostered girls are especially susceptible to sexual exploitation by predator kin (or their acquaintances) away from their natural homes. Some cases have appeared before the South African courts where relatives have exploited fostered children as cheap labour while renting them out to adults for simultaneous sexual services. Both here as well as in other parts of Africa, kinship placement is a potential source of trafficking by erstwhile parents or their friends linked to criminal elements that have penetrated traditional networks. In these extreme cases where fostering situations are 'bastardised', relatives, kin or guardians may exploit the traditional fostering practices by handing children entrusted to their care directly to traffickers who then engage them in forced labour and other violent human rights abuses associated with modern slavery. One global study reports that extended family members did not consider the treatment of children in their care to be exploitative or wrong, even in cases where foster children are subject to extreme violence.

Child trafficking in South Africa also encompasses many especially egregious and hyper-violent practices. Many of these remain largely unexplored by domestic or international writers who feel more 'comfortable' with the 'normal' horrors of child sex trafficking or the exploitation of children for cheap labour.

In the 'moral crisis' of South Africa in the last days of apartheid, children were used, abused and, according to some accounts, murdered for their blood and body parts in satanic rituals and practices. Most of this activity to appease the devil is highly speculative albeit fuelled by deep uncertainty in the white community at the time over the consequences inherent in the transition to democracy. Yet it was surprisingly well documented, especially but by no means exclusively in the white press which reported regularly on the recruitment of children for devil worship, the chilling manner in which they were ostensibly used and the ultimate impact on their victims – brainwashed, abused and in some cases physically sacrificed.[14]

We live at a time when portions of the human body are available for commercialisation. There is a huge lag between the demand and supply of transferable organs and body substances and a growing suspicion among analysts that so-called 'organ harvesting' may be as valuable, if not more so, than sex and labour trafficking. The kidneys, lungs, livers, intestines and corneas of children as well as their blood, ova and skin tissue are especially prized in this bizarre yet expanding market because young body parts are generally healthier and cheaper than those of adults, relatively easier to store pharmacologically-speaking, and more susceptible to immunosuppressive drugs used in transplantation procedures.

Little is known about the dynamics of organ trafficking in South Africa or its neighbours where there is only a single substantial study that is not specifically related to children.[15] Having said this, there is mounting concern among human trafficking analysts that South Africa has been engaged in organ trafficking activity, in one form or another, for at least the last fifteen years. Some of this involves 'transplantation tourism' where foreigners come on 'surgical safaris' to South African hospitals and clinics to circumvent long waiting lists for organs in their countries of origin. In these cases, there are three essential preconditions, namely, patients desperate and willing to travel great distances to more cheaply obtain the transplants that they or their children need, the existence of mobile organ sellers allied to the medical profession, and ultimately, the willingness of surgeons, nurses and other medical personnel to break the law. There is also some evidence of the bodies of stillborn or recently-dead children being used for medical research by local doctors or pharmaceutical companies without the knowledge or consent of their parents – but here again, this is largely a matter of speculation.

Organ trafficking, it should be added, also stands at the complex intersection of culturally induced superstition, witchcraft and in extreme cases, muti murder. Albeit that most indigenous and traditional practices are benign, there are cases of inversion at the frequently thin boundary between culture and criminality. While most *muti* fabricated by traditional healers is based on potions made from anodyne vegetable or animal material, 'black muti', the most powerful (and expensive) involves substances sourced from human material. Here again, the body parts of children are especially prized, particularly in lethal poisons manufactured to cast evil, promote wealth or, perhaps most importantly, increase the fertility and sexual potency of consumers.

In southern Africa, there is concrete evidence of ongoing and successive muti murders where children are mostly hunted for their fingers, feet and, above all, their penises as key elements in sometimes decades-old muti recipes. Male children are, in these circumstances, highly at risk of being abducted, seduced or otherwise lured away from their parents with promises of education and employment. This could lead to mutilation or death where '*umuthi onmyama*' ('black' muti in Zulu) is practised.[16] The areas involved in these atrocities include large swathes of the region including Limpopo, Venda and substantial portions of KwaZulu-Natal (KZN). Child murders of this variety have been systematically documented by anthropologists and criminologists as well as the Roux and subsequent Ralushai Commissions established to investing witch-burning and other pernicious cultural practices in murders in northern areas of South Africa in the 1990s.

Unscrupulous traditional healers or witches in the business of black muti – a very small minority one must add – are normally contracted by 'customers' to procure a victim through a variety of procedures which may involve outright kidnapping. However, like most practices in human trafficking, they include more subtle techniques such as fraudulently purchasing a child from parents, illegal adoption, or stealing children from orphanages and foster parents. The strongest or most 'vital' muti aimed at spiritual intervention characteristically involves the dissection of the victim when still alive, in which case the resulting product can be marketed at very high prices in the market for body parts. Moreover, in many communities, there is the entrenched belief that killing a disabled child as muti can cure people with various maladies, including HIV and AIDS.

In many parts of Africa, including countries like Tanzania and South Africa, organ trafficking frequently involves adolescents suffering from albinism who, along with their parents in some cases, are particularly at risk of being accused of witchcraft, abducted, trafficked and then dismembered in gruesome attempts to appease the spirit.[17] Children with albinism are therefore kept at home, denied education or otherwise segregated from participation in most social affairs. In some cases, muti killings of this type can also be used to increase the good luck, wealth and success of a community, especially its leadership. This acts as a spur to organ trafficking and also inhibits prosecution of offenders. People are mainly terrified of the provision of evidence and there have been suggestions that some members of the police – in Zululand for example – are themselves superstitious and reluctant to go after muti killers for fear of bewitchment. In the circumstances, there is little correlation between the number of muti killings taking place and perpetrators being brought before the courts.

The perpetuation of muti murder of both adults and children has been explained in various ways, including the clash between modernity and traditionalism which effectively undercuts the translation of human rights into domestic action to safeguard children and women at the grassroots more generally. Notwithstanding 'ubuntu' with its connotations of solidarity, tolerance and caring for the needy among other humanitarian values, many gender-based practices on the African continent intermingle with human trafficking. These include forcing young girls into ritual servitude, rendering them as 'slaves to the Gods' ('*Trokosi*'), '*Wahaya*' (the taking of a fifth wife) and female genital cutting to ensure subserviency.

Ukuthwala, involving the forcible marriage of young girls to older men forms part of this sub-set of 'cultural distortions' with implications for human trafficking in South Africa.[18] *Ukuthwala* can involve the kidnapping and rape of young girls, shaming, family stigmatisation and then forced marriage. While largely practised among 'fallen heroines' in isolated areas of KZN and the Eastern Cape, this can also take place in urban communities – so-called 'ethnic villages' – where traditional values devaluating young women continue to dominate family structure and lifestyles.

Not everyone agrees on the purpose of *ukuthwala*.[19] Some see it as a form of coerced marriage and a type of human trafficking while others believe it to be a far less lethal procedure which induces negotiations leading to a customary marriage. The customary marriage is a mock abduction agreed upon by all parties. *Ukuthwala* nonetheless is adaptive and today, in some respects, it 'operates beyond its cultural parameters' as parents accept the right of their daughters to have boyfriends Some girls also conspire with their boyfriends to arrange their 'abduction' to pressure or compel parents into providing a dowery and accepting their marriage. In these types of cases, there is no forced marriage and the custom becomes a device to extort a dowery and induce parental condonation.

There are, nonetheless, cases where *ukuthwala*[20] is not an innocent system for finding a marriage partner as appears in the original custom, but a perversion of a tradition leading to the human rights violations of young girls in the form of forced marriage. Much of this goes unreported in far rural areas, either because victims fear community sanction or because deep rural people do not see the custom as an abuse of child rights, sexual slavery, forced marriage or a trafficking crime involving victims and perpetrators. In some cases, *ukuthwala* is so pronounced that young women are compelled to leave family and homes and migrate to the urban areas.

The illegality of *ukuthwala* is unambiguous. Under customary law, marriage negotiations are acceptable if the bride is not forced into taking a decision. Otherwise: the practice falls within the parameters of global or regional legislation governing human rights and trafficking. Abduction of a child for sexual purposes is a crime under the Sexual Offences Act as well as a violation of the constitutional guarantees which enshrines the rights of all its citizens and affirms the democratic values of human dignity, equality, and freedom. The practice only victimises girls and violates the constitutional provision of gender equality. Forced marriage falls outside the constitutional principles governing customary law.

Most cases of *ukuthwala* involving abuse of women and children by parents, relatives or otherwise colluding in the practice nevertheless go unreported for much the same reason as other crimes involving violence and the sexual exploitation of children. Even fewer go to prosecution for trafficking, even when reported, because prosecutors prefer to bring charges of assault, rape or kidnapping – crimes that are relatively easier to substantiate. The failure of parents to fully understand the true nature of the crime further undermines its severity by allowing perpetrators to avoid the consequences of their actions.

The physical and psychological impacts of trafficking on child victims are immeasurable. In South Africa, as elsewhere, trafficking can result in the death or permanent injury of the trafficked child in the 'exploitation' phase where many are exposed to hazardous conditions. In addition, these children frequently encounter substance abuse and may be given drugs as 'payment' or to ensure that they become addicted and thus dependent on their trafficker(s). As opposed to many other forms of crime, the trauma experienced by children who are trafficked is often prolonged and repeated and lead to severe psychological impacts. The United Nations Global Initiative to Fight Human Trafficking (UNGIFT) reports that trafficked children often suffer from depression, anxiety, and post-traumatic stress disorder, among other conditions.

Effects on families are also severe. Some families believe that sending or allowing their children to relocate to find work will bring in additional income, while in reality, many families will never see their trafficked children again. In addition, UN.GIFT has found that certain forms of trafficking, particularly sexual exploitation of girls, bring 'shame' to families. Thus, in certain cases, children who can escape trafficking may return to their families only to find that they are rejected and ostracised.

There are unfortunate limitations on what can be done about child trafficking. Governments or anti-trafficking agencies cannot prevent parents from handing over their children to live with close relatives, to screen all fostering for potential child exploitation, or to bring the criminal justice system to bear on cases of illegal adoption. Some aspects of child trafficking are insoluble in the short term because of entrenched cultural values and principles that legitimate early childhood marriage, organ trafficking or even muti-murder. The endemic structural features of South African society also pose limitations on policies aimed at undermining the TIP business model by reducing supply and demand along with building an effective network of victim-centred safety nets to lessen risk and ensure children's ability to develop in a safe and healthy environment.

There are, nonetheless, several possible 'solutions' to child trafficking as a human rights problem at the southern tip of Africa. There are infinite ways to improve the protection regime through amendments to the Children's Act to ensure heavier penalties for child desertion. UNICEF, for example, has maintained that successful prosecution of child traffickers is the surest way to send a message that child trafficking will not be tolerated. This means apprehending traffickers at any one of the three steps of trafficking (recruitment, movement, and/or exploitation) and then implementing legal frameworks to both deter and prosecute offenders.

At the preventative level, there is a need for robust action to inhibit child trafficking and the re-trafficking of its victims by curbing to some extent the existing culture of impunity. Since the prevention of child trafficking and its prosecution is inhibited by low levels of public awareness, far more needs to be done to mobilise people with direct contact with children or children at risk. This includes regional authorities, principals of schools, and perhaps most importantly, political leaders, law enforcement and opinion-makers who should ideally have access to both the intelligence around child trafficking and the means to mitigate the recurrence of incidents. Parents and caregivers are critical targets for the dissemination of risk knowledge. Many children are unaware of or do not understand their rights. There is also a need to empower children with information about the sexual exploitation of boys and girls, particularly in vulnerable communities.

Protection begins with efficient processes of victim identification, removal of children from trafficking situations and returning them either to their families or other appropriate settings. This requires extensive training and support for the key stakeholders in counter-trafficking such as law enforcement, justice officials and health and education workers involved in the identification of children at risk and their referral to specialised services. Child survivors of trafficking should also be provided with individualised and supportive physical and psychological rehabilitation. Youth-specific vulnerabilities, such as homelessness, lack of family, mistrust, lack of socialisation, coercive relationships, substance abuse, and lack of education, need to fare better addressed.

In the last analysis, effective anti-trafficking for the relief of children requires a far less dysfunctional system of child protection at all levels. At this state, the DSD suffers all the indicators of poor governmental performance shared with most other elements in the state bureaucracy. This includes, among many others that could be mentioned, a lack of clarity in purpose, poor budgeting (systems, semi-trained and uncommitted personnel, poor lines of internal and external communication and a debilitating lack of awareness about the scale and dynamics of child trafficking. This underperformance runs downwards through the system – what we will call the loss of state agency in a later chapter – to undermine regional structures of the department, At the grassroots level, this underperformance affects social workers, child psychologists and medical and nursing personnel assisting exploited and deprived children from all sectors of society, especially from among the poor who continue to make up the majority of the South African population most vulnerable to human trafficking. There are far too many professionals and other workers at this level who continue to offer protection but know little about human trafficking.

ECPAT has made probably the most thorough study of child trafficking in South Africa.[21] This study concludes with a series of recommendations covering areas such as the requirement to raise awareness about child trafficking, the ongoing necessity to train professionals, better programmes to prioritise SEC and commit resources, the immediate need to enhance collaboration beyond the policy framework (which is analysed in a later chapter), and last, but by no means least, better research and far better data collection systems.

As we have already mentioned there is a lack of public consciousness of trafficking in general and child trafficking in particular. There is a wealth of education still to be done among secondary and primary school children, university students and the multiple children who have drifted outside the education sector. Most programmes run by the state, or more commonly, civil society are neither monitored nor evaluated. There is an urgent need to benchmark the indicators of child trafficking and then address the many areas of weakness that fail to keep children safe from traffickers who use them for sex work, cheap labour, illegal adoption, questionable programmes of fostering and the grotesque murder and extraction of pieces of children to fuel the appetitive organ trafficking market. The media needs to be enlisted in publicising the horrors of child slavery without necessarily using sensationalism. Parents, caregivers and both boys and girls need to be better exposed to information as part of this empowering process ultimately aimed at identifying child trafficking cases and improving care mechanisms.

The ECPAT recommendations quite correctly speak to the lack of training and professionalism not only among psychosocial and welfare organisations involved with anti-trafficking in the child sector but also among law enforcement officials who form part of the process of identifying children at risk. From all accounts, the criminal justice system feels a sense of institutional discomfort in dealing with violated children as opposed to adults accused of a crime. Many policemen on the beat who are otherwise involved with commercial sex trafficking of post-adolescent women feel a sense of shame and incapacity when faced with children who have been subject, in many cases, to even relatively worse exploitation. In South Africa and throughout the region there is a tendency to pass on children to social development authorities as quickly as possible and where these lack capacity the best interests of children necessarily suffer.

We have also highlighted certain areas in child trafficking where children are abused without intervention by law enforcement. This includes cases of illegal adoption, abusive fostering and the continued deviancy of some cultural practices that allow extreme exploitation beyond the reach of the law. At the very minimum, SAPS personnel at the station level need to have an improved understanding of PACOTIP. Finally, the government needs to resource and dedicate public funding necessary for an effective programme to combat CSE and other forms of child trafficking. There is also a need for more intense partnerships where government participates effectively with civil society organisations. There has already been a Childs's Rights Intersectoral Coordinating Committee but this needs enhanced support from the private sector. Corruption and apathy need to be rigorously stamped out among the key stakeholder government committees that participate in these structures at various levels.

CHAPTER 4

Labour trafficking

Labour trafficking is trafficking for economic purposes. This form of trafficking generally but not invariably involves some form of forced labour. Forced or unfree labour driven by the profit motive makes up about two-thirds of all forced labour and is defined as work or service conducted non-consensually and under penalty. Despite being banned in a raft of international laws which guarantee workers the right to work under just and favourable conditions, there were an estimated 21 million people involved in this ultra-exploitative form of work in 2010. Current estimates with increasing globalisation are in the region of 29 million persons entrapped and labouring under compulsion worldwide, mainly recruited by brokers-cum-traffickers in the supply chains of mines, farms, factories, storehouses, homes and commercial enterprises worldwide. 60% of forced labour are men and boys in low-skilled labour sectors including artisanal and illegal mining, agriculture, fisheries, construction or domestic work (which usually involves female servitude). This shows no sign of abating in the foreseeable future, especially in Africa where labour trafficking is preeminent when compared to other forms of trafficking.

There are many aspects of labour trafficking which remain to be understood. This is partially because there is a preference in trafficking research for the sex trafficking of females, and to a lesser extent, children. Research on workplace-related interpersonal violence among migrant male labourers is scarce, while almost no one has explored much in the way of sexual violence against men and boys in all settings, including the workplace. despite the substantial likelihood of injury and enduring health problems in work sectors into which men and boys are commonly trafficked, there are few studies focused on violence, occupational risks, and injuries experienced by male trafficking survivors. While there is a growing body of literature on the health of female trafficking survivors, there is currently little to no evidence on the health needs of trafficked men and boys. Male sex trafficking or labour trafficking with its strong male component remains a 'road less travelled' for a variety of largely methodological reasons including the relative indivisibility of trafficking victims at the dividing line between labour trafficking and simple exploitation.[1]

Yet, trafficking into forced labour is familiar to SA. The 'founder' of South Africa, Jan van Riebeeck, brought two slaves from the Dutch settlements in Batavia, and soon after, the Dutch East India Company introduced slavery as the primary source of menial labour. One of the main reasons for the Great Trek was the abolition of slavery. In the same vein, there is a voluminous literature on the recruitment and exploitation of mine labour following the discovery of diamonds and gold in the late 19th century.

Many factors are still at work in support of labour trafficking in South Africa where an estimated 200 000 people currently exist under conditions of forced labour. Some factors are exogenous and rooted in global production networks; others are intrinsic to the region where characteristically high levels of unemployment sustain a reserve of men, women and children that can be drawn upon by traffickers or their agents to work in various sectors of the economy. Many migrants flowing into the country are undocumented or under pressure to acquire work of any sort at any cost. Overall, there exists what some writers have deemed a 'two-tier allocative regime' that ultimately sorts migrants into a minority of skilled rights-holders with access to social membership and legal citizenship, and a substantially larger unskilled majority with limited, or no rights at all. It is the latter who are typically trafficked into supply chains involving 'heavy' work in dangerous and relatively unregulated sectors, such as agriculture, domestic work, construction, fishing and mining.

Needless to say, some population groups are more vulnerable than others to economic trafficking involving some form of forced labour. Typical victims worldwide are adolescent boys or men in the 18–34 age group fed into various sectors of the formal or informal economy as well as small to large-scale enterprises. Female victims and children are recruited into domestic servitude and some are involved in minor criminal activities, such as house-breaking, car theft or begging. Labour trafficking in South Africa also involves a diversity of people including workers in the process of internal migration from rural poverty nodes to small towns and big cities, relatively static workers hungry for jobs, South African citizens moving across borders, criminals, the politically persecuted, and women in prostitution.

Mixed migrants are especially vulnerable, be they legal or illegal. The undocumented are especially prevalent among the victims of labour trafficking and forced labour. This is at least partially because of language deficits that preclude them from asking questions about the occupational safety and health aspects of their jobs, collective bargaining and their rights under the Constitution. On the other hand, contract workers who are fluent in one or another of the official languages can talk back to managers. When this happens, brokers will usually not re-use a worker and will discharge him or her into a highly competitive labour market – once he has settled his outstanding debts to the broker. Migrants are generally willing to accept unsafe work conditions, extended hours and even concealed injuries for which neither company management nor their brokers take responsibility

There are many cases where locals or migrants have, in desperation, essentially sold themselves into modern slavery as an alternative to competing with local labour on a seasonal or permanent basis. This has been facilitated by the development of what was already termed 'an exponential increase in the use of labour broking' almost ten years ago, which even then resulted in the existence of over 6 000 recruitment centres involving over 500 000 people at a value of R26 billion. Much of this has involved informal broking and currently, a very substantial informal brokerage network exists in tandem with formal placement organisations in the TES (temporary services sector). These work mainly within the law to outsource jobs and services in virtually every area of the economy. Sustained by the requirement of modern production for elastic labour, this informal network at the bottom end of the organisational ladder is attractive to certain business operations which, irrespective of the protective regime, require immediate short-term labour and whose procurement services have contacts outside the mainstream broking system. Current arrangements also suit the business interests of some of the more unscrupulous brokers in this bottom category. These brokers collect an often substantial economic rent from these transactions representing the difference between the costs at which workers are hired out and the amount paid to the sub-contractees. This often works through a cascading system of contracts and sub-contracts where even employers are uncertain about the origins of their workers and the conditions under which they entered the workforce.

The Labour Relations Act of 1995 describes informal brokers as persons who for reward procure for or provide a person to a client to render services or to work. There is virtually nothing systematic written in South Africa about the interface between informal brokers and labour trafficking. We also do not know the size and composition of the 'grey' broking sector in this country, despite several global writings on brokerage, economic trafficking and forced labour within the anthropology of development where most academic mileage has been made on the study of brokers.[2]

The informal workers' brokers are often pejoratively labelled the 'bakkie brigade' because of the small numbers of contractees conveyed in a sociology of the sector, which consists of multilayers of private employment agencies and independent contractors and sub-contractors that in some industries deal with huge numbers of outsourced labour. In line with global practice, most of its more successful members appear to have had a lengthy experience in contracting; many are ex-migrants embedded in the migrant world.

Most brokers near the borders of Limpopo or the Eastern Free State have contacts with the key stakeholders involved in migration. These include the provincial-level police, the border police, immigration officials, local employers and state agencies at provincial levels that are the traditional 'enemies' of migrants. Brokers in these and other areas are normally well-known to bus and taxi drivers. They also sometimes assist the police with extracting bribes from undocumented migrants or in manning checkpoints where they cream off potential 'customers' or negotiate the exchange of sexual favours. Police corruption involving migrants is often filtered through brokers who can bribe law enforcement to look the other way. Some brokers also appear to have considerably higher contacts in the mid to higher levels of the state bureaucracy, especially in the DHA and the Department of Labour. This is especially important for brokers working at the narrow divide between labour recruitment and trafficking who face the prospect of 'wrongful' arrest as an occupational hazard. Cascading broker networks are almost always present in the reception areas of the big cities and towns to which migrants travel. These are inevitably based on corruption, nepotism, back payments and influence-peddling.

Conventional wisdom associated with the 'bakkie' mentality also fails to take account of the multiplicity of functions performed by some brokers or brokering organisations in the 'black box' of migration across the Limpopo or other South African borders and then into the interior. While many informal brokers conform to the stereotype of profiteering, rent seeking, and highly and highly abusive practices, others are in some sense in the migration assistance business. This often includes the provision of translation services to migrants without linguistic skills and information about living conditions in various geographies and the social experiences of others. While brokers accept any type of labour regardless of status, they also participate in assessment exercises to ensure that their clients are not contracted to employers within the regulatory framework who are likely to break the law. Many migrants sent into dangerous work at below legal minimum standards in mines or factories owe this to the largely unilateral choices made by the brokers on the first confrontation.

Contractors working in 'grey' areas are also involved in providing the undocumented with under-the-counter documents from labour authorities or providing the dislocated migrant with medical or housing contacts shortly after arrival in South Africa. In some cases, the brokers act as small-scale banks and extend credit to potential workers, most of whom are already in debt. While most brokers deal in a mix of smuggling, from cigarettes to humans to supplement their labour income, some specialise in certain industries and work designations which ensure a match between migrant skills, if they have any, and the place of work to which they are assigned. With networks in the transport sector, brokers also facilitate movement from the border to the big cities, albeit, as with other services, at a cost. Illegal brokers also often have the positionality necessary to exploit extensive networks of corruption in the law enforcement system. This includes work as informants on border movement as well as negotiating bribes on behalf of itinerant or arrested workers.

Seen in these terms, brokers can be key to the infrastructure of migration, namely, the complex web of persons, objects and practices that define operational space. Consequently, brokering is not necessarily consistent with labour trafficking or forced labour and, in some circumstances, can even assist migrants to navigate between precarious work conditions, unscrupulous employers and predatory officials.

Labour trafficking forced labour and the workplaces to which brokers eventually assign their clients exist along a continuum where relatively normal placement occurs at one end and brutal coercion at the other. In some cases, migrants or locals find themselves in conditions of near slavery following forced recruitment and transportation to the workplace, or more commonly, the site of exploitation. This might involve victims being shackled or chained, burnt, slapped or pushed and beaten by employers, foremen, security staff, enforcers or even co-workers. This is in accordance with what the ILO deems 'actions, incidents or behaviour in which a person is assaulted, threatened, harmed, injured in the course of, or as a direct result of, his or her work'. In the greater majority of trafficking transactions, however, recruitment is by fraud and manipulation of aspirations to earn wages. Compliance in the workplace might then involve the use of a variety of less egregious 'soft' techniques aimed at confining the victim through the confiscation of key documents (identification papers or passports), restrictions on the possibility of exchanging jobs, limited freedom in and outside the workplace, prohibitions on organising, debts incurred, service fraud and simple wage theft.

Having said this, labour trafficking is intrinsically exploitative even in cases where brokers or their agents deal relatively sympathetically with contractees. The economic rent taken by brokers may also vary substantially. Yet this is entirely beyond the agency of victims who all along the constellation of compulsion are basically commodified. This, in many cases, leads to work under hazardous conditions with punishment being meted out when victims are too sick to work, avoid work, work too slowly or where victims fail to follow instructions, in some cases because of language differences.

An estimated one-third of trafficked labour suffers an injury at one time or another because workers entrapped by economic trafficking characteristically work extended hours without breaks, Occupational health and safety (OHS) standards or personal protective equipment (PPE), even in deep underground mines where rockfalls and subsidence are common. Trafficked and forced agricultural workers worldwide are often forced to labour without hats in intensive heat and fishery workers often lose body parts. Medical care is rare and is usually a luxury.

Exiting from these exploitative conditions is normally difficult either because of physical restrictions placed on movement or because workers are owed back pay. Debt repayment obligations, lack of documentation or the inability to reclaim confiscated documents are also used to perpetuate entrapment. This is often backed up by force on the part of both employers and the police threatening sexual violence, extortion or, in the case of the undocumented, arrest for violation of immigration laws and other trumped-up charges.

The space occupied by brokers or contractors between the 'normal' relationship between employee and employer also creates innumerable opportunities for all kinds of manipulations and scams in labour chains throughout the South African economy. Debt is a key instrument in labour trafficking and thousands are working lifelong to pay off cumulative 'loans' from labour brokers and their accomplices. In the least lethal of some cases, the brokerage is simply wage-cheating where victims are offered supposedly high-paying jobs 'on contract' but receive little or nothing of what has been promised. In other cases, victims are charged exorbitant 'recruitment' costs and are required to put down 'safety deposits' to continue working. They could also be victims of unforeseen salary deductions under penalty from enforcers. In some cases, 'contracts' turn out to be fictitious or uncomprehending to victims who lack literacy skills. Undocumented foreigners could be threatened with exposure to the police or immigration authorities should they make complaints against the perpetrators of default on regular payments. There are extraordinary if anecdotal cases of West African traffickers in South Africa approaching teenage footballers with business cards carrying the logos of top European soccer clubs, sending them and their families to Europe for a hefty fee, and then abandoning them.

Labour trafficking in the mainstream of forced labour can be far more vicious. The principle of 'posting' workers across the frontiers to exploitative work in South Africa is deeply ingrained in economic history. Today, much like the subcontinental 'native recruitment' agencies established to filter cheap labour into the mines from the late 19th century, there are brokers, agents or dedicated trafficking syndicates who scout the region and sometimes abduct mainly unskilled victims who are then transported as labour in the lower reaches of the economy. Illegal brokers also work along the borders with gangs awaiting undocumented migrants entering South Africa and with sympathetic members of the transport sector who take their cut as 'finders'.

There are long-standing allegations of forced or bonded labour of undocumented migrants in the lower end of the construction industry and in manufacturing where procurement of casual labour involves shady deals between company officials responsible for procurement and labour brokers whose services have been tried and tested. Here, risks include exposure to harmful chemicals, lifting heavy objects or repetitive motions, overexposure to UV rays, falls from working at heights, crush injuries, being struck by falling objects, and injuries from hand tools Trafficked factory workers are often not provided with protective gear. It has been reported that these labourers could also be physically assaulted by supervisors and management.

As is the case in the illegal mining sector (discussed in more detail later), workers in small-scale manufacturing in the 'townships' are frequently irregular migrants from other parts of Africa and are designated for the worst-work situations. Faced with xenophobia in the competition with local labour for scarce resources, many are obliged to seek employment irrespective of poor pay and poor workplace conditions. Faced with the impossibility of exit, many have structured choices that become, in effect, forced labour. In these cases, OHS is ignored because workers have no collective bargaining power and, as in other sectors, there is insufficient capacity and job dedication on the part of labour inspectors.

The South African agricultural sector currently employs some 880 000 people. A still tentative study suggests that forced labour takes place in the fruit and wine industries of the Western Cape where the workforce is overwhelmingly temporary, undocumented and seasonal. This results in many vulnerable people, especially young females under twenty-five, and undermines the effective implementation of labour legislation. Moreover, throughout the sector, both trafficked and untrafficked labour faces occupational hazards including injuries from heavy farm machinery and chemical hazards that could cause skin and respiratory diseases. As is the case in exploitative agricultural conditions in other countries, the risk is also associated with poor education, lack of machine operating experience, daytime drowsiness brought on by exposure to drugs and alcohol, being in debt and operating under stress.[3]

In Limpopo, for example, there are documented cases of local farmers going to concentration points for cross-border migrants, recruiting on a fraudulent basis and then transporting victims to neighbouring farms. Here they are worked in the fields in abusive conditions and then refused payment on conclusion of their mainly verbal 'contracts'.

Debt bondage then turns into fully-fledged TIP as farmworkers are denied the right to leave their workplace, ostensibly until they have worked off their debts. These forms of illegal detention are frequently overlooked by labour inspectors, the SAPS or local authorities with whom farm owners have close connections. This could also involve payoffs to officials who turn the other cheek in the face of these illegal detentions. The precarious situation is frequently aggravated by the dependency of workers on employers for food, housing and other basic needs in isolated areas. This also undercuts any agency by the workforce in the form of organisation or collective bargaining. In some cases, described as 'legal servitude', it is estimated that farm labourers take anything from months to years to pay off their accumulated debt.

Bondage of this sort is also multifaceted with a range of actors who often unsuspectingly become perpetrators in the process of profiting from the aspiration, needs and earnings of trafficked labour. These include the police, migration officials and rapacious labour brokers as well as transport agents, house owners, shopkeepers, banks and other creditors to whom exploited workers might turn in trying to ease off their debt. Taxi drivers working the routes from Beit Bridge to Gauteng are notorious for assisting urban gangs to meet migrants destined to have their documents confiscated before being sold off to various city enterprises in Pretoria or Johannesburg who specialise in using the skills of the entrapped for a range of dubiously legal business operations. Some of the more small-scale commercial or manufacturing entities are situated in places like the Hillbrow-Berea area, which is a magnet for people coming from places north of the Limpopo. Other places are substantially bigger, for example, the discount houses operated in various Chinatowns.

Domestic work involving tasks such as cooking, cleaning, washing clothes and caring for children and/or the elderly is an important source of employment in developing countries. In South Africa today there are approximately 1 million people – almost 6% of the South African workforce – in the domestic sector. There are approximately 953 000 black women currently active in this sector, which represents approximately 5,84% of the total South African labour and 8% of the informal employment sector. While domestic service does not necessarily imply trafficking or even exploitation, this represents a huge population of uneducated, unskilled, mainly black (or in the Cape 'coloured') females at risk of being manipulated by unscrupulous employers, some of whom are involved in labour brokering on the edges of TIP. The exploitation of this population is deeply entrenched in society and domestic workers are especially vulnerable. Many of the women in the domestic sector are the consequence of apartheid policies delimiting the access of black women to work and education. Today, 25 years after apartheid, domestic workers are still at risk of being trafficked or otherwise exploited because of their low status in the saturated job market and the post-Covid rising costs of living. Most women are denied agency by the precarious nature of their work, which is usually unstable, poorly remunerated, and generally non-compliant with ILO standards for decent work based on freedom and productivity. This situation is widely ignored in many homes, both white and black.[4]

Research also indicates that many domestic workers still experience marginalisation, poor job security, poor wages and working conditions. This leads to a sense of powerlessness that can result in ongoing exploitation either by employers or their agents. Legislative reforms have provided domestic and other low-income workers with protection in the employment sectors where they work. This includes the Basic Conditions of Employment Act (BCEA) dating back to 1997 which regulates the right to decent work and fair labour practices as well as laws which law down minimum wages and working hours. These apply to domestic workers as well as others. In addition, in 2013, South Africa became a signatory to the Domestic Workers Convention promoted by the International Labour Organisation in 2011.

Having said this, protective labour legislation pertaining to domestic workers among others is difficult to enforce. Unemployment levels for unskilled or semi-skilled people have increased during Covid so that after the pandemic domestic work is still largely based on informal arrangements with employers behind closed doors and other places inaccessible to labour inspectors involved in monitoring working conditions at grass roots. An estimated one-in-five employers continue to pay domestic workers less than the minimum wage. Domestic servitude ensues when employers confiscate documents to ensure that often badly treated workers remain in place. This is especially onerous for irregular migrants in the domestic sector who lack any documents to begin with'.

We do not know the prevalence of domestic servitude for these reasons and others. Nonetheless, it is reasonable to assume that because of the deregulation of the domestic sector, there is a substantial 'reserve' of women and younger girls, some local, others undocumented migrants, who are available for entrapment either by their employers seeking cheap and manipulable household labour or by so-called 'maids-and-madams' agencies who reach out to workers using the characteristic forms of labour trafficking, such as debt bondage or document confiscation. Agents mediating between employers and workers are also able to negotiate lower wages and poor working conditions relative to the market because of the economic desperation of unemployed women.

Pre-democracy research on the domestic work sector in South Africa highlights the factors that contribute towards feelings of oppression experienced by domestic workers in conditions of racial inequality. Yet there is no single systematic and contemporary study of domestic servitude in the Republic.

Statistical evidence suggests that 96% of domestic workers are women. Anecdotal evidence also suggests that trafficking for domestic servitude is largely a women-on-women activity since a relatively high proportion of brokers are women. Some brokers work in the domestic market but others travel into adjacent countries to find recruits who are then brought back to the urban areas such as Soweto and sold off for a 'recruitment' or 'finders' fee. There is prolific trafficking of young women domestic workers from the Northern to the Western Cape, many of whom are placed in the homes of Muslim families. Victims are mainly advertised through informal channels including word of mouth. They are invariably childless young black women, some of whom are teenagers, willing to work below legislated minimum wages. They are then put to work on a variety of homogenous but basic household tasks in residential premises where they may be paid a minimal wage or, in some cases, no wages at all. Surveys conducted in South Africa revealed that one out of five participants admitted to paying their domestic workers less than the minimum wage Most are kept secluded behind the high walls characteristic of suburban South Africa at a time of escalating crime including home invasions. Housing is normally the back-room premises associated with the geography of apartheid.

By no means are all domestics in servitude. Servitude experiences also vary, in some respects more so than exploitative farm and factory work, because of the 'intimate' and navigable space between employee and employer. In some cases, domestics are abused in a manner similar to some of the worst forms of forced labour servitude and can be tantamount to the worst types of forced labour. However, at the opposite end of the spectrum, relations between employers and domestic workers can result in some states of mutual tolerance. In some rare cases in South Africa, this may even stretch to a modulated form of servitude where 'live-in' domestic workers, or their children, are 'adopted' into the family.

The basic conditions of employment are nonetheless at the discretion or whims of employers who normally capitalise on power disparities to pay less than the minimum wage and to resist written contracts of employment. Payment of unemployment insurance is very rare because most employers are either unaware or uncaring about the origins of their workers, least of all their prospects. Most writings on the exploitation of domestics focus on the white middle and upper class. As black South Africans have entered into the middle class, however, domestic abuse associated with servitude has spread into black households. Since domestic labour is cheap, even employers on the lower socioeconomic rungs can afford one or more 'girl' who works the interior of the house, with the exterior being reserved for a 'garden boy', often imported trans-frontier with the assistance of human smugglers and their touts from other countries within the region. In worst-case scenarios, there are a variety of potential dangers to which victims of forced labour in the household setting find themselves confronted. These include exposure to hazardous and toxic chemicals, chronic pain and injury, exposure to humiliating and increasingly sophisticated technologies of surveillance, undernourishment and sleep deprivation, and isolation and loneliness. Household discipline can include differential treatment in the provision of food, obliging domestics to eat left-overs, directing meals times and 'determining where and with whom the domestic worker should eat, thus reinforcing a social divide 'Although the 'dompas' system has long since disappeared with apartheid, employers can still enforce their power by calling the police to press charges against undocumented migrants, enlisting 'enforcers' working with brokering entities or threaten workers with dismissal into a bottomless labour market where migrant women are inclined to work at a minimum price. This is an especially cruel restraint for the very large number of domestic workers who are especially vulnerable as household heads or are obliged to support members of their families in rural areas. In South Africa and worldwide, employers of domestic workers lack familiarity with labour legislation There is also some evidence that domestic workers are coerced into sex work as a facet of their servitude. This is less frequent where employees are white and where sexual taboos inherited from apartheid still perhaps apply.

The practice of employing domestic workers in private homes is a long-standing global phenomenon fuelled by factors such as the ageing of the world population; the insufficiency of state care provision for children, the elderly and the infirm; as well as the increased participation of women in the workplace. South Africa is currently the third biggest employer of domestic workers globally. This situation is likely to continue into the indefinite future because of a mixture of household poverty and limited work opportunities for the unskilled, chronic unemployment and a lack of access to finance and education in South Africa. Domestic work will continue to provide an unregulated and potentially exploitative source of employment in the future. Domestic servitude is also likely to continue as long a cheap and manipulable supply of labour continues to exist to service household functions that would otherwise be incumbent on employers. This could also include educated women, regardless of race, who would be prepared to consider domestic work as a source of employment

Labour trafficking is largely absent in the supply chain of mining corporations with global links because of an awareness of reputational costs among corporate leadership. Increased specialisation in extracting ore also precludes the use of unskilled labour in all but the most general types of work, for example, the cleaning of underground workplaces and around the rockface. There are, nevertheless, cases of some of the 'junior' mines using a mixture of legal and unlicensed broker organisations, which have emerged in profusion over the last few years, to deal with the consequences of labour casualisation in small-scale mining. In these mines, there are typically high levels of absenteeism in the workplace due to health issues such as HIV and AIDS or respiratory problems. This makes it difficult for these mines to reach their daily production targets. As in agriculture, procurement officials without the luxury of time to recruit workers through conventional procedures then proceed to approach informal sources of labour supply outside the framework of TES.

The victims vary, as do the actual trafficking processes. In the majority of cases, the victims are migrating (or at least mobile) men suitable for arduous underground work who approach brokers indiscriminately for work based on a referral from a colleague or a 'homeboy' who has experience of a particular person or set-up at one or more mining sites. In some cases, informal labour brokers congregate at reception points for people entering the mining industry where 'assistance' can be provided to workers who would normally fail the battery of psychological and health tests required for mine work. So desperate is the need for employment with the economic constriction following Covid that potential mine labour increasingly interacts with illegal brokers, even when it is known that they are likely to engage in wage fraud or some other form of exploitation even prior to reaching the target mine site. With Covid, the 'opportunities' of labour trafficking of this sort are increasingly 'reserved' for semi- or skilled labour rather than for the 'general' worker as was the case before the onset of the pandemic.

As women have increasingly entered the mining industry on the back of black empowerment legislation and the Mining Charter, brokers have increasingly begun to work on non-gender lines. In the initial instance this involved recruitment of women for surface work or general work – cleaning and clearing underground. With growing numbers of successful women workers at the rockface, the brokers have, to an extent, shifted emphasis.

Underground gender relationships are highly complex, and in some cases, sexual contacts develop between men and women either near the sub-surface workplace or in mining accommodation which runs a range from barracks-like premises to mine housing or living arrangements in the near mine community.[5] Brokers, it appears, value women who can be marketed for parallel sex and industrial labour and are often willing to pay a high premium to female applicants who fit this category. Given that the lines between sex and labour trafficking are always mysterious this supplements the long-standing relations between the brokers and women in prostitution. The latter are trafficked from urban areas on a commercial basis despite often fierce competition in some mines between these imports into the mining market and women brought to the mines from the rural homelands for culturally sanctioned prostitution.

The proliferating illegal gold mining industry, which accounts for millions of rands each year, is a hotbed of labour trafficking at various 'worked-out' mines across the country, in Gauteng, the Northern Cape, north-eastern Mpumalanga and the Free State goldfields. These mines are sub-economic from the point of view of the big mining corporations but still contain residual deposits to justify mining by small-scale entrepreneurs willing to go underground. Illegal or artisanal mining also takes place on huge mine dumps along the Witwatersrand where mainly women sift mining sands, as well as in shafts abutting mainstream mining activity in many areas, such as around Welkom in the Free State.

The labour force involved in these lucrative activities consists of a mix of unemployed but voluntary workers attracted to the prospect of financial gain, as well as labour fraudulently recruited by brokers working various scams both within South Africa and across its borders. Illegal miners in the Free State areas are typically recruited in Lesotho, which is also a hub for migrants coming from all parts of Africa. Trafficking victims are characteristically enticed with false promises of entry to mining, transported across the South African frontier unnoticed by compliant border police and then sent underground at various badly guarded entry points. As is typical with other forms of modern labour slavery, victims find themselves indebted at month's end and are inveigled into long periods of sub-surface labour. There is little possibility for an escape to the surface, even where victims are not closely guarded. On-surface victims face the police, arrest, imprisonment and deportation as illegal immigrants. In the worst-case scenario, they fall into the abusive physical and sexual clutches of mine boss-boys working on a vigilante basis.

In most illegal mines there is a hierarchy dominated by gang leaders who market extracted gold to various local criminal networks with connections to international syndicates who then market this gold to the wider world. Many of these gangs are led by experienced miners made redundant by the mainstream industry and have now become 'Zama-zamas' (the 'chancers').[6] Since underground work often requires continuous activity, which may stretch over many months at a time, the gang leaders also function as procurers of food, equipment, drugs and women, some of whom also engage in sub-surface sex work voluntarily.

In cases where illegal mining takes place in the vicinity of legal operations, miners up to supervisors and middle management are supply channels for various goods and services. Children are often encountered in medium- to deep-level mining where there is a demand for small people to navigate the tortuous channels running to and between gold deposits.

Only the most dreadful of accidents are reported, least of all investigated, such as the recent death of eighty illegal miners. This is at least partially attributable to the pervading culture where violence and death are normalised or ignored. Trafficked labour, however, almost always works on the bottom rung of the organisational pyramid. This means constant exposure to a highly dangerous environment where injury and death are commonplace as a consequence of both geological and human behaviour. This includes risks such as rockfalls, mudslides and exposure to noxious gases leading to silicosis and other respiratory ailments. Trafficked victims with only a few minutes of explosives training sometimes use dynamite to hack out channels in the rockface. Discipline is rigorous and teams are forced to work fast in meeting often humanly impossible production targets. Trafficked labour is generally on the front line of fatalities because involuntary miners are almost always assigned the most primitive stolen, discarded or redundant tools. Trafficked labour is especially prominent in the highly dangerous process of adding acid to unrefined gold as required by the standards of the global market. Underground work of the elementary sort associated with illegal mining also entails labour in dark, dusty and confined spaces which are major stressors for the uninitiated.

Frequent sub-terranean homicides reported by many men who have fallen prey to the Zama-zamas supplements mining injuries as the main cause of death. There are only rudimentary safety standards in this violent situation. PPE is almost exclusively reserved for gang leaders who mainly live above-ground separated from shacks or poorly serviced compounds for workers. Much like undocumented farmworkers in the United States, these barracks are sites of additional violence brought about by living conditions, crowding and the availability of alcohol and drugs like nyaope. Needless to say, all this takes place in an unregulated sector where no one has a voice and all are universal.

There are some variations in this sorry situation. There is less risk for personnel working in above-ground artisanal operations. These include criminal mining for diamonds which may be located on or near the surface, sifting industrial sands for valuable sediments, or open-caste mining. In these cases, however, detection is easier if and when the police or mine security personnel act on intelligence. This is, however, rare because the local police and mine security networks are often penetrated by outside elements working with mining gangs or inside the regular mining establishment. In the Free State and other areas, the SAPS, is reluctant to go deep underground because of ongoing armed conflict between mining gangs who compete for the most profitable seams based on knowledge acquired from mainstream miners and are often ethically divided. Some of the 'criminals' detected by the SAPS turn out to be trafficking victims or, in some cases, victims who have become enforcers. In the circumstances, mine security is often sub-contracted to private concerns who are hired thugs who are not especially sensitive to trafficking while selling their services to the big mining houses at a premium.

The first step forward from a trafficking perspective possibly lies with unionisation. However, the National Union of Mineworkers (NUMSA) and the Association of Mineworkers and Construction Union (AMCU) are unenthusiastic about taking these highly unstable populations into their ranks. Another pathway is through decriminalisation and regulation of illegal mining now that a significant proportion of underground ore processing appears to be in the hands of the zama-zamas. But much like the legalisation of sex work, there are competing visions of whether and how this should be done at a time when 'the glory days of South African gold mining have come to an end'.

Labour trafficking also takes place in more open spaces, such as in the air and on the sea. In the former instance, workers recruited by brokers internationally arrive at one or another of South Africa's major international airports with fake documentation, are met by local agents and then deployed to sites of exploitation – normally places where fellow nationals and sometimes relatives have already arrived and established various forms of business. Some of the Chinatowns that have spawned across the country employ illegal Chinese immigrants who have also entered the country via some of the less-travelled air corridors, such as those running into the Republic from Eswatini and Lesotho. Routes of this type are mainly controlled by Triad gangs operating out of Macau and Hong Kong for whom labour trafficking is only one item on a larger menu that includes the smuggling of drugs, gold, ivory and exotic fauna and flora destined for the 'wet' markets of the People's Republic of China. Commercial labour trafficking also involves young men from South Asia, especially Bangladesh and Pakistan, who come to work in small businesses in or near South Africa's 'townships'.

Because trafficking by air is expensive, this mode of transaction is limited relative to landward trafficking. Improved vigilance by border police at airports such as O.R. Tambo has also reduced couriers coming into the country with labour in tow. Covid and restrictions on aerial movement over the past few years have also disrupted the use of aerial routes by labour traffickers although this has done virtually nothing to halt landward movement between the often vast distances between sealed frontier crossing points.

In line with global patterns, this has induced traffickers and human smugglers to make increasing use of maritime means to enter South Africa. As a result,with the end of lockdown decreases in intensity, there is a greater probability that we will start to see leaky and other unseaworthy boats bringing a mixture of vulnerable economic migrants displaced by the devastation in their countries of origin appearing along our long coastline.

Commercial fishing, among the world's most dangerous occupations, also has a trafficking component.[7] This can take many forms including South Africans working on local vessels or, more frequently, South Africans seeking work opportunities overseas and then falling fall prey to trafficking networks in the worldwide commercial fishing industry. South Africans are known to involuntarily work in often deplorable conditions for weeks and months at a time in such places as South and South-East Asia following document confiscation and debt bondage. Foreign fishermen working long-hauls are also exploited in territorial waters and then, in some cases, off-loaded in South African ports following long periods of egregious abuses, inhuman working hours, lack of access to protective gear, drownings and other serious injuries. There are two well-documented cases of Indonesian and Cambodian fishermen fleeing from their captors in Cape Town and then seeking repatriation following weeks of continuous work cycles without respite, adverse weather conditions, isolation, crew violence and murderous intent on the part of captains.[8]

Yet, dealing with slavery at sea is controversial because the responsibilities of South Africa are unclear. Much depends on where foreign trawlers and other types of vessels carry out their fishing activities, and whether the South African authorities can access the victims of ships that sometimes work for months or even years at sea before coming into port. Even then, there is confusion about what to do about trafficked fishermen of countries that may not be represented diplomatically in South Africa, who speak exotic languages and who lack the means to return to their countries of origin. The tendency has been to treat these cases as labour exploitation rather than TIP or to charge victims as illegal immigrants before deporting them to their home countries.

The Constitution provides provisions pertinent to labour trafficking, such as Section 23 which advocates fair labour practice as defined by South African adherence to the ILO and other major laws and conventions governing TIP and forced labour, such as the Forced Labour Convention of 1930 and the Palermo Protocols. Forced labour is also banned in the Bill of Rights under Section 13, which prohibits slavery and servitude. A swathe of legislative instruments has been brought into existence by the ANC and COSATU to combat forced and exploited labour in the wake of apartheid. These. include the BCEA, which defines exploitative labour as anything over nine hours per day and makes producers jointly and severally liable and responsible if contractors fail to adhere to labour legislation. There are, in addition, the Labour Relations Act, the Extension of Security of Tenure Act, Sectoral Wage Determination, and the Employment Services Act (No. 4 of 2014) (ESA) aimed at providing some measure of relief to the conservatively estimated three million migrants now working in South Africa provided they have a visa. In the agricultural sector, arguably the most exploitative after mining, the ANC has abolished many protections, regulations and subsidies which have traditionally protected white commercial farmers.

Civil society also contributes to the ongoing debate over the social and economic impacts of outsourcing and short-term labour contracts on poverty, employment, worker rights, skills dissemination of skills and the battery of tactics ostensibly used by less reputable employers to use 'atypical' types of employment to escape the regulative framework. There have been parliamentary debates over broking as well as discussions in the National Economic Development and Labour Council (Nedlac) where COSATU has consistently if unrealistically, echoed a wider feeling in civil rights circles that broking is immoral, exploitative and ultimately encourages human trafficking – largely irrespective of its value to employers in providing flexibility in the employment market. Somewhere between these opposites lie a variety of perspectives that define broking as an intermediary mechanism allowing workers into the organised labour market and is generally acceptable subject to substantially greater regulation.

Initiatives to hold corporates to account, targeting buying practices and extending principles of worker protection to incorporate labour intermediaries have also been addressed by the South African branch of the UK-based Stronger Together. This organisation alerts producers to the existence of modern slavery and assists businesses to engage in ethical trade based on responsible supply chain policies. Much of this has followed the UK's Modern Slavery Act of 2015. Unfortunately, initiatives of this type have progressively less impact as one moves down the organisational hierarchy from big corporates to small businesses that are relatively immune to reputational risk. A good example is the agricultural sector in Limpopo where large fruit-growing concerns with export markets in Europe identify with supply chain control, whereas smaller enterprises continue to often rely on dubiously contracted rural labour. Even further up the ladder, these initiatives are only as good as their social audits in identifying characteristically 'disappearing' labour in factories, farms and mines under assessment.

The protective regime with its various laws, however, remains seriously under-capacitated and poorly enforced. While acknowledging that the period since apartheid has witnessed a number of core rights for agricultural workers, a recent study concludes that implementation is uneven and 'many of these rights are unenforced'. Part of the problem is that there are far too few labour inspectors to monitor producers and employers who fail to report accurately. Also, far too few of these officials lack knowledge concerning the interface between labour trafficking and criminality, and far too many take advantage of corruption to look the other way even when encountering forced or deeply exploited labour. In the agricultural sector, for example, there are fewer than 1 000 inspectors in the national and provincial Department of Labour to cover 40 000 farms nationwide. There is limited awareness of labour rights among the populations of most farms and the department is notorious for sole ownership of statistics governing compliance with labour laws. In these circumstances, only third-party interventions can be used to track forced and trafficked labour patterns if and when they are followed up.

CHAPTER 5

Counter-trafficking

Counter-trafficking is a multi-faceted set of activities for which the state is primarily responsible in the process of providing human security for its citizens.[1] In some cases, including South Africa, counter or anti-trafficking may involve a multisectoral partnership, commonly called a counter-trafficking coalition, which transcends the divisions between the public and private sectors.[2] Irrespective of the exact configuration, counter-trafficking aims at establishing what is commonly called a 'prohibitive regime' based on three pillars. Firstly, if not necessarily foremost, counter-trafficking has a preventative function, the central facet of which is to raise public (and sometimes governmental) levels of awareness about the nature and dynamics of TIP as well as possible avenues to stem its tide. In the ideal case, the public becomes an alert and active front-line intelligence source whose existence may even be more critical in preventing trafficking than the scale on which trafficking takes place. Counter-trafficking also involves pinpointing trafficking events, investigation and ultimately prosecution and conviction of perpetrators by the criminal justice system. Thirdly, effective counter-trafficking also has a protective dimension. This can be prophylactic in the sense of offering support to reduce the risk of a vulnerable population, or reactive in assisting victims and survivors of trafficking experiences to once more reintegrate into society.

South Africa's counter-trafficking armoury consists of legal instruments arising out of the Republic's adherence to international and domestic laws. At last count, South Africa had ratified 25 conventions, directions or protocols dealing either directly or indirectly with human trafficking.[3] These include the 'model' Palermo Protocol supplement to the UNTOC of 2001, whose provisions have been largely incorporated into South African law, five international instruments against child trafficking, and two major conventions on gender discrimination and violence.

South Africa also adheres to several milestone instruments in the development of international law as well as a number of regional instruments to combat trafficking.

Neither the Constitution nor the South African Bill of Rights specifically mentions human trafficking. They are, nonetheless, the first line of recourse in dealing with trafficking crimes because of their emphasis on human rights, access to healthcare for all and the protection of adults and children from exploitation. There are, in addition, a variety of inclusive laws to prosecute trafficking, protect witnesses in trafficking cases, address irregular migrants associated with trafficking activity, protect child and adult refugees, and for extraditing traffickers. Labour trafficking, for example, is covered by the BCEA of 1997, which variously disallows the employment of children, bans forced labour of anyone, and also prohibits inappropriate or high-risk work for people under 18. The production of pornography falls within the ambit of the Films and Publications Act. (No. 3 of 2009), which prohibits obscene material along with the sexual exploitation of children.

Under current South African law, witnesses in trafficking cases are protected by the Witness Protection Act (No. 112 of 1998) or the Protection from Harassment Act (No. 17 of 2011). Irregular migrants involved in trafficking can be prosecuted under the provision of the Immigration Act (No. 13 of 2002), which deals with passports, travel documents and the business operations of undocumented foreigners. The Refugees Act (No. 130 of 1998) provides full legal protection and access to services for refugees.

Three laws – or sets of laws – have been especially important legal devices for exacting justice on traffickers since the 'discovery' of trafficking by lawmakers in the late 20th century. These are Section 7(1) and 7(2) of the Criminal Law (Sexual Offences and Related Matters) Amendment Act (No. 32 of 2007); the Children's Act (No. 38 of 2005), which has been progressively amended to include the procurement of children for use in slavery, commercial sexual exploitation, illegal adoption and the repatriation of child victims of cross-border trafficking, and to a lesser extent, the Child Justice Act (No. 75 of 2008); and the Prevention of Organised Crime Act (No. 121 of 1998), which is essential in undermining the economic logic of trafficking insofar as that it controls the proceeds made from human trade. The POCA also contains an extensive list of charges related to trafficking, including money laundering, racketeering and criminal gang activity on a transnational basis. Unlike the other pre-2013 Acts, it specifically mentions trafficking.

The combined impact of these laws is to regulate child protection and welfare, sexual offences and labour codes governing minimum standards of employment. Unlike any of the other domestic laws, POCA explicitly mentions trafficking. In our history of combating trafficking into the second decade of the 21st century, POCA was, in fact, the law most frequently used to punish traffickers. Section 29 of POCA is especially important in that it prohibits people convicted of murder, torture, genocide, narcotics smuggling, money laundering or kidnapping from entry into South Africa and criminalises anyone who assists a person to enter, remain or depart from the Republic.

All of these acts have been progressively amended over the years so that they can, in some respects, accommodate trafficking. Under amendments to the original Children's Act, procuring a child for use in slavery and commercial sex exploitation carries penalties from five years to life imprisonment. Penalties of up to 20 twenty years' imprisonment are also prescribed under the current SOA for sex trafficking and rape. The crime of trafficking can also be linked to common law charges, such as living on the earnings of prostitution (under the SOA), rape, sexual assault, common assault, assault with the intent to cause grievous bodily harm, murder, and even crimen injuria.

In the last analysis, however, the law before 2013 was riddled with loopholes that helped perpetrators escape justice – with a good defence lawyer. Prosecutions could be tailor-made based on selection from the wide legal menu and this almost invariably meant that traffickers facing the courts were convicted of, at most, minor infractions. Traffickers could even escape the laws altogether because of operational dysfunction in the criminal justice system, such as the failure of the SAPS to investigate what appeared to be trafficking crimes. In general, in this early period, the SAPS was reluctant to enforce the laws because of connivance with traffickers behind the excuse that there is 'no trafficking law in place'.

From an interior perspective, the laws were also inconsistent. Under POCA, for example, traffickers are not explicitly prosecuted for their behaviour. Perhaps most importantly, POCA was and is useless when trafficking is incremental, spontaneous and not a specifically 'organised' form of criminality. Since it only applies to children, the Children's Act could also not be logically invoked against adults or persons over 18. The SOA criminalises trafficking for sexual exploitation. The Act also criminalises certain sexual offences involving both children and adults, and the displaying of indecent sexual material to children or their use for purposes of manufacturing pornography. However, the act cannot be used in crimes that do not ultimately involve the commercial usage of victims. This makes it effectively redundant in prosecuting child labour sanctioned by culture or custom, even in cases where there is an identifiable sexual component. Other than the BCEA, there is no alternative instrument to cover labour trafficking in our criminal justice system. Moreover, none of these acts, the SOA excepted, contain provisions commensurate with the egregious nature of human trafficking, which often involves more than a single term of life imprisonment.

Since the turn of the millennium and the signing of the Palermo Protocol, South Africa has been engaged in the search for an over-arching legal solution for counter-trafficking purposes.[4] While this technically began with the Republic becoming a member of the IOM in 1997, the decision of the Republic to sign the Palermo Protocol in June 1999 was decisive. The Protocol, as we have already noted, obliges signatories to incorporate its provision into domestic law and provides a model for doing so. The requirement to do so was reinforced by anti-trafficking legislation in the United States, which established a worldwide barometer operated by its State Department to judge the progress made by countries in complying with its laws and to take economic action against states falling beneath Tier 3 of its 5-Tier system. In the first and second of these reports, in 2001 and 2002 respectively, South Africa was assigned Tier 2 status just behind the major industrialised countries who were, unsurprising, placed on Level 1.

The counter-trafficking momentum was also fuelled by developments within South Africa itself. These include the decision of the IOM to begin an anti-trafficking project in the country along with two major pieces of seminal analysis (2003), South African ratification of Palermo (2004) and a revised Children's Act with anti-trafficking provisions in 2006. In the meantime, research was undertaken to describe and, if possible, accurately measure the extent of trafficking in the country. The most notable of these studies are the two seminal studies generated by the Cape Town based NGO, Molo Songololo. In 2010, the HSRC published its important but flawed Tsiriledzani Report, which extended research from South Africa to trafficking in the wider subcontinent.

Despite these efforts to define the social reality, South Africa was demoted to a Level 2 Watchlist in the US State Department audit in 2007. This was because seven years after Palermo it had still failed to create appropriate national legislation. The SARLC had already begun to examine the possibility of such a systematic and inclusive anti-trafficking law as far back as the turn of the millennium on the heels of South African adherence to Palermo. Yet progress was very slow due to several mitigating factors which surfaced in trafficking debates between key stakeholders at the time and, over twenty years later, are still important for the roll-out of the law that was eventually formulated. These include bureaucratic resistance on the part of the DSD and the DHA, both of whose provincial organs were expected to take responsibility for a range of new functions despite years of funding constraints and organisational incapacity.

Opposition was also encountered from traditional leaders who anticipated the dilution of customs and culture should the proposed new law prohibit such practices as 'ukuthwala'. Parliamentarians were also not especially active in providing support for new legislation, partially because no one could provide exact statistics on the extent of trafficking to justify a slice of the national budget, but more fundamentally because few had any conception as to the nature of trafficking, barring a handful of exceptions.

Given its universally recognised commitment to human rights enshrined in the Constitution and the Bill of Rights, much of this proved embarrassing to the government and the various local NGOs who had become active in the need to concretise action against traffickers. The United States' pressure on the government to be more energetic in developing anti-instruments was also fuelled by the perception in the American foreign policy establishment that TIP was funded by organisations associated with both global terror and trafficking. After 9/11, the American intelligence community made several overtures to encourage law-making against trafficking among their South African counterparts. The 2010 FIFA World Cup also generated a so-called 'moral panic' based on fears that the country was about to witness a massive increase in prostitution with the arrival of sex-cum-sports tourists into the country. Even though this did not ultimately transpire, following the soccer finals, the South African government began to take counter-trafficking with an unpreceded degree of seriousness.

In 2008, the Minister of Justice and Constitutional Development issued a final report on new counter-trafficking legislation for parliamentary consideration. In 2010, the proposed bill was 'noted' in Parliament before referral for comment to the Parliamentary Portfolio Justice Committee where it languished for another two years while representatives of the various parties weighed up the need for further anti-trafficking legislation, the form it should take and the allocation of public funding. The conspicuous debate focused on the role of organised crime as an actor in the trafficking process and appropriations for the compensation of trafficking survivors. In making their representations, government departments expressed fear of setting irreversible precedents, most particularly the DHA which feared that the act might create a legal basis for foreign victims to remain in South Africa.

The Prevention and Combating of Trafficking Act was finally promulgated. in 2013. However, the process leading to this watershed was tedious, slow and complicated. Even after the promulgation of PACOTIP, it took a further two years to take the Act to the point of operationalisation because the DSD and DHA were resistant to making administrative adjustments necessary to the enforcement of the Act. This act was nevertheless a watershed in the history of trafficking in South Africa. It was, in the words of one commentator, a 'sharp sword' to be used in the prosecution of offenders in line with international standards that could be brought to bear on all forms of trafficking.[5]

The Prevention and Combating of Trafficking Act consists of 10 chapters, a miscellaneous 11th chapter and a total of 49 clauses, all of which in combination improve the normative, legal and operational environment for combating trafficking while transcending all other domestic legislation for doing so. The Act begins with a Preamble which underlines the inadequacy of current common and statutory law to deal with human trafficking. It notes the provision of the Bill of Rights in the Constitution, which enshrines the right to human dignity, freedom and security of the person, including the right not to be arbitrarily deprived of freedom without just cause; the right not to be subjected to slavery, servitude or forced labour; and the right of children to be protected from maltreatment, neglect, abuse and degradation. The Act intends to give effect to the Palermo Protocol in South Africa by aligning domestic law with international standards. It means to define trafficking as a criminal offence, specify appropriate penalties and provide the means to prevent it. It also aims to provide measures to protect and assist victims, provide effective enforcement measures and facilitate the establishment of an inter-sectoral mechanism that combats trafficking in a coordinated manner.

Key definitions go beyond Palermo to whose adherence South Africa agrees to work hand-in-hand with the global community to combat trafficking. This is defined as the physical and psychological 'abuse of vulnerability' that leads a person to believe that he or she has no reasonable alternative but to submit to exploitation. Vulnerability is taken to derive from the illegal presence of a person in the Republic, pregnancy, disability, addiction to a dependency-producing substance, childhood status and/ or socioeconomic circumstances. Exploitation is associated with, inter alia, slavery, which is defined as a 'state of submitting to the control of another person as if the other person were the owner of that person'.

The PACOTIP is victim-centred and maps out an exact programme for the protection and repatriation of both domestic and foreign trafficking victims. The Act states that all trafficking victims must be certified for assistance by a service organisation accredited by the DSD within 24 hours of being informed of a case by the SAPS. All must be informed of their rights, and in the case of foreign trafficking victims, informed of the right to apply for a period of 'recovery and reflection' in the Republic of up to 90 days. During these 90 days, the DSD is given 30 days to investigate whether it is safe for the victim of trafficking (VOT) to be repatriated to his/ her country of origin. If this cannot be completed during the 90 days, the DSD can request the DHA to extend the stay of the repatriation period to six months. The process applies irrespective of whether the VOT is willing to cooperate with the prosecuting and law enforcement authorities.

Trafficking victims who cannot be returned or who agree to cooperate with the prosecuting authorities in the investigation of a case may be granted temporary residence by the DHA for the duration of a case. The victims may work or study during this period and can apply for permanent residence after five years. In this case, the victims must supply proof to the satisfaction of the Director-General of Home Affairs that they may be harmed, killed or trafficked again if they are returned to their countries of origin or the countries from where they have been trafficked. Certified foreign trafficking victims are also entitled to the same healthcare as South African citizens and may not be prosecuted for violation of the Immigration Act, possessing a false passport or any other illegal activity taking place under compulsion.

Similar protections are offered to internal trafficking victims, all of whom must be informed of their rights. Immigration officers, labour inspectors, social workers, medical practitioners, nurses, teachers and traditional healers and leaders are obliged to report to the police for investigation any suspicion on reasonable grounds that a person is a VOT. If police to whom a report has been made suspect that a person is a VOT, he/she must be referred within 24 hours to an accredited organisation of the provincial DSD, pending investigation

PACOTIP also takes note of the contributory role of socioeconomic opportunities in inducing victims' vulnerability. All certified trafficking victims, both domestic and foreign, are immune from prosecution for 'certain offences' committed by them as a direct consequence of their situation. This will enable them to be used as witnesses for the prosecution. Certified trafficking victims are to be assisted by accredited service providers identified by the DSD who can provide services to adult trafficking victims and who qualify for possible financial assistance. Certification is to be based on quality assurance control and performance monitoring based on minimum standards developed in consultation with stakeholder departments, for example, the SAPS, Department of Health (DOH), DOL and the DJCD. Based on information from the accredited service providers, both the service providers and the DSD are obliged to maintain an information system on trafficking victims including the number of foreign victims and South African citizens (including trafficking victims not referred through the SAPS), the countries of origin of foreigners, the destinations to which South African are trafficked, the purpose for which victims are trafficked, the methods of recruitment and transport, routes, and types of travel documents used to cross SA's frontiers and how these were obtained.

Neither the DSD nor the DHA may return any person without due regard to that person's safety during the repatriation process, their safety on return or the possibility that he or she will be harmed, killed or trafficked again. Summary deportation of a VOT is prohibited but the VOT may exercise the voluntary return notwithstanding. The Department of International Relations and Cooperation (DIRCO) is obliged to participate in this assessment while the DHA deals with practical arrangements regarding the safety of trafficking victims during their return.

A broad definition of 'perpetration' includes not only people guilty under the Act but also persons conspiring to commit an offence or inciting, aiding, advising, encouraging or procuring any person to commit an offence. Colluding carriers who assist the entry or exit of trafficking victims from the Republic knowing that the victim does not have the required passport are liable to prosecution. Measures to combat the demand for the services provided by trafficking victims include the criminalisation of users who financially or otherwise benefit from an association with a known VOT or someone who ought reasonably to have been known as a VOT. This includes the intentional lease of property for services provided by trafficking victims. Conduct causing another person to enter into debt bondage is also criminalised.

PACOTIP includes the global principle that it is no defence for a child or those in authority to provide consent to intended exploitation. In the case of children, reporting is obligatory 'despite any law, policy or code of conduct' to enable professional persons to report child trafficking victims without violating professional standards. These protective measures for child trafficking victims are those set out in the Child Care Act (No. 74 of 1983) and the Children's Act but do not apply to persons over 18. Excepting police, immigration, labour officials, mentally disabled persons and those in an 'altered state of consciousness', the written consent of adults must be obtained in reporting to ensure that he/she can lay a charge against the perpetrator.

The chapter dealing with offences and penalties specifies that persons guilty of trafficking are liable to a fine or imprisonment for life, imprisonment without the option of a fine, or both. Factors to be considered in sentencing for various acts involving the deprivation of human rights include the significance of the role of the person in the trafficking process, previous convictions for human trafficking, whether the perpetrators caused the victim to become addicted to a dependence-producing substance, the conditions and time of captivity, the psychological and physical effects suffered by the VOT, whether the VOT was a child and whether there is/was involvement by organised crime.

Persons convicted under the Act may be obliged to pay the VOT compensation for, inter alia, loss of property and/or income, physical and psychological injury or for being infected with a life-threatening disease. Chapter 7 dealing with this in alignment with the provision of Palermo represents an important extension to our criminal law, which has no provisions for damages to be paid to trafficking victims. Penalties are also laid down for persons who intentionally destroy, confiscate or tamper with travel documents of trafficking victims as well as persons benefiting, financially or otherwise from the services of a VOT and who 'knows or ought reasonably to have known' that such a person is a VOT.

The criminalisation of debt bondage is an important device for dealing with labour trafficking.

Media as well as internet service providers 'operating in the Republic' must take 'reasonable steps' to prevent their service from being used to advertise or promote trafficking and failure to report a site is an offence liable for a fine or imprisonment. Since trafficking in persons is an international crime, Clause 10 gives the High Court universal jurisdiction, irrespective of where the offence was committed, by whom and against whom.

Police officials are expected to report details on their execution of the Act. This includes the division/s to be tasked with investigating human trafficking, the general management of trafficking cases from reporting to referral, measures to be taken at ports of entry and borders, and the development of information systems. Similar directives apply to Home Affairs, Labour, the DSD and the NPA. Disciplinary steps are to be taken against any police official, prosecutor or another functionary who fails to comply with any duty imposed on him or her in terms of this Act or the national instructions or directives issued in terms of this Act.

PACOTIP reinforces the principles of the Service Charter for the Victims of Crime and also maps out a concrete plan to deal with trafficking which overarches governmental departments with their silo approaches in doing so. This is effected through the establishment of an Inter-Sectoral Committee composed of representatives of the DJCD, the SAPS, the DHA, the IRC, the DSD, the DOH, the DOL, the National Intelligence Agency, the NPA and Government Communications. The committee may co-opt representatives of civil society as necessary. The key stakeholder departments are to develop a national policy framework to plan implementation and ensure coordination. Under the administrative provision of PACOTIP, they are also obliged to develop training courses and promote the use of uniform norms, standards and procedures to ensure appropriate, efficient and sensitive trafficking management.

Of particular importance is that PACOTIP takes cognisance of multisectoral institutions already in operation before its promulgation to endorse an inter-sectoral device to facilitate its enforcement. This is now encapsulated in the National Policy Framework that was established in 2019 following various private-public sector consultations to give concrete content to the new law, which has been labelled a 'sharp sword against trafficking' in line with, and in some senses, exceeding global prosecutorial stands.[6]

As it currently stands, the 2019 'system' is headed by a National Anti-Trafficking Coordinator to coordinate, monitor and report on the implementation of the policy framework. The coordinator is responsible to the Chief Director of the DJCD, and ultimately to the Minister of Justice and Constitutional Development. The coordinator also heads up a National Inter-Sectoral Committee on Trafficking in Persons (NICTIP) to facilitate and support execution of the policy framework ensuring that the relevant departments of government (and other stakeholders) fulfil their respective obligations.[7]

The NICTIP has several sub-committees and in order 'to promote a cooperative and aligned response' it establishes in association with provincial structures in each of South Africa's nine provinces. Each is equipped with a response team to deal with operational matters. These response teams are expected to function as 'front-liners' in providing a coordinated and rapid response when suspected cases of TIP are reported. This includes 'swiftly setting into motion the coordinated and multi-disciplinary management' of TIP cases; identifying, supporting and protecting victims; prosecuting traffickers; assisting in the case-flow process; updating provincial structures on the progress of pending cases, and allocating and using available resources both efficiently and effectively.

The provincial structures together constitute what is termed South Africa's National Coordination Referral Mechanism.

It must be emphasised that this entire system is not necessarily unique or indigenous to South Africa. Counter-trafficking through multistakeholder arrangements bridging the state and civil society is the prevalent paradigm in many countries and there are dozens if not hundreds of counter- trafficking coalitions currently at work to stem TIP based on this model. Some function at the national level and can be used as a comparative tool for South Africa's new policy framework – while some are sub-national. These include the Enhanced Collaborative Model in the United States, which is strikingly similar to the policy framework in both structure and intention. This works under the Federal Bureau of Justice Affairs and the Office for Victims of Crime.

Irrespective of its internal excellence, PACOTIP, as well as other legislation that can be brought to bear on offenders, shares problems of enforcement common to anti-trafficking legislation and criminal justice systems worldwide, as well as in Africa and on its southern subcontinent. This extensive catalogue of operational constraints includes major problems of policing that undermine investigative efficiency, widespread corruption at all levels in law enforcement, dysfunctional data management systems and serious inconsistencies in the prosecution and conviction process.[8]

Given the intrinsic interconnection between PACOTIP and the policy framework whose provincial structures and response teams are meant, among other responsibilities, to interdict criminals, deficiencies in the PACOTIP create dysfunctionality in its key implementation vehicle. There are many deficiencies in so-called national policy frameworks worldwide and, overall, the policy framework is at this point in its existence is a very weak tool for catching traffickers. This is not necessarily conceded by governmental departments participating in the policy framework, many of whom resent external monitoring of underperformance. This is, however, not necessarily the case with CSOs that are available to speak and are highly critical of the workings of the policy framework based on their roughly two-year experience.

Effective multisectoral counter-trafficking organisations, of which the policy framework is one manifestation, generally require certain virtually decisive preconditions to make the transition from creation to 'take-off'. For the most part, these are absent in the sociological environment of the current provincial structures.[9] These include prior experience with multi-stakeholders as a tool for resolving policy conflict, effective leadership to ignite and then crystallise the foundation process, an energetic civil society with dedicated counter-trafficking organisations, a relatively high level of urbanisation in the target areas, and levels of literacy and education consistent with the circulation of social messages and other trafficking information. Other than KwaZulu-Natal – which is by consensus the

far-and-away best example of a provincial approach to TIP at present –
only Gauteng and the Western Cape possess elements of these critical
pre-dispositions, each of which is a necessary but insufficient element in
the recipe for an effective counter-trafficking operation in contemporary
South Africa.

The present South African state also has serious problems of 'agency
loss' because of corruption that allows trafficking interests to undermine
'local and regional authorities, border officials, labour regulators,
immigration personnel and law enforcement officials' to the advantage
of trafficking interests.[10] Agency loss also impacts the transmission of
policy from the centre to the grassroots so that the policy framework
organograms do not necessarily describe the way the policy framework
actually functions.

The regional representatives of the key governmental departments
designated for service in the provincial structures are a case in point.
Outside of the policy framework, whose senior personnel chair the
provincial structures, the great majority of these departments, so
CSOs complain, are mainly absent from the meetings of the provincial
bodies to which they have, for the most part, merely instrumental
connections. Officials are frequently 'unavailable' for meetings because
of other bureaucratic engagements, sheer laziness, or because they have
other priorities that exclude trafficking and are better placed to ensure
promotion. It seems that departmental incapacity undermines the
availability of officials for anything outside their core functions. This
includes such critical participants as the regional representatives of the
DOH, the DSD and above all, DHA officials who often change between
meetings in a way that undermines coherence and continuity. Despite
the importance of trafficking from rural to urban areas, it is extremely
rare to find provincial representatives of, for instance, the Department
of Agriculture, Land Reform and Rural Development attending sessions
regularly. The intelligence organs of the state are almost always absent
notwithstanding their core function in dealing with the interface between
trafficking and organised crime. The policy framework design mentions
traditional authorities but it is again extremely rare to find them in a
session of a provincial structure. As with many other critical provincial

players, their officials often justify non-involvement with the policy framework because 'we know little about trafficking'.

Sustainability of the policy framework and its provincial structures also requires effective adequate finance and far more overall effort to address serious and systemic incoordination. Yet, two years after its elaboration in governmental circles, the lack of financial capacity in the policy framework 'system' remains a major problem for provincial structures that receive no central government funding. Planning for preventative work becomes extremely difficult in these cases where provincial structures experience ongoing 'fund-swings' between coffers that are reasonably full or, more invariably, empty. The CSOs providing support to the task teams do so on a gratis basis despite their financial constraints. The constant state of near or virtual indebtedness facing each PPT also has major impacts on protective activity in the service network of safe houses, repatriation facilities, and other physical and mental health institutions to which victims are referred.

Coordination problems leading to jurisdiction overlaps are almost always among the primary problems confronting nascent counter-trafficking coalitions involved in counter-trafficking via complex systems of interacting institutions, networks, policy frameworks and governance structures. In South Africa's case, inter-agency cooperation, or lack thereof, is also a major stumbling block in attempting to provide a coordinated response to trafficking under the auspices of the policy framework. Plans to create a Secretariat as an arch-mechanism for the system have failed to materialise for a mixture of financial and political reasons and there is an urgent requirement for improved communication, both horizontal and vertical between the various stakeholders.

The process by which civil society is incorporated into each provincial structure designated by the policy framework is also variable because of the failure of the policy, as with many other counter-trafficking coalitions, to define the key term, 'civil society participation'. In actuality, there are no hard-and-fast rules for admission of civil society representatives into the various provincial bodies. In some cases, or so it appears, NGOs and other CSOs are chosen according to DSD accreditation, which, as we shall see, is problematic. However, in other cases, NGOs become members upon simple recognition by the chairperson 'in consultation' with sitting members. This opens up the dire possibility that the inclusion or exclusion of NGOs in provincial structures can end up being the choices of chairpersons or by the existing 'ethos' in a committee with their values, attitudes and perceptions framed around a particular discourse, such as sex or child trafficking.

Even more egregious are cases where civil society 'representatives' are chosen at random or where an ostensible member is a person simply walking through the door claiming NGO representation and is 'recognised' by the meeting or its chairperson. In these cases, of which there are some outside the elite provincial structure triad of KZN, Gauteng and the Western Cape, a member may or may not be a respected member of a society, may represent no one or, worst-of-all, be an actual informant working for networks of trafficking perpetrators.

The attendance of CSOs at provincial structure meetings is also discontinuous with organisations coming or going as their sentiments and interests dictate. While the National Freedom Network (NFN) coordinates most CSOs with a counter-trafficking disposition, it does not control their membership in the provincial structures. This is decided by the leaders of each of the roughly 100 organisations belonging to the NFN, the main vehicle for aggregating anti-trafficking responses. Many members are unable to be sustainable members of the provincial structures because of logistic and financial problems. In some provincial structures, certain CSOs regularly attend meetings of the provincial structure because they believe attendance to be of importance in principle. This is characteristic of the bigger and more established anti-trafficking organisations as such as A21, or Love Justice, among a few others that (perhaps inadvertently) shape the CSO 'culture' at the provincial level. More frequently, however, attendance ebbs and flows for several reasons including secretarial failures that preclude members from diarising future meetings, member frustration over decisions and proceedings, or in some cases, the prospects for the personal company and a free beer. For every civil society organisation that values participation in the local provincial structure as a matter of civic responsibility there are almost always others – so some CSOs allege – whose involvement is simply unadulterated self-interest.

Accreditation by the DSD is also technically required for CSOs to participate in the provincial structures. This is also problematic for a number of NGOs that would otherwise welcome the opportunity to sit on the provincial structures as a means to acquire status and possible funding for their work at local level. Many civil society organisations simply do not participate in the policy framework because they believe, rightly or wrongly, that they will not meet DSD recognition criteria, because the terms of accreditation seem daunting, because there is an information gap around counter-trafficking policy or because of previous experiences of the DSD in discouraging dissent. In some cases, this feeds into the broader view that the provincial structures are simply compliant 'instruments' of government.

The performance of the response teams working at the interface between policy and the hard reality of trafficking is an additional problem triggered when suspected trafficking cases are brought to light at the provincial level by the SAPS, the intelligence agencies or some other third party. The response team is then, at least theoretically, activated and sent on-site to the nodal point of TIP activity where it performs an extrication function. Should victims be encountered and injured physically, they are treated by paramedics mainly from the local DOH, simultaneously identified and then sent into DSD assistance networks – shelters or safe houses – where they receive trauma and other forms of counselling designed to re-empower and re-integrate them into the social mainstream in either the short or (in most cases), longer term.

There have been few response team interventions, partially because of the unfortunate coincidence between the roll-out of the policy framework and the pandemic. The seemingly simple process of AER, namely, activation of the response team, extrication of victims and their referral or rehabilitation is, however, complicated in reality by several factors that characterise the 'normal' raids conducted by the authorities in the general enforcement of PACOTIP.

Much like admissions of CSOs to membership of the provincial structures, there are no hard-and-fast guidelines as to the composition of the response teams other than what emerges from negotiations between potential actors on a case-by-case basis. Thus, the response team may or may not include para-medical personnel, social workers or other forms of critical immediate assistance to victims on site. There are cases where victims have suffered secondary traumatisation at the point of contact with their ostensible 'rescuers' because psychological services are not in place.

In far too many cases, the role of the SAPS as support services for the response teams and as an entry point for the referral of victims into DSD assistance channels is also problematic. When response teams raid brothels, for example, the SAPS may (or may not) appear because their commanders have been bribed by the owners of enterprises where the police are colloquial, 'in their pockets'. Far too many members of the SAPS are reluctant to intervene in cases where young women are employed involuntarily to provide sexual services. They prefer to work on large-scale drug busts that are bound to be registered for a promotion. While many SAPS members are 'hardened' through the career-long experience of atrocity crimes, others, especially newer recruits, are reluctant to participate in situations where evidence exists of young women and even children being abused and force-fed narcotics.

There are numerous cases where the provincial structure has become a site of struggle over ostensible TIP crimes. This is because of the reluctance of the SAPS to provide what it deems 'sensitive' information, the inaccuracy of police data or the failure of law enforcement to prioritise TIP crimes among others. In some provinces, such as the Eastern Cape, the response teams are largely dormant precisely because of differences between the local SAPS and other stakeholders over membership of the response teams. In other provinces, the response teams remain semi-functional because of continuous staff turnover among SAPS members liaising with the provincial structures. There has been at least one case where differences between the SAPS and other provincial structure members on responses to a trafficking case have seriously prejudiced the rights of a child trafficking victim.

Much of this depends on the caseload and availability of SAPS personnel, the degree to which provincial commanders at mid-level have experienced counter-trafficking training, and various idiosyncratic factors beyond the purvey of the national framework. The personal connection between provincial structure members and mid-level officials is especially important when deciding whether the local SAPS is willing to accommodate response teams work on an otherwise busy agenda. This personal connection can also make the critical difference between provincial structures that have relatively succeeded (such as KZN) and those that have failed in performance practice.

Accurate victim identification is always a hazardous aspect of the interdiction and extraction process carried out at the nodes between provinces and perpetrators. This is especially relevant where victims are profoundly traumatised by the experience, rendered incoherent as a result of drug force-feeding by their perpetrators or are otherwise averse to cooperation with a response team that may, or may not, arrive at crime scenes on a consistent basis. There are cases described by response team personnel where victims have refused to cooperate with their rescuers for a variety of reasons including fear of their perpetrators or fear that their perpetrators are entangled in corrupt relationships with the SAPS that will reverberate back on the life chances of the victim. One such case involving commercial sex trafficking has seen Thai women in prostitution rejecting overtures of assistance because of monetary awards and ostensible job satisfaction.

The position of foreign victims, either documented or, in the majority of cases, undocumented, is especially problematic. This is because victims fear repatriation in a situation where PACOTIP, seven years on, has failed to legislate key immigration provisions, or because of the fear that the SAPS will desist from deportation unless they cooperate with the police on TIP investigations. While this is patently illegal under the existing PACOTIP provisions, considerations of this nature inevitably define boundaries for response team action largely irrespective of what the provincial structure has decided. All of this is aggravated by the general lack of translators to work hand-in-hand with the response teams where foreigners do not speak one of the official South African languages. In this case, what transpires at the nodal point where the response team meets the victims depends on how many speakers of foreign languages are able in the immediate geography to service the response team, the provincial structures and the local SAPS division.

There is some evidence of demoralisation in the response teams bred by the often traumatic work they are required to do as well as their involvement at the interface where perpetrators are either not brought to justice or are slapped lightly on their wrists. While there is firm evidence that prosecutions (and even convictions) are increasing under the umbrella of PACOTIP, statistics of this type are of little assistance to workers at the coalface of human degradation. There are some anecdotal and indicative cases where response team members (along with those of the SAPS) are referred to the counselling services along with the victims they have rescued. At the same time, the risk factor in response team work has increased with the growing involvement of international syndicates in South Africa's commercial sex industry. In these circumstances, every response team worker has to consider that his work will run into the hard-edged face of professional criminals.

The 'provinciality' of the provincial structures is also problematic because many, if not most, trafficking problems have a national as opposed to local dimension. Some of these already mentioned include widespread corruption in law enforcement, the flow of highly vulnerable foreign migrants across South Africa's frontiers, increased labour trafficking associated with illegal mining operations, the penetration of South Africa's political economy by transnational criminal networks, the relative absence of political will and capacity in many state institutions concerned with TIP, the poverty of resources in rehabilitation systems geared to re-integrating victims of TIP into the social mainstream, and a criminal justice system reluctant to punish perpetrators to the extent commensurate with the seriousness of their crimes.

These trans-provincial considerations impact different provincial structures in different ways. In the mining sectors in Gauteng and the Free State, there is a substantial flow of trafficked persons that challenge counter-trafficking capacity in all of its manifestations. In Gauteng, labour trafficking in the residual mines of the West and East Rand takes place untrammelled a few kilometres away from the provincial structure headquarters, which is relatively silent about the perpetration of serious crimes against human dignity in both artisanal and shallow sub-subsurface surroundings. In the Free State, where residual gold mining still takes place around Welkom there is no provincial structure to speak of other than an ostensible 'committee' that meets on an occasional basis. This means that the large numbers of young men trafficked across the porous borders with Lesotho into deep underground operations for months at a time continue largely unabated.

Further north, there is little resembling a fully functioning provincial structure in Limpopo, which plays host to the operations at the narrow boundary between human smuggling and outright trafficking of both undocumented and questionably 'legal' foreigners entering the Republic across the north and north-eastern borders. Since the majority of these people who are not criminally recruited into local agricultural activity head for Johannesburg or even Cape Town, the problem is displaced onto the Gauteng and Western Cape provincial structures, which are busy.

In the North-West there is only a smidgeon of what could be termed a functional provincial structure. This is at a time when Rustenburg has become a distribution point for legions of fly-by-night labour brokers supplying workers to mines across the platinum belt. These include a large number of women in prostitution whose role is to service the sexual needs of men living in near-mine communities or, in some cases, within the dormitory accommodation of mines.

The focus of the provincial structures is also selective relative to the real-time complexity of trafficking issues. The PACOTIP and policy framework aim to deal with all forms of trafficking yet labour trafficking is largely neglected because of general conflation at the provincial level of trafficking with sex trafficking. This may be attributable to the high proportion of women in the civil society organisation component of each provincial structure, because of broader ideological orientations brought into the provincial structure system by its members or because of the utility of sex trafficking narratives to mobilise counter-trafficking sentiments among the greater mass of the population. Either way far more needs to be done to alter this perspective in line with the very substantial degree of forced and bonded labour used in South Africa's manufacturing, mining and agricultural sectors. Other than in the Western Cape where many young 'coloured' women are involuntarily indentured, the issue of domestic servitude is almost absent from provincial structure agendas.

Much the same applies to organ trafficking, illegal adoption, child-briding, *ukuthwala* (outside the Eastern Cape) and other 'minor' forms of TIP.

At this early stage, the exact impact of the policy framework, least of all its provincial structures, cannot be exactly determined because the entire system is still in its nascency. Overall, however, the establishment of the National Policy Framework as the implementing arm of the PACOTIP has led to the upgrading of South Africa to Tier Two in the United States' annual audit of global counter-trafficking. By mid-2020, there were ostensibly increased prosecutions and conviction of traffickers relative to the previous year, more counter-trafficking training of front-line responders at the national and provincial levels and greater numbers of victims being identified and referred to care. The policy framework labelled as 'a strategic plan to improve capacity and coordination among government agencies', also increased awareness of trafficking among the general public and stimulated South African adherence to the SADC regional data collection tool. In the period 2019/20, the DJCD included, for the first time, an indicator of trafficking in its annual performance plan, the department's strategic plan through which Parliament held it accountable.

Having said this, the emergence of the policy framework has done little to address some of the key problems inhibiting effective counter-trafficking. These include corruption among law enforcement officials (including border police), greater investment of resources to inhibit labour trafficking, training new labour inspectors, and investigating the use of child labour and adults trafficked into various sectors of the economy, such as in the agricultural, mining, construction, and fishing sectors. The advent of the policy framework also seems to have done little to encourage the government, especially the DHA, to implement the immigration provisions of the PACOTIP that have been in abeyance for the last seven to eight years. Roughly a year after the advent of the policy framework, much remains to be done to address the lack of capacity in the SAPS, enhanced mechanisms to screen traffickers among vulnerable populations, amend PACOTIP to remove sentencing provisions allowing fines instead of imprisonment for some sex trafficking crimes, and to extend the network of dedicated trafficking facilities for both men and women trafficking.

As already implied, many critical issues simply escape the policy framework and continued to do so immediately after its creation. These include the failure of the LRA to inhibit worker abuse in the informal sector and efforts to amend the birth registration process which underwrites the ongoing abuse of children. Many suggestions fed into the framework at the centre or through regional mechanisms by NGOs go unregistered in the feedback loop between civil society and government.

Public awareness to prevent trafficking also remains tentative and the goal of developing widespread public consciousness as an intelligence tool for counter-trafficking is still chimerical. Notwithstanding the activities of provincial structures acting under the aegis of the policy framework to engage in a range of activities, such as pamphlet distribution, releases of news to local media, distribution of DVDs about TIP and many other counter-trafficking initiatives under the preventative function, the greater majority of people remain relatively unaware of key issues. These include the malignant relationship between sex work and trafficking, the role of drugs in sexual exploitation, the variety of mechanisms used to groom trafficked children, the pernicious role of pornography and the internet in fuelling activity, the policy framework and the PACOTIP, least of all its key provisions.

While training programmes of law enforcement officials appeared to have increased in the first year after the establishment of the policy framework, very much remains to be done to conscientise and mobilise government personnel on the provincial task teams to trafficking as a crisis issue. This especially applies to the SAPS who remain generally insensitive to the interface between culture and trafficking in the case of undocumented foreigners. Far more needs to be done within the policy framework to develop translator resources to identify trafficking victims and promote cooperation between the SAPS and the DSD in the referral process system. Instances, where trafficking victims are arrested and then shoved back across the borders, are especially egregious

Notwithstanding the advent of the policy framework, the situation of trafficking victims beyond extrication from points of exploitation remains a nightmare. In most cases, the AER activity at the nodal points between victims and frontline responders still involves victims in a bureaucratic maze where what is to be done, and how, remains generally uncertain. The emergence of the policy framework has not seen the development of an effective sheltering

National policy framework structures at the highest level remained fractured during the first year after the introduction of the new system. According to the 2021 State Department audit, 'both the NICTIP and the provincial task teams often exhibited poor coordination and communication'. 'Some of the provincial task teams ceased meeting or functioning' for reasons we have already articulated. According to the audit, there was 'no accountability' to require these groups (namely, the provincial structures), to function. Officials in positions of authority with the ability to facilitate change, it adds, 'rarely attended meetings'.

Critics of the policy framework have also suggested that the marginally increased prosecution levels of traffickers in the dawn of the national framework may be illusory and unsustainable in the absence of structural reform in the criminal justice system. This includes the prosecution of law enforcers and other government officials who take bribes from criminal syndicates in the execution of their duty, capacity-building to ensure the safety of officials who become whistle-blowers, and dedicated counter-trafficking investigative procedures. As of 2020, none of these changes in police management had been even remotely accomplished.

All this reflects the fact that inter-organisational cooperation is always a risky business, especially collaborative ventures between government and civil society where interactions change and evolve, circumstances and responses to opportunities. Most counter-trafficking coalitions fail after two or three years and the average lifespan, in all but exceptional cases is five years (which coincides with the policy framework's projected cycle).[11] This reflects complexity of factors from historic background to geography but is most often associated with failures to fully develop an embracing multisectoral ethic that transcends the often different agendas of government departments and civil society organisations locked into a multisectoral modality.

There are other ecological challenges facing states in a counter-trafficking posture like the policy framework.[12] Bureaucratic efficiency and adequate finance are critical predeterminants of performance in counter-trafficking coalitions designed along the lines of the policy framework because anti-trafficking initiatives are almost always cost-intensive. counter-trafficking coalitions only function effectively within the framework of 'relatively stable political institutions and highly developed infrastructure'. Trafficking along the lines of the policy framework almost inevitably fails when 'zones of impunity' emerge in cases where the minorities are abused and, once again, corruption is ingrained.

There are no 'once-and-for-all' solutions to human trafficking. An overall recipe probably involves a mix of international legislation, criminal sanctions and law enforcement officials with credibility among the general public. The latter is, of course, problematic for the policy framework in South Africa. Much like its predecessor the PACOTIP, the policy framework represents a step forward on the very long and rocky road to effectively manage trafficking in the Republic. Its intentions are good and it also constitutes a role model in some respects for similar national anti-trafficking initiatives in the Republic's neighbouring states. It demonstrates both what and what not to do in creating and then attempting to run an anti-trafficking mechanism with all its inherent problems. This being said, there is a huge discrepancy between the goals expected of the PACOTIP, the policy framework and the hard operational realities, the 'facts on the ground' to which some of the more vocal critics in civil society quietly speak. From what we can see from the vantage point of 2022, the policy framework is deficient in many respects from what is taken as an effective counter-trafficking coalition. There are intellectual, motivational and organisational chasms between the government bureaucrats largely responsible for the current form of the policy framework irrespective of 'widespread inter-sectoral consultation much like those between the legal minds behind PACOTIP and the institutions deemed responsible for its execution. The organogram sketched out in the initial stages of the policy framework does not reflect what is taking place at central and, for the most part, in the provincial structures The policy framework may not be an especially good example of a 'national policy framework', when referenced against the dozen global criteria for effective public policy, the United Nations sustainable development goals or even the 2020 National Development Plan forming part of the background to the spawning of a younger cousin.[13]

The global pandemic has, in the meantime, led to massive organisational failures in both governmental and NGO sectors, both worldwide and in South Africa. This has major implications for counter-trafficking governance in South Africa and the abutting region. The following two chapters discuss some of these issues.

CHAPTER
6

The regional framework

South Africa is the core of a constellation of states to which it is linked by a dense network of political, cultural and socioeconomic connections. This includes six states on its immediate borders – Lesotho (enclaved within the Republic), Botswana (to the north-east), Eswatini (formally Swaziland in the south-east, Namibia (to the north-west), Mozambique (along the eastern border), and Zimbabwe (across the Limpopo to the north). While neither Zambia nor Malawi are direct neighbours of the Republic, both have historic connections to the Republic and are normally included in definitions of the southern African subcontinent. All nine countries including South Africa are members of SADC and, perhaps more importantly, are described by the United States' Department of State annual barometer of human trafficking as countries whose track record on human trade since 2015 as troubling. (See Appendix A.)

In the absence of statistics, there is uncertainty about the prevalence of human trafficking in the region. Much as in South Africa, we lack data on the extent of TIP, both in the region as a whole and in the eight states which constitute our focus in this chapter. The US State Department barometer of trafficking across the world is not especially helpful since it is only a grading tool with various indicators of counter-trafficking, unpopulated by statistics. This is also true of other audits such as the Global Slavery Index and the Counter Trafficking Data Collaborative whose figures are, at best, empirically unproved estimations.

In South Africa itself, trans-frontier trafficking is the focal point for the majority of studies that consequentially underestimate internal or domestic trafficking. We, however, suggest the trafficking across the borders into the neighbouring states, Africa and further beyond possibly accounts for some 40% of the total number of victims imported, exported or in transit across the territorial boundaries of the Republic. Over and beyond these, there is a constant human spill over of trafficking activities in and between other southern African states, which are, from a trafficking perspective, interdependent with each other. This means that at a time of globalisation we cannot comprehensively understand trafficking within the Republic without reference to what takes place immediately outside its territory. By the same token, regional trafficking provides an important backdrop against which South African TIP can be loosely compared.[1]

A cursory regional perspective also reveals that the forces behind trafficking are, in most respects, similar in both the subcontinent and its core. These invariably include poverty, economic inequality, unemployment, gender violence, or lack of access to education, housing, and other community services. In Eswatini and other countries in the region, traffickers also target poor communities with high infection levels of the HIV epidemic in the process of identifying potential victims. Family breakdown, which is both a cause and a consequence of unaccompanied children moving across borders, is also important. Other factors coming to the fore include customary laws bent to the perverse purpose of human trade. *Ukuthwala*, which we have already identified as a source of forced marriage on the part of young women in the Republic, also sometimes carries across national boundaries from the Eastern Cape into Lesotho, KZN and further afield.[2]

The region is also home to substantial numbers of displaced men, women and children who, like their counterparts in other regions of the world, are highly at risk of TIP. Unaccompanied children frequently move across regional borders in search of families or friends who may have moved earlier, or employment and opportunity. Many live on the streets of small towns where they eke out a marginal existence. Others subsist in the bush in places like northern Mozambique, which has been rocked by a mixture of political violence caused by the intrusion of Islamist rebels as well as the destruction caused by two tropical cyclones over the last two years. According to international estimates, as of April 2021, there are more than 700 000 internally displaced persons (IDPs) in the so-called 'resettlement' camps in the area where non-state armed groups traffic for sexual purposes and forced labour.[3]

There are other concentrations of IDPs in resettlement camps susceptible to trafficking. These include Dukwe, where thousands of inhabitants are restricted in their freedom of movement because of ongoing delays in obtaining refugee status. This makes them vulnerable to small-scale traffickers as well as syndicates offering 'liberation'. Much the same occurs in the much larger Dzakela refugee camp and at Tongorora near Harare.[4] The former houses almost 50 000 refugees and asylum seekers from many countries including Congo, Rwanda, Burundi and Somalia. Many of these are stateless women who are used by consortia of traffickers both inside the camp in areas adjacent to the camp or further afield. Tongariro in turn contains legions of young Somali and DRC girls whose statelessness is manipulated by a variety of strangers who subsequently despatch them into involuntary sex networks throughout the region.[5]

Patterns of perpetration and victimhood are also not dissimilar to those found in the South African epicentre. Most traffickers of the minority who are intercepted appear to be locals given to recruitment and exploitation of their fellow nationals, but there are also perpetrators from other parts of Africa and even from as far away as Asia. In Malawi, for example, the national complement of perpetrators is accompanied by foreign nationals from Zambia, Mozambique as well as Pakistan and China. Malawian victims of labour and sex trafficking work far afield in Kenya, Mozambique, South Africa, Tanzania, and Zambia.[6] Others are sold trans-continentally for domestic servitude in the Gulf states, especially Kuwait and Saudi. Young men, women and children from East Africa are also sent via Zimbabwe to South Africa in a mixture of human smuggling-cum -trafficking operations. Child labour, involving some of the worst practices, is widespread in agriculture and especially pronounced in the Malawi tobacco industry.[7]

Trafficking occurs even in the smaller southern African states where victims may be moved surreptitiously across borders, between regions within states or held in temporary transit facilities before transportation to eventual sites of exploitation. In Malawi, trafficking flows mainly but not exclusively involve the movement of victims from the southern to the central and northern regions of the country.[8] Many trafficking victims are held for long periods in transit before eventual deployment. In Botswana, Central and West Africa, migrants are frequently intercepted by Zimbabwean gangs while crossing Botswana for South Africa.[9] Zimbabweans involved in labour and sex trafficking use much the same route for transporting Somalis and Ethiopians en route to the Republic.[10]

Recruitment characteristically involves fraud rather than violence. In Mozambique, young women are approached in the rural areas, promised false jobs in Maputo or Beira and then find themselves in brothels on arrival.[11] Victims characteristically include a mixture of men, women and children recruited and subsequently exploited for an array of purposes similar to those encountered in the Republic. Although we cannot strictly compare prevalence within and between South Africa and its neighbours because of the all-round absence of statistics, sexual exploitation, involuntary prostitution and child trafficking appear rampant across the region.

The trafficking and exploitation of children are also widespread, especially in cases where children are in ongoing movement between transnational households, or as a consequence of illegal child placement through adoption and informal fostering arrangements.[12] This is especially acute, but by no means confined to the Botswana-Zimbabwe and South African-Zimbabwe borders where traffickers are alert to the presence of unaccompanied adolescents.

Forced labour occurs throughout rural areas, in many cases because of a mixture of culture and customs.[13]

Child labour persists in the region. This is mainly because of limited public awareness; limited state capacity to enforce existing laws; poor school transportation, infrastructure and material conditions in rural areas; a lack of vocational primary and secondary educational opportunities for street children, abandoned children, child-headed households, pregnant girls, teenage mothers, children of migrant workers, orphans affected by HIV, and many others.[14] In cities like Gaborone or Lusaka as well as in smaller towns like Mbabane or Maseru, small businesses exploit teenage or pre-teen children as delivery boys or storekeepers with minimal wages. Some also work as babysitters, houseboys, gardeners and in other forms of domestic labour.

The forced labour of children occurs in the agricultural sector in all the states in the subcontinent.[15] This includes Malawi, where children, some as young as five, are used in herding goats and doing back-breaking work, such as brickmaking. These children are denied education and access to health facilities and many are trafficked to tobacco farms within Malawi and in the neighbouring countries of Zambia, Tanzania and Mozambique to work as tobacco pickers. As in South Africa, albino women and children are always at risk of being violently trafficked or killed according to local customs.[16]

According to the United States annual barometer Country Studies, 9% of children in Botswana are engaged in some of the worst forms of child labour. Most cattle herders are children forced to work by their relatives and family in remote farming areas[17]. In Eswatini, Swati boys are found on small marijuana farms in rural areas.[18] In Zambia, child labour is present in agriculture, textile production, mining, construction, and small businesses such as bakeries. Orphans and street children are also used for forced begging in the cities.

Zambian children are trafficked from the depressed western areas into Namibia.[19] There are also so-called 'jerabo' gangs who force Zambian children in the Copperbelt into illegal mining operations, such as loading stolen copper or crushing rocks. Solwezi is an especially dangerous site for child sex and labour exploitation.[20]

Throughout the subcontinent, poor families inadvertently assist sex and labour traffickers by sending their children to work in the cities, which is seen as relatively lucrative and higher in status than labouring on farms. In Botswana, as well as in other countries throughout the region, there is a general reluctance to intervene in sometimes distorted cultural practices governing the use of children in working on farms at an early age.[21] Meanwhile, some parents in poor, rural Batswana families – particularly the San people – send their children to work as domestic servants in towns and cities where they are confined, subjected to abuse and denied education.[22]

Throughout the region, this situation is reinforced by rules governing school admission that require an identity document or birth certificate, which few rural children have. This means that for many children, exploitative farm work is the only option.[23] In Namibia, where children are exploited in the fishing industry alongside the country's extended coastline, fostered children and children of certain ethnic groups are also at risk. These include San children, as in Botswana, as well as children of Zemba extraction.[24] Both adults and children in Malawi are either imported or imported for forced labour from Mozambique, Zambia, the Great Lakes region or, further afield, the Horn of Africa.[25]

The local fishing industry is also a potential site for trafficked children who are coerced into begging and committing minor crimes. In Zimbabwe, forced child begging by Mozambican children takes place in Mbare and other towns and cities. Indian-Zambian consortia also exist to traffic children for sex and domestic work in Zambia and South Asia more generally.[26] In an age of digital communication, online pornography is widely used to 'groom' children in Zambia and more widely afield in the region.[27]

Several factors, including poverty, absentee parenting, peer pressure and exposure to risky lifestyles, encourage child prostitution. In some parts of Zimbabwe, child prostitutes make up a fifth of the overall child population. This figure is increasing as the country remains in an economic crisis.[28]

Despite its relative success as a southern African country dealing with trafficking forced sex work involving women and children is widely prevalent in Namibia in places such as Windhoek and Swakopmund.[29] This is often facilitated by domestic and trans-frontier transport networks, taxis or bus drivers complicit with traffickers. Many Zimbabwean children (and adults) are, for example, taken to Beit Bridge or nearby unofficial crossing locations by Zimbabwean bus drivers where they are transferred to their South African counterparts linked to criminal gangs working outwards into the Republic from Musina and, more generally, the Limpopo River.[30]

Truck drivers are also notorious for exploiting Zambian boys and girls in sex trafficking in towns along the Zimbabwean and Tanzanian borders, and miners exploit them in Solwezi.[31]

Highly mobile child populations available for sex trafficking are also of concern in Mozambique cities such as Beira, Chimoio, Tete and Nacala, which also have high concentrations of truck drivers. There are also reports of child refugees in Botswana being exploited in sex trafficking, including by South African truck drivers transiting the country. Sex trafficking within and over borders is prolific as desperately poor women succumb to false promises of a better life in the large urban centres or neighbouring countries. In Mozambique, large numbers of women leave their residential areas in the interior in the hope of social integration through paid work but then fall into the hands of traffickers who use them as sex slaves or sell them to third parties.[32]

Mozambican towns along the South African frontier are major jump-off points for exporting women for a mixture of purposes including sex and labour trafficking in the Republic. Transit points, such as bus stations, rail depots and border areas, are hotbeds of sexual trafficking. In Mpumalanga, makeshift brothels with a variety of women of all nationalities pepper the border areas. Many are staffed by Zimbabwean women and children of all ages. Many bars and nightclubs throughout the subcontinent house brothels cater to a variety of clients, including passing long-distance truck drivers.

Some traffickers force young Eswatini girls coming undocumented into South Africa into commercial sex work under the pretence of offering lucrative job opportunities. Targets of choice include orphans and girls precluded from returning to their families by poverty in their country of origin. Other girls from Eswatini are channelled into a mixture of 'survival' sex work and domestic servitude where they are economically and physically abused by their South African employers.[33]

The transport corridors between Maputo, Johannesburg and Mbabane are notorious for Mozambican prostitutes with their pimps found in roadside clubs, bars and overnight stopping points. Many of the prostitutes have been recruited by perpetrators disguised as normal employers over the internet and other social media. Cross-border trafficking into Zambia often entails Rwandan women offered refugee status as DRC nationals, exploited in sex work, and threatened with possible reports to police or immigration authorities.[34]

Other sex workers in Zambia, including Chinese women working in Lusaka massage parlours, come from far distant areas. In these cases, the perpetrators are normally Zambian-Chinese consortiums. On the other hand, Zambian women on the move as undocumented migrants have been reported as being trafficked to the DRC, as well as in the Middle East and Cyprus.[35] This often involves fraudulent 'scholarships' followed by sex work and forced labour at the places of destination. In nearby Malawi, most of the young women forced into involuntary sex rings are highly vulnerable, including women from refugee camps in the country.[36]

The movement of Basotho women seeking sex work across the Lesotho border is legion. Many are destined for illegal Free State mines where they work as underground sex slaves in mine hostels or near mine communities. This is especially common along the Western Platinum Belt in the vicinity of Rustenburg.[37] Prostitutes from Basotho are an important source of HIV and AIDS in all of these areas.[38] Organised sex trafficking rings, some of whom are Bangladeshi in origin, work along the Zimbabwean-southeast African axis.

Labour trafficking in its many forms is the most prevalent form of trafficking in southern Africa. This contrasts with other areas of the world where sex trafficking is predominant. In southern Africa, labour trafficking often involves family members working as primary facilitators, especially in the rural areas of places like Malawi where children and adults are offered fake employment opportunities on farms, clothing, and lodging. Failure to pay exorbitant 'transaction fees' to traffickers may result in victims being forced into sex, domestic servitude or other types of forced labour.[39]

Traffickers increasingly exploit victims from Tanzania and Malawi in the Zambian timber industry, while Zimbabweans are often subjected to labour without pay throughout the region. In South Africa, this includes working on farms and construction sites and in factories, mines and businesses in the hospitality industry.[40] Malawi tenant farmers are often exploited by groups of landowners and traffickers who purposely call in debts at times of a poor harvest. On a wider front, there is a healthy trade in forced labour victims from Zimbabwe, primarily to Kuwait, but also to China and Saudi Arabia.[41]

In some countries in the region where there are concentrations of Chinese or North Koreans involved in big infrastructure projects commissioned by governments, workers live in closely guarded premises and are paid very little, even by local standards. This applies, for example, to North Koreans working on contract in Zambia as well as Chinese nationals in the construction, mining, and services sectors.[42] Chinese construction and mining companies in Zimbabwe reportedly employ practices indicative of forced labour, including verbal, physical, and sexual abuse, as well as various means of coercion to induce work in unsafe or otherwise undesirable conditions. Traffickers also force Chinese nationals to work in restaurants in various Zimbabwean towns including Harare.[43] North Korean nationals and Cuban medical professionals working in Mozambique 'may have been forced to work' by the North Korean and Cuban governments.[44]

Swati students are also known to be exploited in Taiwanese chicken factors as a result of bilateral relations between the Taiwanese and Eswatini governments. Swati nationals are often recruited as cheap labour in the South African mining sector by a variety of unregistered labour brokers working either in Eswatini or across the South African or Mozambique borders. Swati nationals are also forcibly recruited into the South African timber industry in Mpumalanga.[45]

Men and boys from Mozambique are also found in the South African agricultural sector where they work under coercive conditions with little or no pay before being deported as undocumented migrants back to their rural origins.[46] Mozambicans also work for small-time trafficking rings in eSwatini car washes as well as in the agricultural sector where they mainly herd animals. Cheap labour from the country is also exported for sex and domestic work in Angola, Portugal and Italy. In Botswana, the size of the country precludes effective monitoring of forced labour even if proper systems were in place to finance labour inspection. There has been exploitation of the local San people by cattle farmers in rural western Ghanzi province since 2014, however, visits to the area by labour inspectors have been routinely blocked by political connections between local white farmers (many of whom are white emigres from South Africa) and local government. Botswana laws also allow political prisoners to be contracted by private persons, some of whom are believed to be running lucrative businesses as facilitators between shady broker organisations and prison authorities.[47]

Lesser forms of trafficking also occur. Forced marriage of young women to older men is widespread and is possibly the fourth most prevalent form of trafficking (after labour, sex and child trafficking, which can also encompass forced marriage). Organ trafficking, sometimes based on the muti murder of adults or children, is also relatively prolific in all SADC countries.[48]

None of the states in the region condones TIP, if only because governments desperately need the developmental assistance which would not go to criminal states monitored by the global community. Given that some states in the subcontinent are among the most destitute in the world, international partnerships have also been forged with foreign aid donors or international organisations who track the impacts of their assistance and social services to victims where the local state is effectively absent.

All the regional role-players have promulgated national anti-trafficking laws in line with aim of the Palermo Protocol to translate international law into domestic instruments. These may be overarching laws similar to South Africa's PACOTIP or more specific laws aimed at particular forms of trafficking. To adjudicate trafficking cases more effectively, Botswana, for example, has had anti-trafficking legislation criminalising sex, forced labour and child labour since 2014 – a year after South Africa's PACOTIP. Amendments to laws in Botswana are currently being drafted to make it easier for judges and prosecutors to work in more coordination with the country's Anti-human Trafficking Committee (AHTC).[49]

Lesotho's anti-trafficking act and its implementing regulations from even earlier prohibit the prosecution of victims for unlawful acts that traffickers compelled them to commit. The act also allows foreign victims to elect permanent residency as a legal alternative to their removal and encourages victims to assist in the investigation of traffickers.[50] In 2009, Eswatini promulgated a People Trafficking and People Smuggling (Prohibition) Act (2009), which criminalises sex and labour.[51] Namibia's Combating of Trafficking in Persons Act (2018) is one of the best in the region because it fully complies with international law, criminalises all sex and labour trafficking and has stringently prescribed penalties of up to 30 years imprisonment and a fine of one million Namibian dollars (approximately US$68 000) for trafficking offences.[52] Mozambique has an anti-trafficking law dating as far back as 2008. Zimbabwe is currently amending its 2014 Trafficking in Persons Act to fully align with global standards. In several states, such as Lesotho, efforts are now being made to plug the 'gaps' between domestic legislation and international law. In Zambia, draft amendments are, as we speak, in the process of being ratified by parliament.[53]

Certain legislation which does not necessarily pertain to trafficking can also be used in a counter-trafficking capacity. In Zimbabwe, for example, the local Employment Act contains regulations for labour broking and prohibits brokers from charging prospective employees for any services.[54] In Lesotho, labour recruitment agencies have to be registered under local labour laws to mitigate fraudulent recruitment for mining work in South Africa.[55] Botswana, on the other hand, does not prohibit labour recruitment practices which traffickers commonly exploit, including recruitment fees, confiscation of workers' passports, unilateral contract switching and withholding wages.[56]

Other states, but by no means all, have established standard operational procedures, national referral mechanisms and other policy frameworks to materialise anti-trafficking laws in practice. Human rights commissions have been set up in various states but these are often useless in dealing with trafficking, particularly in cases of transnational networking.[57] Penalties for trafficking have also been increased to be commensurate with the serious nature of the crime and in line with global standards.

Various oversight mechanisms to track the trafficking scene have also been established but many are unable to provide a true picture of the trafficking landscape. The implementation of counter-trafficking policy in places such as Mozambique is stymied by many of the problems which confound South Africa's policy framework in translating Palermo-style values into domestic counter-trafficking procedures.[58] Botswana, for example, does not screen for labour traffickers and relies mainly on brokers to self-report should they encounter trafficking. This is fairly useless because some brokers are commercially linked to traffickers. In many countries, if not all, in the subcontinent, counter-trafficking activism is stymied by regressive attitudes towards gender.[59]

Implementation of the existing laws and legal instruments to detect trafficking are ineffective, so much so that no state in the region, with the notable exception of Namibia, has been ranked in the forefront of the United States' audit on counter-trafficking. Some move up in the gradings over the years and some don't. All are in the language of the audit, 'still trying'. This is because southern African states are, to differing degrees, underdeveloped and lack institutional capacity, accountability and a political culture that explicitly emphasises counter-trafficking. There are, unsurprisingly, many problems in trafficking governance, with law enforcement necessary to ensure victims' access to justice. There are also problems concerning victim alleviation policies and the level of inter-state cooperation.

There are various inconsistencies in the body of law applicable to counter-trafficking. Lesotho has had an Anti-Trafficking Law for over a decade but it is sub-standard in relation to international law because it fails to criminalise all forms of sex trafficking. Its provisions on child sex trafficking are also out of kilter with global norms in that there has to be fraud, force or coercion to constitute a child trafficking offence. The penalties in Section 77 of the Children's Protection and Welfare Act – a fine or 30 months imprisonment – are also insufficiently stringent.[60]

Much the same 'gaps' in anti-trafficking law exist in the Botswana legal system where the penalties for child prostitution prescribed under Section 57 of the Children's Act are significantly lower than in the 2014 anti-trafficking act. Legal systems are poorly crafted to deal with human trafficking and criminal justice responses throughout the region are generally grossly inadequate, mainly because of administrative capacities and widespread corruption.[61]

Criminal justice responses are generally inadequate in South Africa and throughout the region. Although the number of perpetrators who are investigated, arrested and successfully convicted of trafficking in regional courts is growing annually, the percentage of those apprehended often is also still minuscule relative to what analysts in civil society and government believe to be the scale of the problem. During the 2021–22 period, for example, Malawi failed to apprehend a single case of sex trafficking despite reports that the country is, like many others in the region, a site for both domestic and trans-border trafficking involving multiple numbers of young women. Many tentative prosecutions never reach take-off or come to successful conclusions because victims are reluctant to testify against perpetrators of whom a growing number are associated with organised crime dealing in a mix of drugs, arms and human trafficking.[62] Although some countries have adopted special procedures to shield witnesses from retribution should they testify, witness protection programmes in most countries are weak to non-existent. Some have clearly been 'penetrated' by a mixture of police personnel and government officials who are themselves auxiliaries of trafficking networks. Inevitably this places whistle-blowers at risk of detection and retribution.

Borders are poorly patrolled throughout the region and this acts to the advantage of illegal immigrants as well as trafficking consortia. In countries like Zimbabwe, inter-state collaboration at the multilateral level is compromised by corruption, double agendas, distrust and an overall lack of organisational will.[63]

Many tentative prosecutions are reactive in the sense that persons are charged with a lesser offence out of which some evidence of trafficking arises. This is at least partially because law enforcement in states such as Lesotho, Eswatini or Malawi lacks investigative capacity despite years of training programmes aimed at turning law enforcers into efficient policemen/women. In these and other cases, intelligence gathering is also haphazard and information management in underdeveloped police systems is often so poor as to preclude convictable evidence for scrutiny by magistrates and judges. Trafficking infractions are, in any case, invariably more complex than most other crimes and require reserves of time, energy and dedication that are simply beyond those available to these relatively small police forces.

There are frequent acquittals for blatant trafficking crimes, either because of insufficient evidence, because the police have withdrawn a case to avoid public embarrassment, they have lost or otherwise misfiled key documentation, or because members of law enforcement are placed under pressure by criminal syndicates with links to police leadership. Although there is detection, investigation and sometimes prosecution, convictions are rarely secured, especially in labour exploitation.

Sentencing, if and when it occurs, is often too lenient, especially where clear-cut traffickers are charged with lesser crimes found in the sexual calendar, such as rape or sexual assault. Zimbabwe's Labour Relations Amendment Act criminalises labour trafficking with prescribed penalties of up to two years' imprisonment but this is insufficient against the backdrop of international standards.[64]

Notwithstanding the theoretical gravity with which TIP has come to be viewed in both governmental and criminal justice, in some southern African countries, such as Zimbabwe, it is still possible for perpetrators to escape with a fine instead of imprisonment, even in cases of sex offences.[65] This is at the very time when no regional role-player, South Africa included, is making any discernible effort to address the demand for sexual services.

Considerable efforts have been made to conform with the principle in the TIP audit to prohibit government officials and others from participating in, facilitating, or condoning such trafficking, As part of this, some countries have set up counter-trafficking coalitions with multi-stakeholder participation analogous to South Africa's policy framework.

Botswana currently has a four-year implementation plan backed by almost US$100 000 per annum, This plan is regulated by an AHTC established under the auspices of the Ministry of Defence, Justice and Security (MDJS).[66] Working closely with the local Directorate of Public Prosecution (DPP) efforts are currently being made to monitor the impact of the anti-trafficking policy and the work of specialised units with the first of a series of biannual reports appearing this year.

In 2017, Malawi launched its National Plan of Action against Trafficking in Persons. This plan provided for the establishment of a National Coordination Committee Against Trafficking in Persons led by the Ministry of Security. In 2021, new district committees were established in Dedza, Karonga, Mangochi and Mzimba to supplement those already in Mchinji and Phalombe. District-level plans are being drawn up in alignment with, among others, the Malawi Network Against Child Trafficking. This grouping comprises government officials, religious leaders, NGOs and international organisations working in the country to train police and social welfare officials and to raise awareness to counter trafficking in a preventative capacity. Some of this work is aimed at the Dzaleka refugee camp.[67]

Similar mechanisms have been developed in Lesotho where the business of coordinating implementation has been devolved to a multisectoral committee led by the Ministry of Home Affairs. A new four-year action plan is pending following feedback from civil society and international organisations. In the meantime, a special smuggling and trafficking unit has been established in the Lesotho Mounted Police.[68]

In Zimbabwe, the Trafficking in Persons National Action Plan established in July 2019 has spawned an Anti-Trafficking Inter-Ministerial Committee (ATIMC) which, one year later, adopted guidelines for a National Coordinating Forum to engage the government with civil society actors. Seven provincial task teams have now been established to assist with targeted training and improve public consciousness.[69]

In 2019, Namibia adopted a four-year National Action Plan to address both trafficking and GBV, and a five-year dedicated anti-trafficking action plan is currently under discussion. This system works reasonably well in currently coordinating anti-trafficking responses.[70]

Mozambique, by way of contrast, has had a Law on Preventing and Combating the Trafficking of People since 2008 but has gone no further than a draft National Action Plan that the government has still not adopted.[71]

In some other cases, however, anti-trafficking arrangements are more impressive on paper than in practice. Governmental departments identified as key stakeholders in many states often lack the commitment and capacity required for effective participation with anti-trafficking committees in various states and only meet infrequently. High levels of absenteeism occur at many counter-trafficking coalition -designated meetings and discussions within the occasional get-togethers are often of low quality with one or two 'experts' recirculated between meetings. These are not necessarily people informed about trafficking but individuals reflecting power in local networks.[72]

8   HUMAN TRAFFICKING IN SOUTH AFRICA

Botswana, whose anti-trafficking structures are reasonably well publicly funded, is more the exception than the rule. Most provincial structures working within national frameworks are dependent on what they can raise ad hoc from other governmental departments or privately. This necessarily undermines continuity in the execution of public policy. As in the policy framework, both vertical and horizontal communication is inconsistent in governmental systems throughout the region. Some provincial structures are no more than paper creations without the capability to implement national policy or established counter-trafficking laws.

Policy impacts in most states of the region are mainly minimal and much more needs to be done to educate state bureaucracies in developing specialist knowledge about counter-trafficking. With this in mind, Lesotho has established a cabinet-level sub-committee of six ministers to supplement the MDC in drafting added anti-trafficking legislation

Eswatini has also seen shifts in power from counter-trafficking coalitions and their secretariats to more centralised cabinet-level involvement in developing upward communications.[73] Civil society involvement in counter-trafficking coalitions is often patchy because of limited human, administrative and financial resources in the non-governmental sector. In far too many cases, civil society is excluded from these key debates on trafficking policy or informed ex-post-facto decisions taken unilaterally.

Most states have made efforts to gather data from district-level police stations. In Malawi, for instance, some improvement has taken place during the last calendar year. But, as we have already, inferred, police mobilisation behind counter-trafficking purposes is extremely difficult in some of these countries which are either very large (like Namibia) or contain terrain that is difficult to negotiate. In Lesotho, for example, the centralisation of the (CGPU) in Maseru means that the capability to deal with trafficking, smuggling or even more minor crimes is very limited in all of the country's ten districts.[74] In most cases, little more than guidance in managing crime is given by the central authorities to outlying units. In some countries, a majority of police, despite training offered by international organisations fail to use standard operating procedures for pinpointing traffickers and indiscriminately arrest victims and their perpetrators. Police frequently conflate gender-based violence with trafficking and in places such as Lesotho are insensitive towards child victims of sexual abuse.

There is, in addition, widespread corruption throughout the state bureaucracy in many southern African states and the police (including the SAPS) are known to turn a blind eye to trafficking. There are cases where rogue elements in local police forces have been complicit with traffickers before raids on brothels, farms, factories and other establishments where trafficking is flagrant. Police officials are poorly paid, which renders them vulnerable to overtures from traffickers. In Zimbabwe, corruption has effectively undermined the referral process governing the protection of trafficking victims after identification.[75] This includes corrupt border police who are characteristically 'elastic' with law enforcement. There are many cases in the region where visible cooperation between trafficking gangs and the police goes unprosecuted, for example, in Lesotho, Nigerians linked to regional gangs operate with relative impunity. In some cases, victims are jeopardised when reporting a trafficking crime because police are in cahoots with traffickers.[76]

Much as in South Africa, undocumented migrants can acquire visas and residence permits with under-the-counter payments to officials in government departments dealing with the execution of the trafficking laws. Labour inspectors in some states are notorious for deporting migrants so that farm or factory managers can avoid paying their workers. Failure to cooperate with organised crime can also result in retribution against both members of law enforcement and the government.

Enforcement of labour laws involving child labour is especially inadequate in most countries. In Eswatini, the labour inspectorate has no dedicated funds for inspection and has to rely on ad-hoc transfers from the Department of Labour.[77] As in other states, violations in the formal sector are given priority while forced labour is almost exclusively found in the informal sector. Despite officials' acknowledgement of forced and child labour among the San community on cattle farms in Botswana, neither law enforcement nor labour inspectors make concerted efforts to investigate or address the issue.[78]

Some southern African states, to their credit, have developed referral mechanisms that fine tune standard operating procedures for the identification of victims and their onward transference for social assistance. Zimbabwe's ATIMC, for example, has such an instrument for governing the often-extended process from when victims are first encountered by front-line responders in provincial task teams to their eventual housing, rehabilitation and reintegration into the social mainstream.[79] In some countries, such as Namibia, this works relatively well (by regional standards) and the local Ministry of Labour, Industrial and Employment have a well-integrated system of social workers, labour inspectors and residential care centres where children can be educated.[80]

Referral systems throughout the region are fraught with difficulty. Despite training, ongoing screening for trafficking indicators among vulnerable populations, such as women in commercial sex, migrants, and potential deportees, are a rarity. Frontline responders who come into trafficking situations often lack resources and training in victim identification, particularly in cases where child victims are encountered. Training in standard operational procedures often means little in the field and much more remains to be done to train frontline responders to understand the push-pull dynamics of TIP victim-centred interview techniques and the investigation of TIP offences according to local counter-trafficking legislation.

First encounters between victims and their 'rescuers' are also often compromised by language differences. Despite plans to develop a regional translator database some years ago, interpreters are often in short supply. This negatively impacts the pinpointing of victims. It also impacts the psychological support provided by services-providers, negotiations over the certification of foreign victims as required by the law in some countries, transfers to places of safety, an investigation by the criminal justice system and, ultimately, the victim-preparation for court proceedings and/or repatriation. In some cases, victims have to pay a fee for interpretation services, despite the governments reporting these facilities as being available free of charge.

In places like Zambia, access to medical care and counselling by survivors of trafficking are frequently minimal to non-existent outside the capital cities and major towns.[81] In Lesotho, the mountainous topography largely precludes victim care in the deep rural areas. Even where accessible, sheltering facilities are generally poor, modest or so insecure that there are many cases where perpetrators have recaptured and then re-used their victims, even after they have been placed under state protection.[82] Few dedicated safe houses are available on call when victims are encountered. Malawi, for example only established its first four licensed shelters in 2020. Before this, victims were simply housed, denied basic services, ill-fed and re-traumatised in police detention. Even now, outside of victim protection in the form of counselling or specialised services is basic, especially for child trafficking victims.[83]

There are very few multipurpose facilities for such highly vulnerable groups as men, (especially if disabled), prostituted children who mainly vanish under the radar, or LGBT persons who remain profoundly stigmatised. Taken jointly or several, the nine countries in our regional survey have seriously limited treatment facilities for survivors of drug and alcohol addiction or with a variety of psycho-social conditions associated with the experience of being trafficked. There are very few dedicated shelters for separately assisting men, women, or children. Counselling services are hard to procure and most treatment is outpatient even when residential assistance is required. In some countries, like South Africa, shelters and safehouses receive a per-person stipend from the government. But throughout the region, most shelters and safe houses receive little to no regular and sustainable funding from state sources and are entirely or partially dependent on international organisations or foreign donors.

In most southern African countries, referral to protective care has remained static or even declined over the last few years. Meanwhile, a great deal more needs to be done to upgrade the accreditation process for service providers originating in civil society, to improve communication between state authorities and civil society organisations, to increase the number of locations to which victims are assigned after identification, as well as to monitor the quality of counselling and other the services provided by NGOs in shelter conditions.

Secondary victimisation in violation of humanitarian principles on victim treatment is also widespread if not rampant in many southern

African countries, at least in part, because front-line personnel – social workers, police or paramedics – are unfamiliar with victim needs or with trafficking more generally. The 2015 anti-trafficking law in Malawi explicitly directs courts to provide immunity to victims forced by perpetrators to commit crimes including potential immigration violations. The courts also guarantee temporary residence. In reality, however, foreign victims are almost automatically deported before they even come to court. In Mozambique especially, severe re-traumatisation occurs when victims are penalised for crimes traffickers compelled them to commit.[84]

Police in other southern African countries often expel victims across borders. This is done unilaterally and without consultation with social services in violation of protective legislation. Victims are sometimes held in custody with their perpetrators and threatened with deportation if they refuse to cooperate with prosecutors. In some states, victims of TIP are required to testify against perpetrators before being assisted in obtaining temporary immigration papers. In some southern African countries, there are also cases where victims have assisted the local police in the hope of avoiding deportation but have been deported anyway after criminal proceedings against the perpetrators. Deportation is often too dangerous countries of origin without any evaluation of the victims' safety once across the border.

Government departments in the regions have conducted many activities to proactively prevent trafficking by raising public consciousness about TIP, including advertisements, leaflets, outreach, orientation programmes and public broadcasts. These aim to sensitise stakeholders in the public sector and civil society, especially doctors, nurses, social workers and community leaders, to the complexity of TIP. Yet the impacts of these initiatives on perception and behaviour have not been systematically monitored or evaluated. Much more could be made of hotlines as both preventative and reporting mechanisms.

Most of these initiatives may make no difference, least of all according to some commentators who believe that TIP in southern Africa is likely to worsen rather than improve in the foreseeable future under the multiple impacts of inter-state migration, the inability of states to coordinate security policy along national borders, internal systems which disseminate trafficking activities within states, and other socio-political developments giving rise to the refugee populations especially vulnerable to trafficking activity.[85]

While the SADC may or may not rise to higher levels of inter-state integration in the years to come, more effective and sustainable counter-trafficking in the immediate future requires at least improved multilateral or bilateral inter-state collaboration by regional police forces, in some cases, backed up by the national militaries. Some of this is already in place with the SADC regional trafficking tool to which most southern African states subscribe, but this needs to be taken many steps further despite a history where inter-state activity has been undermined by a mixture of in inter-agency competition, corruption on the part of border police, the predominancy of national interests and intelligence failures that have allowed syndicates to penetrate national security systems.

Trafficking poses enormous threats to peace and security in the southern African subcontinent and Africa as a whole. Major problems remain to be confronted in effectively managing trafficking in the subcontinent. This demands proactive and enduring measures to address those age-long root causes behind trafficking as an egregious crime. State response to human trafficking in contemporary African states will not be successful unless policy reaches far deeper into the socioeconomic, political cultural milieus of the states, and there is a collective responsibility of all relevant stakeholders, including the government, NGOs, civil societies, religious and educational institutions, human rights groups and parents.

In many cases, access to justice for victims is difficult despite the existence of criminal legislation for the accountability of offenders, as well as the provision of specific legal measures for the protection and assistance of victims. However, there are difficulties in the social reintegration of victims since there are no concrete programmes for this purpose and institutional conditions for monitoring them.

Mass undocumented migration, which curates trafficking, is a problem with which all SADC members struggle. Unfortunately, it is difficult to see how trans-border human movement can be curbed in places like Zimbabwe or Zambia where hundreds of migrants cross borders without valid travel documents each day. In other regional states, much like South Africa, there are large concentrations of people, several million in some cases, who live within states, without official recognition on a semi-permanent basis. Many are susceptible to police harassment, trafficking and other forms of exploitation because of their irregular legal status.

Governmental and most political leaders throughout the region concur that trafficking poses a threat to effective state-building at all levels. This includes regional integration, which has been pursued by southern African states for many years; regional development, which necessitates crime control across borders; and the building of socioeconomic connections to address the pervasive problems of poverty. A 2016 SADC report, for example, states that human trafficking also leads to human rights violations with the potential to break down the social fabric and human capital. TIP also has implications for governmental authority as well as public health.

The recognition by all states in the region that inter-state action that complements national-level interventions is critical has given rise to a dense network of policies, laws and organisational structures designed to facilitate joint counter-trafficking action. Some of these take the form of bilateral arrangements, such as the deliberations in the Joint Permanent Commissions on Defence and Security set up by several regional actors. Human trafficking was on the agenda at the Zimbabwe-Mozambique meeting at Harare in 2019, in a similar meeting held between Botswana and Nambia in Gabarone in February 2020, and in a similar get together between Zimbabwe and Zambia held at Victoria Falls shortly thereafter. Mozambique, Eswatini, Zambia and South Africa also have a Memorandum of Understanding for cooperation in trafficking cases.

South African states also adhere to the many international conventions related to human trafficking, including the Convention on the Elimination of All Forms of Discrimination Against Women (CEDAW) and the United Nations Convention on Transnational Organised Crime (UNTOC) where Articles 27 and 28 advocates regional partnership and cross-border coordination against human trafficking. This is supplemented by several African instruments which southern African states have either acceded to or ratified, all of which underline the significance of coordinating national and regional resources in the fight against TIP. The African Union is also finalising a Ten-Year Action Plan on the Eradication of Child Labour, Forced Labour, Modern Slavery and Human Trafficking in Africa designed to run until 2030.

The SADC has undertaken a number of research-type studies and has adopted a variety of instruments to combat trafficking in the region.[86] These include a Ten Year Strategic Plan of Action on Combating Trafficking in Persons, especially Women and Children. This plan was in effect between 2009 and 2019 and identified several strategic policy areas, including skills enhancement and capacity building, victim support and the raising of public awareness.

During the 2016–2020 period there were other initiatives with similar strategic objectives. The SADC adopted a harmonised SADC Regional Plan on Combating Illegal Migration, the Smuggling of Migrants. It also adopted a Trafficking in Persons and a Strategic Indicative Plan, which underlines the threat of TIP. This latter plan was prepared for SIPO (the Organ on Police, Defence and Security Cooperation) under the authority of the SIPO Public Security Sector dealing with justice, immigration and organised crime. In addition, the Protocol on Gender and Development of 2008 as amended in 2016 identifies trafficking as an emerging threat to all SADC members. Under Article 1 of that Protocol, all member states undertake to adopt policies, legislation and other instruments in a counter-trafficking capacity.

The Protocol urges all states to enact and adopt anti-trafficking laws and, as we have noted, this milestone as well as national plans for the implementation of these laws has, to a great extent been realised. SADC has also generated a number of knowledge products of which the SADC Regional Trafficking in Persons Data Collection System aimed at assisting states to collect reliable and verifiable data on trafficking patterns is the most important. This has now been supplemented by a SADC Trafficking in Persons Network to allow for more effective monitoring. Various programmes to build capacity under the aegis of SADC have been running for a number of years as have several enabling mechanisms. These include the Joint Permanent Commissions on Defence Security whose purpose is to provide a platform to discuss human trafficking problems and approaches to cooperation. In addition, the Southern African Regional Police Chiefs Cooperation Organisation (SARPCCO) reports to the Inter-State Defence and Security Committee of the Organ on Politics, Defence and Security Cooperation, which liaises with the International Criminal Police Organisation (INTERPOL) to detect human trafficking and initiate action against transnational syndicates.

It is by no means clear that the SADC is in the process of reaching its major counter-trafficking objectives in the face of the structural forces behind trafficking. These included such powerful drivers as poverty, gender violence, under-education, discrimination, food insecurity and unemployment. As long as these issues remain problematic, the SADC will continue to have difficulty in establishing a solid evidence base from which date-driven, multi-sector and cross-sectoral responses to trafficking can be extracted.

Ultimately, the member-states of the SADC are all 'developing' or low-income countries with some being landlocked with all the attendant economic disadvantages. The IMF and the World Bank list these countries as some of the poorest in the world. This implies not only a major lack of human, administrative and financial capacity in dealing with fundamental indeterminants of trafficking but also deep-rooted problems in practically executing the SADC policies and plans, no matter their elaboration. Innovation receptiveness is limited at the bottom end of the global economic hierarchy so new anti-trafficking initiatives often fail to take root beyond the halls of government. Most initiatives to investigate and prosecute trafficking crimes founder on administrative dysfunctionality, failures in governmental infrastructure, corruption and nepotism at all levels of state bureaucracies, self-interested political leadership, and poor inter-institutional communication. Cross-border migration is largely unmitigated, and citizenship is 'ineffective' in the sense that there is a gap between what laws proclaim as their objectives and what happens in practice.

Notwithstanding development aid and collaboration in the form of partnerships between global and local counter-trafficking organisations such as the UN or the EU, both human and social capital is seriously under-resourced. A widespread lack of confidence in governance undermines messaging to raise public awareness. In inter-governmental relations national interest mainly supersedes regional obligations.

The indicators of these failures are manifest and mainly reflect problems at the national level. Some states have not signed or ratified the many global, African or even SADC treaties, conventions or protocols, either in whole or in part. This is often the result of internal political competition, double agendas on the part of the bureaucratic establishments, a simple lack of energy among officials or even plain oversight. Given that the SADC has no power to induce compliance other than through diplomacy or persuasion, the delinquent states go unpunished.

Since national information on trafficking patterns is poor, to begin with, it is unrealistic to believe that a regional instrument will be effective The regional data collection tool is unsurprisingly dogged by the reluctance of officials to share information for a variety of reasons ranging from politically sensitive disclosure problems through to basic incompetence in the collection and management of often-complex data. As we have already noted, there is considerable corruption in the criminal justice systems of the various SADC member countries. This corruption promotes selectivity in what is transmitted for data collection and how information is subsequently programmed and used or managed. Either way, there is still a lack of information on trafficking patterns, traffickers or victims several years into the existence of the regional service.

The problems of the data collection tool reflect wider technological shortages, which undermine the SADC's ability to keep track of increasingly sophisticated trafficking systems used by transnational syndicates. There is evidence that Chinese traffickers are now using drones to detect counter-trafficking operations along many borders and/or that comparable activities by other global players have long since penetrated the databanks that individual states or the SACD have collected.

The whole SADC system is top-heavy and massively over-complicated. Counter-trafficking initiatives have to surmount huge bureaucratic obstacles to obtain clearance and the often complex logistic and material resources required for cross-border operations. Most of the enabling organisations for the implementation of plans and policies from the national to the local level have suffered from intelligence failures that have cleared the way for trafficking gangs to operate with impunity. There are multiple cases where ostensibly top-secret information has been leaked by one or another of the member state's police forces and action by the police to sabotage counter-trafficking 'stings' across frontiers as a result of complicity with trafficking networks is far from unknown. Mutual hostility between officials or police forces frequently aggravates the situation. Border control processes in the SADC are not consistent or standardised, which undermines proper migration management and governance.

Major problems remain to be confronted in effectively managing trafficking in the southern African subcontinent. Proactive and enduring measures need to be put in place to address those age-long root causes and factors behind trafficking as an egregious crime. State response to human trafficking in contemporary African states will not be successful unless there is a collective responsibility of all relevant stakeholders.

Human trafficking in the region is, like anywhere else, a crime-within-crimes, so that dealing with associate offences such as money laundering and various types of petty or grand bureaucratic corruption is part-and-parcel of the management formulae which requires adoption by the SADC and the individual states in the region.

Trafficking is also inextricable interwoven with the resolution of several complex, multi-layered political issues in various places like Cabo Delgado in northern Mozambique, where extremist Islamic fighters and perpetrators of trafficking crimes work hand-in-hand to recruit a mixture of supporters and victims from the hundreds of thousands of people displaced by violence since 2017.

Given that this site of IS resurgence in Africa also involves the historically unequal distribution of political and economic power among the predominant ethnic groups in the area, TIP will take an inordinately long time to manage, least of all root out.[87]

Mass undocumented migration, which in turn curates trafficking, is a problem for all states where, like in Zambia, either dozens or more were being intercepted and arrested at the border when entering the country without valid travel documents or staying in the country without required documents.

But there are severe challenges to the collective management of the migration problem, which include long stretches of borders to which some were porous, lack of political will, lack of manpower for immigration officers, absence of migration policy, bribery/corruption, inadequate sensitisation, and lack of skill. Effectively dealing with migration in the form of a labour regime also requires the adoption of a still politically absent mind-shift from seeing human movement less as a security issue than a socioeconomic and developmental problem in line with continental and global trends associated with the African Union Protocol to the Treaty Establishing the African Economic Community Relating to Free Movement of Persons, Right of Residence and Right of Establishment in January 2018 and the Global Compact for Safe, Orderly and Regular Migration.

As discussed in the chapter to follow, there are reasons to believe that the degree of trafficking in South Africa has increased during the last two years of the Covid pandemic. Many smaller to medium-sized communities are experiencing human trade in one or another of its malignant manifestations to the extent that law enforcement has gone public with its organisational problems in meeting the requirements of the current situation. Because of the close linkages between South Africa and its subcontinental neighbours, some of this has cascaded onto other regional actors who have little capacity to initiate and sustainably maintain counter-trafficking, even in the best of situations. In these cases, it is optimistic to believe that we are likely to see a downturn in sub-regional trafficking in the short-to-medium term.

CHAPTER
7

Conclusion:
Beyond
Covid

Covid has had major implications for victims of human trafficking worldwide, including in South Africa and southern Africa. The global opinion is that the numbers of people falling victim to sex, labour, child and organ trafficking are unlikely to decrease in the foreseeable future.[1]

There are several reasons for this. Firstly, the extent of trafficking continued unabated during the pandemic. War and the quest for improved economic opportunities, two of the key drivers of human migration, have continued since the beginning of 2020. Climate change, which also drives immigration, has also impacted movement and has created many new business opportunities for traffickers.

Despite a slight lag in early 2020, trans-frontier trafficking in southern Africa continues despite periodic closures of international border points for long periods.[2] This is because most undocumented migrants susceptible to traffickers do not come into South Africa through the official crossing points, which were monitored for the spread of Covid, but on foot through the veld in many places. The number of potential victims arriving at border points concealed in the compartments of trucks, freight vehicles and cargo trains at Beit Bridge and our other major border points has also escalated as lockdowns have been lifted.

There is also some evidence that limitations placed on landward movement as well as the intensified examination of travellers arriving from abroad have encouraged traffickers to turn their attention to maritime routes. One consequence is that in the immediate future we will see, as in the Mediterranean, leaky boats with migrants arriving along our extended coastline. These carry mainly refugees and economic migrants from further afield in Africa pushed into the Republic by the economic devastation associated with Covid in their countries of origin. In many cases, this is propelled by human smugglers and/or traffickers exploiting the business opportunities inherent in the pandemic.

Intra-country trafficking has also continued because restrictions on inter-regional trafficking introduced in large countries like South Africa during the Covid epidemic were not effectively implemented. Our main trajectory for trafficking along internal routes from impoverished rural nodes to the cities has only been partially impeded by now-lapsed restrictions on inter-regional travel. The lifting of these regulations means business as usual in the form of men, women and children lured into involuntary and exploitative sex work as well as an unremitting stream of labour trafficking into most sectors of the economy, especially mining and agriculture. In the illegal mining sector, many young men and women will continue to be recruited for slavery at the interface between sex and labour.

Because the pandemic assisted a substantial worldwide growth in illegal economies, including transnational syndicates dealing in everything saleable from exotic animals to human beings, trafficking in all cases (land, sea or air) has been only temporarily disrupted. A surge in trafficking from jumping-off points in the region is expected as Covid restrictions are done away with.

On the supply side, human smugglers and traffickers have devised new methods to circumvent travel restrictions and border controls. Traffickers now make more use of less observable transportation methods such as bicycles and motorbikes as opposed to trucks and buses to transport their potential victims. In line with international trends where trafficking has been digitalised, online trafficking brought about by the closure of international borders will, if anything, intensify as a mode for victim recruitment at the southern tip of the African continent. In Namibia, for example, traffickers are reportedly increasingly using online tools such as social media to avoid movement restrictions.[3] Although the use of chatrooms, advertisement sites, social media and the dark web has at least a fifteen-year history, high-technology communications designed to limit the distance between victims and perpetrators will increasingly be used for criminal purposes in the future.

Trafficking has become more lucrative as perpetrators take on increased risks for increased premiums. Higher prices for victims are likely to continue dominating the market into the intermediate term with the introduction of green cards or other travel documents aimed at officially restricting cross-border movement.

Child trafficking in places such as South Africa continued unabated during the pandemic period. Local trafficking continues to exploit pre-teenagers while *ukuthwala* persists to legitimise the abduction and forced marriage of young girls in remote villages of the Eastern Cape and KZN. Pre-pandemic forced labour by children in domestic service, mining, begging, street vending, food services, criminal activities, agriculture, and the fishing sector is still in evidence as Covid fades away.[4] During 2020, one NGO reported an increase in children forced into commercial sex or labour by their families and this is likely to continue.[5]

Little has been done in South or southern Africa to curb the demand for commercial sex. The police and other public officials continue to take advantage of women and young girls enlisted by traffickers. The complicity of some SAPS members who either own or support notorious brothels in the main urban areas remains unchecked as does the flow of young women entrapped by traffickers in movement from poor rural areas. While the supply of victims has shifted marginally away from recruitment in Europe or Asia due to restrictions on air traffic, syndicated trafficking rings based in the DRC, Cameroon, Ghana and especially Nigeria have continued to feed the local sex market.

The prosecution of offenders, one of the main weapons in counter-trafficking has ground to a virtual halt throughout the subcontinent. Notorious brothels well-known to traffickers, law enforcement and the mass public have continued to thrive despite lockdowns on freedom of movement over the last two years. This is in line with global patterns indicating that sex trafficking has become increasingly 'privatised' in many countries. In South Africa, as well as countries like Zimbabwe,

Zambia and Malawi, this connotes prostitution moving away from closed restaurants and bars that have been traditional gathering points for sex trafficking into suburban housing, apartments in the central city areas or cheap bed-and-breakfasts and other tourist accommodation emptied by restrictions on international travel destined for the southern African market.[6] The red listing of these countries in the forefront of the recent Omicron wave has even seen some remote game lodges being used for commercial sex activity. 'Localised' sex-and-safari trips involving the use of women and children from remote rural areas have also been reported by observers of the trafficking scene.

Most of this goes undetected and police complicity in trafficking crimes appears to have increased rather than declined over the pandemic period. The Covid lockdowns were generally poorly policed and inter-regional movement has often been facilitated by corruption at the local level. This is in line with what we have previously termed 'loss of agency' by the South African state – the failure of policy to translate from the centre to the periphery or grassroots implementation. Investigations of trafficking offences became impossibly difficult with social distancing and restrictions on all movement.

In the wider region, the situation has been far worse in countries with a limited state capacity to manage trafficking. In some southern African countries, such as Botswana, courts either stopped operating for long periods or convened infrequently over the 2020–21 period. Law enforcement and investigations of trafficking across the board have slowed because of travel limitations and border regulations have excluded the participation of foreign witnesses who are often required for trans-frontier trafficking cases. In Mozambique, both government and civil society stakeholder capacity in local counter-trafficking coalitions have been curbed by a mixture of travel restrictions within the country, curfews and border closures.[7] In some cases, judicial backlogs have been aggravated. Much as in the Republic itself, criminal justice systems have become clogged with thousands of violators of lockdown regulations. Arrests and conviction rates for trafficking have plummeted in all countries and there is some anecdotal evidence that traffickers took advantage of the confusion during South Africa's recent 'insurrection'.

Either way, the prison population has been even further increased by looters now awaiting trial for murders and property violations during the mid-2012 'insurrection'.

Covid vastly broadened the pool of potential victims while trafficking remains cruel. There are many manifestations of this including the continued use of LGBT persons, albinos, the very young, and drug-induced adults for coercive labour in the sex sectors of major cities such as Johannesburg, Cape Town, Durban and Bloemfontein. Irrespective of lockdowns, the drift of vulnerable rural populations with the potential to be trafficked has largely continued, especially into Gauteng province. The mobilisation of the SANDF to assist with maintaining public order has not necessarily led to the identification of traffickers among criminal elements who have been hard at work both around and during curfews.

Women and girls forced to work at home have become more vulnerable to recruitment by domestic predators, especially in the high-rise flatlands of South African cities. Lengthy school closures along with demoralisation among learners have also put more children at risk of sex grooming and forced labour in the agricultural sector. Child begging and minor crime have become more prevalent in inner-city areas where children form gangs as opposed to attending closed-down schools.

Many victims of trafficking who have endured stay-at-home orders, isolation and lockdowns in dangerously crowded circumstances have themselves become victims of the virus. These include the marginalised youth who are at additional risk of depression, suicidal ideation and self-harming behaviour. due to the stresses and instability posed by Covid. In line with international experience, increasing numbers of young women and girls have turned to traffickers and survival sex work, which in turn becomes an inadvertent transmission belt for the perpetuation of our social problems.

Exploitation and servitude in the domestic sector worsened during the Covid epidemic. Many domestic workers were fired during the first phases of the pandemic, rendering them vulnerable to traffickers.[8] Others were restricted at their worksite, thereby increasing vulnerability to forced labour and abuse by employers. The intra-regional trafficking of young men for farm labour remains an opportunistic source of income for labour traffickers. The United States State Department Annual Audit also notes a variety of other continuities in South African forced labour practices from the pre-Covid period. These include the exploitation of victims on fishing vessels in South African territorial waters and forced labour based on debt coercion. Traffickers subject Pakistanis and Bangladeshis to forced labour through debt-based coercion in businesses owned by their co-nationals. In one case, a Nepali trafficker fraudulently recruited a Nepali man to South Africa and exploited him in forced labour. Chinese businessmen recruited workers to South Africa and forced them to work in factories.

Some arrests for using forced labour were made during the 2020–21 period but overall, the inconsistencies in the inspectorate of South Africa's DOL, have continued. Albeit we lack the statistics, the monitoring of forced labour in the informal and agricultural sectors has largely been precluded as lockdown restrictions have compounded the 'normal' problems faced by labour inspectors in gaining access to private property. Despite these challenges, however, inspectors made some notable efforts, including raiding a Chinese-owned factory in Durban, where 14 local workers were forced to manufacture face masks; and discovering two makeshift factories where 105 Ethiopians were forced to make counterfeit goods

According to various sources, such as the United Nations High Commission for Refugees (UNHCR), the United Nations Office on Drugs and Crime (UNODC), INTERPOL and the IOM, the risks for population groups vulnerable to the poly-victimisations of modern slavery also worsened over the last year of pandemic.[9] This pool now includes women and girls trapped by social distancing in the face of ongoing exposure to gender violence and domestic abuse, migrants from poor communities embarking on journeys driven by the economic collapse in their home countries, gender-non-conforming youth, the homeless, children in foster care susceptible to child trafficking, and survivors of slavery struggling with post-traumatic stress disorder (PTSD) and substance abuse, among many others. According to some analysts, female victims of trafficking will disproportionately increase among the world's victims because women in poor communities are marginalised, participate in hazardous labour and always struggle to make a living.

The fragile pre-COVID southern African network to manage trafficking is currently on the brink of unravelling at a time when the vulnerability of many populations will extend far beyond the pandemic itself. Normal governmental activity has been disturbed or even halted in many states as the bureaucracies struggle to deal with lockdowns and spatial restrictions. This has inevitably impacted service delivery not only to trafficking victims but also populations susceptible to victimisation. In several countries, the problems facing migrants in obtaining identity papers required for employment have multiplied. In South Africa, the protective provisions of the PACOTIP pertaining to the right of immigrants to work with appropriate documentation have largely lapsed because of severe staff incapacities in major state departments, such as the DHA where personnel have worked either irregularly as a result of lockdowns or, in some, cases, not at all.

While the government took steps to increase data collection and sharing regarding trafficking at the beginning of 2020, much of this was put on hold with the outbreak of the pandemic in South Africa. Since then, data collection from its internal hotline operated by the NGO-run National Human Trafficking Resource or other resources linked to criminal intelligence has been haphazard. The DJCD efforts to address the knowledge gap in TIP with a new integrated management system to collect data and improve responses have also been delayed, while a Department of Science project backed by USAID to develop the first baseline study of the scale and human trafficking has been put on hold, partially because of operational difficulties in conducting research in the virtual world. Many officials remain resistant to recognition of trafficking as a South and southern African problem. One consequence of all is that the SAPS has been confined to using redundant pre-pandemic intelligence in a decentralised data management system that seriously needs updating.

Front-line operations by some of these organisations working with the SAPS have been disrupted to the point of non-existence in most of the provinces where the provincial task teams, the building blocks of the policy framework against trafficking, have been effectively suspended virtually since the onset of Covid. The KZN, Western Cape and Gauteng task teams, generally recognised as being at the forefront, have only recently convened regularly. It remains to be seen whether these mostly shaky structures can effectively function in a virtual world devoid of face-to-face contact.

Referral services based on standard operating procedures (SOPs) in the nexus between frontline encounters with trafficking victims and the state have collapsed in many countries because of communication breakdowns between key stakeholders. Victim identification, always problematic, has worsened. Many child-protection services along with medical and mental health providers have been rendered inaccessible or de-staffed, in many cases irrecoverably. Countries throughout the region have been unable to access the limited public funding available. The shelters and safehouses for trafficking victims run by the DSD in South Africa in most cases became dysfunctional because of lockdowns, social distancing regulations and fear of admitting patients without Covid testing or, more recently, vaccination. Since testing and vaccination rates are lower amongst the poor, this has seriously impacted victims who would sometimes be admitted.

Repatriation of victims which is central to anti-trafficking strategy across the board has been seriously disrupted by border closures and travel restrictions stemming from the pandemic. In most cases, this has put added strain on service networks run by NGOs and the government, which were poor even before the virus. The limited funding for counter-trafficking across the region has also dried up as public funds have been diverted to anti-Covid activities. In a representative case, In 2021, the US$434 000 normally assigned to NGOs by the Botswana government dropped to US$60 000.[10]

Civil society organisations involved in the prevention of TIP and the protection of victims have been badly hit as instruments of victim care. Even better-funded organisations, of which there are few, have a huge backlog and victim identification has become even more difficult than usual due to fear of social contact and social distancing regulations.

The training of government officials, police, members of the judiciary and social workers aimed at promoting an understanding of trafficking has been put back across the region. The rollout of the South African government's new training manual has been stymied as part of a wider halt in operationalising national anti-trafficking plans throughout the subcontinent. Public awareness campaigns involving groups of people have effectively ground to a halt while the training of officials for capacity-building has now been suspended in most southern African countries not only because of pandemic-related restrictions but also because of widespread infection among officials in many countries. In Botswana, most planned counter-trafficking training of police, prosecutors, immigration officers and social workers has been indefinitely postponed.[11]

Covid challenges multiple stakeholders in TIP including officials in government departments, such as the DOH, which otherwise figures in the policy framework, security organisations, and border and immigration officers, all of whom are expected to play a role in managing the public health crisis. Unfortunately, some of the key stakeholders in trafficking have failed to adopt creative solutions to counter-trafficking under pandemic conditions used in some other countries. These include the widespread use of tele-medicine and tele-counselling to create an alternative health and emotional safety net for survivors. Far more use could have been made of virtual reality communications as a means of raising public consciousness about trafficking, especially in law enforcement and the criminal justice system. This includes the SAPS, prosecutors, magistrates, and members of the legal fraternity, all of whom must now adapt to a crisis far from over.

As of the middle of 2022, a year after the pandemic, none of the states in the southern African region were reaching their trafficking goals. While, according to the United States State Department's worldwide annual barometer of trafficking, there was no significant improvement in performance in the previous calendar year (2021–22) nor the year before. Excepting for Namibia, no state in the region was meeting the minimum standards for the elimination of trafficking, and, in many respects, most were doing worse than under Covid. Namibia alone maintained Level 1 status in the US audit while South Africa and the other states in the region were variously consigned to Level 2, or even Level 2 Watchlist.[12] Even though all countries had some legal infrastructure to prosecute trafficking (in South Africa, the PACOTIP, sexual offences legislation, the Children's Act, the BCEA and the POCA), the implementation of the counter-trafficking policy was, for the most part, inconsistent, poor and rudimentary.

In late 2022 South Africa, if not its neighbours, was also moving assertively forward towards decriminalising sex work in one modality or another. This has major implications for trafficking throughout the region given the high-level of trans-border circulation of people, including undocumented migrants amenable to participate in sex work, as well as their and perpetrators. Given that the essential pre-conditions for legalising sex work – good governance, accountable law enforcement and a network of functional social services – are largely absent in South Africa, there is reason to believe that the new order is unlikely to assist the moral quality of society, the interests of sex workers, or government in its management of counter-trafficking policies. To the contrary, based on the international experience discussed in an earlier chapter, it is fairly probably that the incidence of trafficking is likely to increase along with the widely documented emotional, psychological, and physical impacts on participants in sex work, victims and survivors. This posits various challenges to public health derived from an increased incidence of HIV and Aids and the transmission of sexual diseases. Given that trafficking also has a wide variety of psychological concomitants we will probably also see a rise in mental health disorders such as depression, anxiety, posttraumatic stress disorder (PTSD), substance abuse, and suicidality to name but a few. Since many victimised sex workers characteristically experience trauma, most will continue to face risk factors including sexual abuse, physical abuse, emotional abuse, neglect, intimate partner violence, homelessness, and social marginalisation.

Having said this, several inter-connected processes or policies need to be emplaced in the foreseeable future, both in South Africa and the surrounding region, if counter-trafficking initiatives are to be optimised.

Ten-point counter-trafficking strategy
- Increase arrests, prosecution, and conviction of traffickers to the full extent of the law.
- Build enhanced capacity in law enforcement.
- Confront corruption and complicity by law enforcement and government personnel.
- Improve assistance and social services for vulnerable populations and trafficking survivors.
- Enhance national policy frameworks and multisectoral counter-trafficking coalitions.
- Train for effective counter-trafficking in the criminal justice system.
- Mobilise civil society.
- Promote transnational activity.
- Utilise the financial sector to combat money laundering.
- Encourage foreign investors to undertake human trafficking mitigation in labour supply chains.

1. INCREASE ARRESTS, PROSECUTION AND CONVICTION OF TRAFFICKERS TO THE FULL LETTER OF THE LAW

Judges in southern African states are now able to sentence traffickers to life or very long terms of imprisonment. Nonetheless, there are few convictions for trafficking. In South Africa, for example, despite the variety of laws in place to bring traffickers to court and face justice, there were only eleven convictions for trafficking last year.[13] Throughout the region, there is a necessity to identify more traffickers and institute more prosecutions, ideally backed up with national plans and public funding. Moreover, while convictions can carry severe penalties, the greater majority are slapped on the wrist. This is especially the case with sex trafficking where sentencing is not commensurate with the seriousness of the crime and where it is still possible for traffickers to face the option of a fine instead of imprisonment.

Overall, the number of traffickers arrested is tiny in relation to the large numbers of people believed to be involved in trafficking in all its complex manifestations. The number of detected or identified victims, normally in the dozens, is correspondingly minuscule. Cases of trafficking during 2021–2022 involved 426 survivors which, as the US audit notes, 'did not reflect the scope of trafficking' according to reports from NGOs.[14] Many, if not most of the crimes perpetrated against victims of trafficking thus go unreported.

Sentencing of convicted offenders under the trafficking laws of the various southern African states also needs to be made fully commensurate with the global understanding of trafficking as a serious criminal offence. While there are several cases where offenders have been subject to the full letter of the law and received lengthy or life terms in jail, it is still possible in some countries (not excluding South Africa) to negotiate a fine in place of imprisonment or obtain a plea deal resulting in no prison time at all for some trafficking-related sexual offences. In Lesotho, ten magistrates are being trained to hear trafficking cases, but only three are currently operational. Fines are often imposed for labour trafficking and there is a Subordinate Court Act which precludes magistrates from issuing maximum penalties for trafficking crimes.[15] In Botswana, the sentencing of traffickers to adequate prison terms is a relatively recent innovation in the criminal justice system. Section 57 of the Botswana 2009 Children's Act prescribes a penalty of two-to-five-year imprisonment for encouraging a child to engage in prostitution, which is far too lenient for an especially egregious crime.[16] There are long-standing inconsistencies between international and domestic laws on trafficking in Mozambique where redrafting has now gone on for several years.[17] In Zambia, moreover the legal system does not cover all forms of child trafficking.[18] In Zimbabwe, no traffickers were convicted during 2022.[19] Countries throughout the entire region suffer from a shortage of interpreters in their respective criminal justice systems. In Botswana, for example, this seriously hinders the process of convicting traffickers.[20]

2. BUILD ENHANCED CAPACITY IN LAW ENFORCEMENT

There are no dedicated investigators on human trafficking in law enforcement in southern Africa, nor are there specialists in computer forensics to investigate online exploitation. Most investigations into trafficking are compromised by poor data management techniques. In South Africa, the SAPS, like their counterparts in other regional countries, lack responsiveness when confronted with trafficking, especially in cases where victims refuse to testify because of the shame or fear of their perpetrators. Because trafficking cases are intrinsically complex, police officials throughout the region prefer to work on easier non-trafficking cases that guarantee a promotion. There are very few police in the subcontinent who work proactively on trafficking cases, especially where these involve perpetrators linked to organised crime.[21]

In South Africa, victims must report to law enforcement and the DSD to access government services. This can be highly problematic because of poor or broken communication between the SAPs and the DSD or, more fundamentally because many members of the SAPs do not fully comprehend trafficking as a criminal activity.

Throughout the region, police forces rely too heavily on victim testimony in the process of case-building as opposed to material generated by investigations. This undermines testimony in courts because of recall problems on the part of traumatised victims. Far more work needs to be done to acquaint police officials with victim-identification techniques and the standard operating procedures for the referral of victims into the social services network.[22]

3. CONFRONT CORRUPTION AND COMPLICITY BY LAW ENFORCEMENT AND GOVERNMENT PERSONNEL

While southern African governments have recognised official complicity as a key challenge in addressing all transnational crimes including human trafficking, only the South African government has gone so far as to investigate, prosecute and convict some government officials. Much remains to be done throughout southern Africa to address corruption among law enforcement and immigration officials who casually elicit bribes from both perpetrators and victims of trafficking, exchange sexual favours for non-reporting of offences, or otherwise manipulate the lives of immigrants. Particularly delinquent are border police who frequently turn a blind eye to both sex and labour trafficking.

Corruption is, of course, not the monopoly of law enforcement. At a time when corruption has become a structural problem for governance more generally, agencies such as South Africa's DSD and DHA are notoriously corrupt at all levels.[23] Officials in the DHA have an especially long history of accepting under-the-counter payments by undocumented immigrants seeking working permits or residence status and this continues uncurbed. During 2021/22, there were cases of DSD officials being bribed to return victims in care to their perpetrators

Similar patterns are detectable in other areas of the region. In Eswatini, for example, serious allegations of trafficking and abuse of trafficking victims by senior government officials in protection roles have remained pending for multiple years.[24] In Zambia, police, military and security personnel are reported to be in the trafficking business.[25] In Zimbabwe, officials, including those at the senior level, are implicated in child labour trafficking and exploitation in the Mazowe district as well as in other areas.[26] Soldiers on the South African border at Beit Bridge are notorious for ignoring traffickers and there are cases where they have allowed organised criminal gangs safe passage into South Africa.[27] In Lesotho, attempts are being made to address corruption among immigration officials through a system of rotation on border duty.[28]

4. IMPROVE ASSISTANCE AND SOCIAL SERVICES TO VULNERABLE POPULATIONS AND TRAFFICKING SURVIVORS

South Africa has established an extensive support network for victims of trafficking. This network consists of 18 multipurpose accredited NGO-operated shelters, one government-run multipurpose shelter, 88 semi-accredited shelters providing emergency accommodation to victims for up to 72 hours, and 55 Thuthuzela Care Centres full service crisis geared to assisting victims of gender-based violence (GBV), including trafficking victims. There are also several unaccredited shelters run by NGOs.[29] Despite this, there are several outstanding problems. South Africa still needs to put into effect the immigration provisions of PACOTIP (sections 15, 16 and 31(2)(b)(9ii)). Its persistent failure to do so over many years has left foreigners largely unprotected and is indicative of what the United States audit terms the South African government's 'poor understanding' of TIP issues.[30] This should ideally go together with streamlining access to documentation for migrants, greater latitude for families and their dependents and more humane implementation of the Refugees Act.

In South Africa, and more widely in the region, there are several inconsistencies and shortfalls in dealing with vulnerable populations and trafficking victims. The referral process by which trafficking victims are inducted into the assistance network is often complicated by problems related to the identification of victims, and secondary traumatisation due to the inability of the SAPS and other frontline responders to fully comprehend the emotional consequences of trafficking.[31] Trafficking victims in Malawi are often kept in police custody because of the absence of sheltering facilities and this often results in added trauma.[32] Botswana has no formal system for identifying victims and then referring them to care.[33] Very little, if any, work is done to proactively screen victims in Mozambique where, unlike anywhere else in the region, victims from the northern border include child soldiers.[34] Work on counter-trafficking in 2021 is described as 'minimal' – no more than a handful of victims were encountered and these were the result of normal criminal investigations.

Trafficking victims in the rural areas of Zambia and Zimbabwe often encounter long delays in obtaining services and gaining admission to shelters.[35] In the safe houses and shelters throughout the region there is frequent confusion over victims of GBV and trafficking victims, each of whom requires tailored forms of treatment. Security of victims declines as one moves into the non-accredited division where there are high risks that perpetrators will establish contacts with their erstwhile victims.[36] Across the region there is an urgent requirement for accredited and dedicated shelters offering intensive counselling, and treatment for drug and alcohol addiction as well as a variety of psychiatric conditions.[37] There is a widespread need for specialised facilities dealing with male, transgender and child victims, as well as sustainable finance to maintain momentum in the assistance system.[38] In South Africa, this means, at minimum, increases in government-funded per-person-per-night stipends at accredited shelters.

Civil society participation should be encouraged and diversified, especially in countries like Lesotho where all counter-trafficking activity and assistance relies on a single NGO.[39] In Zimbabwe, the situation is dire since no victim was sent for care in the country's one shelter during the last calendar year.[40] Eswatini also has a single shelter for trafficking victims, but it needs extensive refurbishment.

5. ENHANCE NATIONAL POLICY FRAMEWORKS AND MULTISECTORAL COUNTER-TRAFFICKING COALITIONS

Throughout the region, 'national policy frameworks' of various sorts have been established to deal with trafficking on a multisectoral basis. Few meet regularly and few invoke civil society participation in accordance with the driving principles of counter-trafficking coalitions. Many lack the dedicated and sustainable finance necessary to ensure effective responsiveness to all potential trafficking cases. In Lesotho, for example, human trafficking investigations in all ten of its districts are difficult given the limited funds of the Anti-Trafficking and Migrant Control Unit.[41] Many countries suffer from problems regarding inter-institutional coordination. In Eswatini, for example, counter-trafficking activity is seriously impeded by breakdowns in communication between the local Inter-Agency Task Force for the Prevention of People Trafficking on one hand, and People Smuggling Task Force and the Prevention of People Trafficking and People Smuggling Secretariat on the other.[42]

In some respects, the policy framework in South Africa is comparatively superior to these other subcontinental mechanisms. Yet here, as elsewhere, there is a need to further institutionalise the system and deal with a variety of problems confronting the renewal of the policy now that South Africa has moved past Covid.

These challenges involve building greater capacity in provincial counter-trafficking structures and their first-line responders to conduct effective screening procedures among populations at risk – for example, sex workers, children, members of the LGBT community and migrants.[43] This should ideally include ways to distinguish between GBV and trafficking. There is also a need for enhanced collaboration at all levels. Vertical collaboration between the NICTIP and the provincial structures and within these structures would ensure greater identification with the multisectoral ethic between representatives of civil society and various governmental departments at a regional level. Horizontal collaboration between provinces will assist in the sharing of operational experience. Greater consistency of action and social responsibility needs to be encouraged given the current high level of irregularity of participation in most provincial structures beyond KZN, Mpumalanga, and the Western Cape, and in their use of SOPs for identification and referral. Greater care needs to be exercised to ensure the bona fides are genuinely representative of anti-trafficking civil society groupings. The NICTIP (currently chaired by the DJCD) needs to provide more leadership to combat serial absenteeism in provincial structures on the part of the SAPs and representatives from the DOL and the DHA.

6. TRAIN FOR EFFECTIVE COUNTER-TRAFFICKING IN THE CRIMINAL JUSTICE SYSTEM

Training focused on the role of law enforcement can minimise some of the derelictions of duty on the part of the SAPs and other regional police forces. Ideally, this should focus on, inter alia, the push-pull factors in TIP, the identification and protection of victims, victim-centred interview techniques, the dynamics of investigating trafficking cases and advanced forensics to pinpoint trafficking crimes. A segment of the training curriculum should be geared toward the role of the police in the standard operating procedures for victim referral into the assistance network.

Police forces in the region need to be better equipped to discriminate between perpetrators, victims, traffickers and human smugglers as part of the process of building better information systems. Portions of this syllabus should be used to train government officials as well as civil society stakeholders working within the frameworks of national policy frameworks. This includes frontline responders (including doctors, nurses and social workers) as well as civil society organisations involved in nascent multisectoral counter-trafficking coalitions in several southern African countries.

Given the high proportion of foreigners moving across borders in the region, far more translators are required to assist frontline responders and support the criminal justice system in its investigation and prosecutorial functions. This should ideally be benchmarked, monitored and evaluated to ensure sustainability and self-reinforcement. The development of a translator database, called for several years ago, is an important element in assisting foreigners in various countries to access justice. Enhanced language training would also assist the SAPS and other regional police forces in screening trafficking victims in various southern African countries. In South Africa in particular, there needs to be improved communication between the SAPS and the DSD in the referral process. The frequent practice of arresting victims alongside their perpetrators also needs to end in compliance with the 2013 legislation

7. MOBILISE CIVIL SOCIETY

More general awareness training needs to be conducted among vulnerable populations such as migrants, commercial sex workers, rural communities and foreign migrants in all southern African countries. In some countries, like Namibia, ethnic communities, like San or Zemba children, are especially at risk. In all[44] cases, general awareness training can be especially potent if run in tandem with a 'hotline' that facilitates the transmission of information on a secure and confidential basis, especially reports on official corruption and complicity.

In the interests of developing a nationwide network for intelligence, public awareness-raising initiatives should go beyond vulnerable groups to encompass just about everyone in the region. Programmes along these lines should ideally be benchmarked, monitored and evaluated in a way that ensures sustainability and the self-reinforcement of attitudes. Educators in thousands of South African schools are, for example, anxious about the 'human trafficking' of children, yet there are relatively few interventions aimed at communicating information about the scale, nature, and dynamics of the human trade of people under the official age of eighteen. Much like society more widely, child trafficking is almost inordinately stereotyped as sex exploitation and seldom considers the diversity of horrors to which children are exposed in the form of child labour, illegal adoption, baby farming, sex tourism (CST), criminal activities associated with drug crimes or victims of muti murder. Few teachers in South African schools are even aware of the proliferation of organ harvesting throughout the subcontinent, even while recoiling once acquainted with the high incidence or the murder, dissection and sale of very young children in meeting the demands of the global medical market. Several of the major stakeholders in education, such as SADTU (the South African Democratic Teachers Union), NAPTOSA (the National Association of Teachers of South Africa) and the ISSASA (the Independent Schools of Association of Southern Africa) need to 'run with the ball' on these issues and 'come to the table'.

Social workers and psychologists who are cardinal stakeholders in the treatment of survivors have absolutely no training aimed at equipping them to deal with the therapeutic demands of deeply traumatised victims, men, women and children. Much like their counterparts in the public sector, most outside the DSD in private practice, lack the tools for identifying trafficking survivors, least of all the methodologies for ensuring their possible re-integration into the mainstream of society. This melds with a nationwide inclination of even well-mean social service providers to ignore the special requirements of trafficked people as opposed to lumping them into inappropriate programs dealing with addiction and general psychiatric conditions Relative to the paediatric profession in many other countries, there is an urgent requirement for front-line nurses and doctors to be both conscientious and trained for counter-trafficking purposes if only to ensure the functionality of the provincial structures established by the NPF. The many international organisations present in South Africa need to fine-tune their activities to take more account of indigenous conditions while entering into more sustainable partnerships with local organisations.

Human trafficking risk assessment based on indicative factors and subsequent mitigation are powerful tools for use on a multi-sectoral basis.[45] Everyone from individual schools to large-scale business corporations remains to benefit from identifying the many 'red flags' of trafficking activity and then moving to reduce risk through planned or bespoke interventions. Given the pervasive incidence of labour trafficking in all sectors of the South African economy, in industry, commerce, tourism, agriculture, and mining, it is extraordinary that chambers of commerce and industry remain ignorant of human trade and do little if anything to address trafficked labour in their supply chains relative to their counterparts in other areas of the globe. While there is an understandable reluctance on the part of many constituencies to admit to trafficking as an intrinsic part of operations, corporate leaders need to take far more responsibility in addressing the 'business model' of traffickers, if only as a matter of self-interest to counter the social, economic, and reputational costs associated with evidence of trafficking activity.

Illicit mining or small-scale (junior) mining is a proven hotbed of trafficking driven by rapacious brokers and the mainstream mines need to resolve such long-outstanding issues as the legality of the artisanal sector and its relationship to mainstream mining activity. The hospitality industry and tourism more widely is an important site for trafficking and key players, here as elsewhere, need to learn about human trade, conduct risk assessments and then move towards a variety of programs for risk mitigation. Many victims enter the countries of the region using air transport and airline companies should undertake programs for risk assessment along with the whole transport sector. At another level, young entrepreneurs also require much greater exposure to trafficking-oriented programs geared to the requirements of an ethical and legally compliant business.

8. PROMOTE TRANSNATIONAL ACTIVITY

Many trafficking issues in the region are intrinsically cross-border. Over the last year for example, there has been a movement of refugees fleeing southern Angola into Namibia where some are exploited in domestic work or cattle-herding. Regionalising cross-border collaboration on a bi- or multilateral basis with a view to information sharing and coordination on investigations by judiciaries and law enforcement agencies is essential in an age of transnationalism. Given the capability of traffickers to work trans-frontier there also needs to be more regional policing activity – if and when regional actors can share intelligence and avoid the inter-agency competition that has dogged similar initiatives in the past. More use needs to be made of the SADC data tool and opportunities to interdict syndicates that have penetrated the criminal justice system in various countries. A more effective transnational response to trafficking linked to border security also needs to be developed, either bilaterally between states, or under SADC auspices. This is again dependent on genuinely joint police-military initiatives on the part of regional governments, effective intelligence sharing and greater use of SADC resources such as its regional data collection tool. Operations to interdict traffickers at or near border crossings should also invest greater resources in syndicates who have penetrated the various police, military and para-military forces in some cases. In South Africa, in particular, there is a requirement for improved planning and usage of SANDF members currently deployed near or at our international frontiers.

9. UTILISE THE FINANCIAL SECTOR TO COMBAT MONEY LAUNDERING

Opponents of trafficking have long since argued that one of the best ways to inhibit human trade is through the management of supply and demand. In the case of commercial sex trafficking, for example, this involves disrupting the business model by containing the supply of sex workers amenable to recruitment for trafficking purposes and, in tandem, curbing the number of consumers for sexual services.[46]

Unfortunately, this is a very long-term project and probably unrealistic in societies such as South Africa where the reserve army for trafficking is supported by such factors such as poverty, lack of alternative job opportunities, widespread family dysfunction, poor child protection services, and GBV rooted in patriarchal values.

Having said this, banks and downstream financial services such as real estate agencies, casinos and insurance brokers need to act more emphatically for counter-trafficking and their touch points with traffickers. South Africa is a member of the Eastern and Southern African Anti-Money Laundering Group (ESAAMLG) Eastern and Southern Africa Money Laundering Group and also has financial legislation to track suspicious transactions associated with terrorism and, more recently, human trafficking.[47] There is also a South African Anti-Money Laundering Integrated Task Force, which is a private-public sector partnership responsible for monitoring money banked for trafficking purposes and which has an expert working group (EWG) concerned with finance and modern slavery working to some extent with the Finance Against Slavery and Trafficking (FAST) initiative of the United Nations.[48] Money laundering activity is also subject to oversight by the Paris-based FATF (Financial Action Task Force) which has, along with other organisations such as the OSCE, developed a variety of 'red flag' batteries which can be deployed to detect suspicious financial transactions in the banking system.

South African attempts to address money laundering date back to the nineties. Unfortunately, South Africa remains a high-risk country for money laundering related to trafficking because most transactions involve cash, Banks still fall short of international standards for human trafficking risk assessment and mitigation. In 2019 the FATF issued a report that threatened South Africa with demotion to its grey list and, in the face of the reputational and economic costs this would involve, the government has introduced new legislation, (most notably amendments to anti-money laundering laws), most of which appear to meet the requirements of the FHFT.[49] The translation of the financial system to an effective counter-trafficking instrument depends on various factors that go beyond the law. These include arming the Directorate for Priority Crime Investigation (the

Hawks) with greater forensic accounting skills, enhanced communication between the South African Anti-Money Laundering Integrated Task Force and the various law enforcement agencies, capacity-building in the expert working group of task force, and a greater understanding of the social context of money laundering in financial circles. A shift in focus from the funding of terrorist organisations to the proceeds of trafficking would also be valuable in upgrading the role of the financial sector in the trafficking arena.

10. ENCOURAGE FOREIGN INVESTORS TO UNDERTAKE HUMAN TRAFFICKING MITIGATION IN LABOUR SUPPLY CHAINS

All business in South Africa is obliged to conform to local counter-trafficking legislation such as PACOTIP and the Financial Intelligence Centre Act. Foreign corporations and investors in South Africa that make up a substantial component of the industrial, commercial and manufacturing sectors also fall into the category of, loosely speaking, 'accountable institutions' or 'beneficial owners', and are expected, albeit voluntarily, to identify with South African laws and, more widely, the spirit of UN prescriptions for the increased incorporation of ESG (environmental, social and governance provisions) into investment decisions. A growing number of the many international corporates in South Africa have, in turn, identified with worldwide principles for responsible investment, and, in 2011 a Code for Responsible Investing in South Africa (CRISA) was created on the back of the various provisions of the King Commission for effective governance in the corporate sector. This has now been superseded by CRISA2, which represents an advanced version of the 2011 code and comes into operation in February 2023. Although still voluntary, this holds out many still incipient prospects for integrating international business with building a multisectoral coalition for counter-trafficking in South Africa.

About the author

Philip Frankel is a political scientist and professor in the Department of Social Sciences at St Augustine College of South Africa in Victory Park, Johannesburg.

Frankel was educated at the University of the Witwatersrand in Johannesburg where he obtained a Master of Arts. He then obtained a second Master of Arts and a Doctorate in Philosophy from Princeton University in the USA.

Previously Head of the Department of Political Studies at the University of the Witwatersrand, he is the author of countless articles and studies on various topics that have appeared in peer-reviewed journals, conference papers and the South African and international media.

He is the author of 11 books published by such prestigious houses as Cambridge University Press and Yale University Press. These include three books on the role of the military in South African politics, (he is currently working on the fourth, which examines the post-apartheid SANDF), three books on the mining industry, one on human trafficking as well as various studies of political change and public policymaking.

His book on human trafficking, *Long walk to nowhere, Human trafficking in post-Mandela South Africa* was published by Routledge Press (London and New York) in 2016. It remains the only systematic book on trafficking in persons in South Africa and is cited worldwide. It examines the rollout of counter-trafficking strategy since South Africa's first national legislation (the Prevention and Combating of Trafficking in Persons Act of 2013) as well as the major forms of trafficking, such as commercial sex trafficking and child trafficking. Part of the book is devoted to forced and bonded labour in the domestic, mining, and agricultural sectors – which is again ground-breaking.

Professor Frankel came to issues of labour trafficking as a result of over 10 years as a lead consultant to the mining industry where he first encountered modern slavery in formal as well as illegal or artisanal mining.

During this period when his work focussed on human behaviour and risk issues in the underground workplace, he consulted to all the major role-players in the industry. These include BHP Billiton, Impala Platinum, Gold Fields and the Department of Minerals and Energy Resources. He was a lead consultant to all four divisions of Anglo-American PLC and worked in Latin America with Vale and Rio Tinto. He is the co-author of the National Mining Health and Safety Report commissioned by the Office of the President in 2008.

Outside of trafficking in persons and mining, Frankel has worked as a political consultant to various clients on a range of issues from national security and organisational transformation to local economic development. His clients have included most of the line departments of the central government in South Africa, the South African National Defence Force, the South African Police Force, as well as provincial and local authorities throughout the Republic. He has worked extensively on research, community facilitation and project management for various non-government organisations including USAID, DIFD and AUSAID.

He is currently working as a human trafficking specialist to mobilise opinion in civil society, especially among teachers, in social services and in the private sector.

Notes

PREFACE

1   Havocscope (2015) *Human trafficking: Prices and statistics of the modern-day slavery*. London: Havocscope. On various business 'models' of trafficking see also Kara S (2009) *Sex trafficking: Inside the business of modern slavery*. New York: Columbia University Press.

2   See Rights First, an international organisation based in New York and Washington.

3   There are a handful of global barometers measuring trafficking worldwide and, in some cases, country by country. These include the Annual Report on Human Trafficking compiled by the US State Department and issued annually, the Global Slavery Index (GSI) published by Walk Free in Australia, and the relatively new CTDC (Counter-Trafficking Data Collaborative). Other major sources of information are reports by the United Nations Office on Drugs and Organised Crime (UNODC), frequently referred to as GLOTIP. In the US audit, target countries are ranked on a scale from 1 to 5 where 1 = very good in prosecuting trafficking offences, protecting victims and preventing trafficking. 2 roughly corresponds with 'still trying' and 5 is a country where nothing substantive is being done. South Africa is currently on Level 2 Watchlist, between levels 2 and 3.

4   Frankel P (2016) *Long walk to nowhere: Human trafficking in post-Mandela South Africa*. London and New York: Routledge.

5   The Prevention and Combating of Trafficking in Persons Act (No. 7 of 2013) (PACOTIP). This is South Africa's one and only national and systematic piece of anti-trafficking legislation.

6   The Prevention and Combating of Trafficking in Persons National Policy Framework (NPF), 2 May 2019. The NPF flows from the PACOTIP and constitutes its execution arm.

CHAPTER 1 HUMAN TRAFFICKING: AN OVERVIEW

1   See, for example, Shelley L (2010) *Human trafficking: A global perspective*. New York: Cambridge University Press. This is a valuable general reader among the early works.

2   Kara S (2009) *Sex trafficking*. This book explores the various 'business models' used in trafficking.

3   The United Nations Convention against Transnational Crime (UNCTOC) was passed by the General Assembly in 2000 (55/25). It has three supplementary protocols, the so-called Palermo Protocol to Suppress and Punish Trafficking in Persons, especially Women and Children; the Protocol against the Smuggling of Migrants by Land, Sea and Air; and the Protocol

against the Illicit Manufacture and Trafficking in Firearms. Of these, the first and second are mostly evoked in discussions about human trade.

4   Laczko F & Gramega M (2003) Developing better indicators of human trafficking. *Brown Journal of World Affairs* X(1): 179–194.

5   See PACOTIP.

6   South African peacekeepers in Africa, among other forces under United Nations auspices, have been frequently accused of sexual crimes including human trafficking. As of 30 October 2021, the United Nations reported three allegations against South African peacekeepers – a reduction from six allegations in 2019. According to the *Conduct in UN Field Missions* online portal, since 2015 there have been 37 allegations of sexual exploitation and abuse against 43 peacekeepers from South African units deployed to the UN Stabilization Mission in the Democratic Republic of the Congo. Of the 37 allegations, the South African government had not reported taking accountability measures in 12 of the cases, including the three cases reported during the year, three from 2019, three from 2018, and three from 2017. One of these cases involved the rape of a child, four involved transactional sex with one or more adults, six involved an exploitative relationship with an adult, and one involved sexual assault of an adult. In six of the open cases, the South African government, the United Nations, or both, substantiated the allegations and the United Nations had repatriated the peacekeepers. According to the United Nations, South African authorities continued to investigate the other six open cases.

7   On 'opportunity structures' see Cockbain E (2018) Offender and victim networks in human trafficking. London & New York: Routledge; Allais C, et al. (2010) *Tsireledzani: Understanding the dimensions of human trafficking in southern Africa*. Pretoria: Human Sciences Research Council.

8   Allais C (2013) The profile less considered: The trafficking of men in South Africa. *South African Review of Sociology* 44(1): 40–54.

9   GLOTIP, 2020; UNODC, January 2021.

10   On some of the earliest trafficking cases, some before the promulgation of the PACOTIP, see Frankel, *Long walk to nowhere.*

11   Allais C, et al., *Tsireledzani.*

12   Bermudez L (2008) *'No experience necessary': The internal trafficking of persons in South Africa.* Pretoria International Organization for Migration (IOM) Regional Office for Southern Africa; Kropiwnicki, Z de S (2010) *Wolves in sheep's skin: A rapid assessment of human trafficking in Musina, Limpopo Province of South Africa.* Geneva: International Organisation for Migration.

13   Walker R, Mahati S & Magaya I (2019) *Child trafficking in South Africa: Exploring the myths and realities.* Pretoria: Centre for Child Law, University of Pretoria.

14   GLOTIP; Walker, Mahati & Magaya, *Child trafficking in South Africa.*

15   GLOTIP; Walker, Mahati & Magaya, *Child trafficking in South Africa.*

16   GLOTIP; Walker, Mahati & Magaya, *Child trafficking in South Africa*; Robins

S (2002) At the limits of special governmentality: A message from the tip of Africa. *Third World Quarterly* 23(4): 665–689

17   Van der Watt M (2020) Child trafficking and children in South Africa's sex trade: Evidence, undercounting and obfuscations. *Child Abuse Research in South Africa: A South African Journal* (21)1. https://hdl.handle.net/10520/EJC-1d47701005.

18   Again, on the early cases, see Frankel, *Long walk to nowhere.*

19   There is an ongoing debate about the prevalence of human trafficking and its implications for the victims especially children. See, inter alia, Van der Watt M (2015) Human trafficking in South Africa: An elusive statistical nightmare. *The Conversation*, 16 July; Van der Watt, Child trafficking.

21   The period around the 2010 World Cup spawned a substantial literature on its implications for human trafficking. See, for example, Gould C (2010) Moral panic, human trafficking and the 2010 Soccer World Cup. *Agenda* (85): 31–44.

22   Allais et al., *Tsireledzani*; Molo Songololo (2000) *The trafficking of women into the South African sex industry.* Cape Town: Molo Songololo.

CHAPTER 2 SEX TRAFFICKING

1   On this point see Moore A & Goldberg E (2015) Victims, perpetrators, and the limits of human rights discourse in post-Palermo fiction about sex trafficking. *The International Journal of Human Rights* 19(1): 16–31.

2   See Frankel, *Long walk to nowhere.* Frankel P (2013) *Between the rainbows and the rain: Marikana, mining, migration and the crisis of modern South Africa.* Johannesburg: ASR Press.

3   Ronald Weitzer is widely regarded as one of the pioneers in the analysis of sex work and, less so, sex trafficking. In this regard see Weitzer R (2010) The mythology of prostitution: Advocacy, research and public policy. *Sexuality Research and Social Policy* 7(1): 15–29; Weitzer R (2012) Sex trafficking and the sex industry: The need for evidence-based theory and legislation. *Journal of Criminal Law and Criminology* 101(4):1337–1370; Weitzer R (2015) Researching prostitution and sex trafficking comparatively. *Sexuality Research and Social Policy* 12(2): 81–91.

4   Allais et al., *Tsireledzani*; Songololo, The trafficking of women.

5   Among the leading works on sex trafficking in South Africa over and above the Molo Songolo and HSRC studies are Gould C & Fick N (2008) *Selling sex in Cape Town: Sex work and human trafficking in a South African city.* Pretoria: Institute for Security Studies; Gould C (2014) Sex trafficking and prostitution in South Africa. *American Academy of Political and Social Science* 653(1): 183–201; Horne J (2014) A critical analysis of human trafficking for sexual exploitation. PhD thesis, University of South Africa; Leggett T (2002) *Rainbow vice: The drug and sex industries in the new South Africa.* Cape Town: David Philip; Makhubela J (2019) Substance abuse and sex work: Protracting the potential of risky sexual behaviors among commercial sex workers in Musina, Limpopo Province of South Africa. *Trames: A Journal of the Humanities and Social*

Sciences 23(1): 29; Van der Watt M (2018) Investigating human trafficking for sexual exploitation: From 'lived experience': Towards a complex system understanding. PhD thesis, University of South Africa; Lutya TM (2009) Epi-criminological responses to human trafficking of young women and girls for involuntary prostitution in South Africa. *Journal of Scandinavian Studies in Criminology and Crime*: 10(1): 59–78.

6   See Frankel, *Long walk to nowhere*.

7   Much as in other countries, the role of men in sex work and sex trafficking is relatively small in relation to women. See Allais, The profile less considered.

8   Elizabeth Maswanganye recruited, transported and lured into prostitution through false promises young women and girls looking for employment in Pretoria. She was charged with running a brothel and with soliciting girls for carnal intercourse under sections 2 and 14 of the Sexual Offences Act (No. 23 of 1957) and sentenced to five years' imprisonment. This was one of the first successfully prosecuted human trafficking cases.

9   Amien Andrews lured young women and girls looking for a good time at shopping malls into brothels. He was charged with kidnapping, assault to do grievous bodily harm, indecent assault and rape. He was sentenced to 17 years imprisonment in, again, one of the first successfully prosecuted human trafficking cases.

10   Lutya, Epi-criminological responses.

11   Lutya, Epi-criminological responses.

12   Bermudez, 'No experience necessary'.

13   On the relationship between migration and sex work, see Walker R & Oliveira E (2015) Contested spaces: Exploring the intersection of migration, sex work, and trafficking in South Africa. *Graduate Journal of Social Science* 11(2): 129–153.

14   On the general dynamics of sex work and trafficking, see, inter alia, Van der Watt, Investigating human trafficking.

15   Van der Watt, Investigating human trafficking.

16   On the internet and sex trafficking, see, among many other writings, Dixon H (2013) Human trafficking and the internet* (*and other technologies, too). *The Judges' Journal* 52(1): 36–29.

17   Frankel P (2016) *Long walk to nowhere*.

18   Van der Watt, Investigating human trafficking.

19   Van der Watt, Investigating human trafficking.

20   Among other key documents on the decriminalisation of sex work in South Africa see Commission for Gender Equality (2013) *Decriminalizing sex work in South Africa: 2013*. Accessed January 2023. http://cge.org. za/wp-content/uploads/2021/01/CGE-Decr.pdf; PMG (Parliamentary Monitoring Group) (2018) *South African Law Reform Commission Report: Adult prostitution: Response by stakeholders*. Accessed January 2023. https:// pmg.org.za/committee-meeting/25902/; SWEAT (Sex Workers Education and Advocacy Taskforce). (2019) *Submission to: the CEDAW Committee re: General recommendation on trafficking in women & girls in the context of global*

migration. Accessed February 2023. https://www.ohchr.org/sites/default/
files/Documents/HRBodies/CEDAW/GRTrafficking/Sex_Workers_
Education_Advocacy_Taskforce_SWEAT.docx; UN Human Rights Council
(2016) *Report of the Special Rapporteur on violence against women, its causes and
consequences on her mission to South Africa*, 14 June 2016. Accessed February
2023. A/HRC/32/42/Add.2. There are also various reports of the South
African Law Reform Commission: see, for example, SALRC (South African
Law Reform Commission) (2021) *Project 107: Sexual offences (pornography and
children (June 2021).* Pretoria: SALRC.

21   Hedlin S (2016) The relationship between prostitution laws and sex
trafficking: Theory and evidence on scale, substitution, and replacement
effects. *University of Michigan Journal of Law Reform* 50(2): 329–386; Coontz P
& Griebel C (2004) International approaches to human trafficking:
The call for a gender-sensitive perspective in international law. *Women's
Health Journal* (4)1: 47–58; Brents B (2016) Neo-liberalism's market morality
and heteroflexibility: Protectionist and free market discourses in debates
for legal prostitution. *Sexuality Research and Social Policy* 13(1): 402–416;
and Farrell A & Cronin S (2015) Policing prostitution in an era of human
trafficking law enforcement. *Crime, Law, and Social Change* 64(1): 211–228.

22   The Nordic countries and the Netherlands have been widely used as
case studies. On the Netherlands, see, for example, Wagenaar H (2006)
Democracy and prostitution: Deliberating the legalization of brothels in
the Netherlands. *Administration and Society* 38(2): 198–235; Outshoorn J
(2012) Policy change in prostitution in the Netherlands: From legalization
to strict control. *Sexuality Research and Social Policy* 9(1): 233–243; Smit
M (2011) Trafficking in human beings for labor exploitation: The case of
the Netherlands. *Trends in Organized Crime* 14(1): 184–197; Huisman W
& Klemmans E (2014) The challenges of fighting sex trafficking in the
legalized prostitution market of the Netherlands. *Crime, Law, and Social
Change* 61(2): 215–228; Boutellier J (1991) Prostitution, criminal law, and
morality in the Netherlands. *Crime, Law, and Social Change* 15(1): 201–211.

23   On the role of governance in combating sex trafficking see Emser M (2013)
The politics of human trafficking in South Africa: A case study of the
KwaZulu-Natal Intersectoral Task Team and South African counter-trafficking
governance. PhD thesis, University of KwaZulu-Natal; Emser M & Francis S
(2017) Counter-trafficking governance In South Africa: An analysis of the role of
the KwaZulu-Natal human trafficking, prostitution, pornography and brothels
task team. *Journal of Contemporary African Studies* 35(2): 190–211.

CHAPTER 3 CHILD TRAFFICKING

1   PACOTIP.
2   Walker R. Mahati S and Magaya I (2019) Child trafficking in South Africa:
The landscape of the sexual exploitation of children in South Africa.
Bangkok: ECPAT.

3   Emser M and Van der Watt M (2019) '#Stillnotfound: Missing children in South Africa. *Alternation* 26(1): 89–120.
4   Allais C, et al. (2010) *Tsireledzani*; Molo Songololo (2000). The trafficking of children for purposes of sexual exploitation. Cape Town: Molo Songololo.
5   Walker R, Mahati, S and Magaya I (2020) *Child Trafficking in South Africa: Exploring the Myths and Realities*; Centre for Child Law, University of Pretoria.
6   Van der Watt, M (2020) *A holistic Approach* (4th ed.). Pretoria: Van Schaik.
7   ibid.
8   United States Department of Labour: Bureau of International Labour Affairs (n.d.) – *Child Labour and Forced Labour Report: South Africa.*
9   ibid
10   On sex tourism in South Africa, see Mpapa N (2016) Child sex tourism in South Africa: A children's rights perspective. MA thesis, University of the Western Cape; O'Connell Davidson J & Sánchez Taylor J (1996) *Child prostitution and sex tourism in South Africa.* Research Paper. Bangkok: ECPAT.
11   On illegal adoption, Cantwell N (2017) *The sale of children and illegal adoption.* Den Haag: Terre des Hommes.
12   Nothing substantive has yet been written on the relationship between child fostering and trafficking in South Africa. There is, however, a huge literature on the subject in the African context upon whose concepts new South African research can draw. Representative works in this category include Ballet J (2016) Recruitment patterns of child trafficking in Madagascar: An analysis based on missing and recovered children. *Journal of Human Trafficking* 2(3): 235-254; Bledsoe C (1990) No success without struggle: Social mobility and hardship for foster children in Sierra Leone. MAN 25 (1): 70–88; Case A, Paxson C & Ableidinger J (2004) Orphans in Africa: Parental death, poverty, and school enrolment. *Demography*, 41(3): 483–508; Davidson J (2011) Moving children? Child trafficking, child migration, and child rights. *Critical Social Policy* 31(3): 454–477; Godziak E (2008) On challenges, dilemmas, and opportunities in studying trafficked children. *Anthropological Quarterly* 81(4): 903–923; Howard N. (2011) Is child placement trafficking? Questioning the validity of an accepted discourse. *Anthropology Today*, 27(6), 3–7; Mbakogu I (2015) Understanding child trafficking from the point of view of trafficked children. PhD thesis, McGill University.
13   The Hague Convention of 29 May 1993 on *The Protection of Children and Co-operation in Respect of Intercountry Adoption* protects children and their families against the risks of illegal, irregular, premature or ill-prepared adoptions abroad. This convention, which operates through a system of national central authorities, reinforces the UN Convention on the Rights of the Child (Art. 21) and seeks to ensure that intercountry adoptions are made in the best interests of the child and with respect for his or her fundamental rights. It also seeks to prevent the abduction of, the sale of, or traffic in, children.
14   See Dunbar D & Swart S (2012) 'No less a foe than Satan himself': The devil, transition and moral panic in white South Africa, 1989–1993. *Journal*

of Southern African Studies 38(3): 601–662. Also, Els L & Jonker K (2000)
Satanism in South Africa. Pretoria: Amabukhu Publications

15   Watson C (2016) The organised crime of organ trafficking. Master's thesis,
University of the Free State.

16   Among the many studies on muti murder, see Bhootra BL & Weiss E (2006)
Muti killing: A case report. *Medical Science and the Law* 46(3): 255–259;
Bukuluki P (2014) Child sacrifice: Myth or reality. *International Letters of Social
and Humanistic Sciences* 30(1): 1–11; Cohan H (2011) The problem of witchcraft
violence in Africa. *Suffolk University Law Review* 44(4): 803–872; Labuschagne
G (2004) Features and investigative implications of Muti murder in South
Africa. *Journal of Investigative Psychology and Offender Profiling* 1(3): 191;206.

17   Human rights violations perpetrated on albinos in Africa, including their
murder and trafficking, are covered in Taylor J (2019) Witchcraft-related
abuse and murder of children with albinism in sub-Saharan Africa: A
conceptual review 2019. *Child Abuse Review* 28(1): 13–26. On albinism and
trafficking, see Mbatha S (2021) Trafficking in persons living with albinism
in South Africa. Master's thesis, University of KwaZulu-Natal; Kromberg
J (2018) *Albinism in Africa*. Massachusetts: Academic Press; Bruynell M
(2012) The dangerous modern day belief in the supernatural: International
perceptions of witches and albinos. *Suffolk Transnational Law Review* 35(2):
393–420.

18   Msuya NH (2017) Tradition and culture in Africa: Practices that facilitate
trafficking of women and children. *Dignity: A Journal on Sexual Exploitation
and Violence* 2(1) Article 3. DOI:10.23860/dignity.2017.02.01.03.

19   There is a substantial literature on *Ukuthwala* despite its cultural
obscurantism. See, inter alia, Van der Watt M & Ovens M (2012)
Contextualising the practice of *Ukuthwala* within South Africa. *Child Abuse
Research: A South African Journal* 13(1): 11–26; Prinsloo J & Ovens M (2015)
Ukuthwala as an aberrant traditional practice: The State versus Nvumeleni
Jezile, 2014. *Acta Criminologica: Southern African Journal of Criminology*.
Special Edition No. 4; Mwambene L & Sloth-Nielsen J (2011) Benign
accommodation? *Ukuthwala*, 'forced marriage' and the South African
Children's Act'. *African Human Rights Law Journal* 11: 1–22; Mason D (2009)
The practice of *Ukuthwala*, the Constitution and the Criminal Law (Sexual
Offences and related matters) Amendment Act. *Obiter* 716–723.

20   The illegality of *Ukuthwala* is unambiguous: under customary law marriage
negotiations are acceptable if the bride is not forced into taking a decision.
(FN108 Sections 1(c), 2 and 7. Since the practice only victimises girls it
violates the constitutional provision of gender equality. (FN109 Sections
9/10 109). Forced marriage falls outside the constitutional principles
governing customary law. See also Prinsloo, *Ukuthwala* as an aberrant
traditional practice.

21   ECPAT International. (2019) The landscape of sexual exploitation of children
in South Africa. Bangkok: ECPAT International.

CHAPTER 4 LABOUR TRAFFICKING

1   The literature on labour trafficking in South Africa is relatively small and often fairly old. See, however, Ally S (1979) *From servants to workers: South African domestic workers and the democratic state.* Ithaca, NY: Cornell University Press; and Frankel, *Between the rainbows and the rain.* See also, Naidoo R (1919) Labour broking: The smoke and mirrors industry. Accessed January 2023, https://www.southafricanlabourbulletin.org.za/labour-broking-the-smoke-and-mirrors-industry/; Steele S (2013) Human trafficking, labor brokering, and mining in southern Africa: Responding to a decentralized and hidden public health disaster. *International Journal of Health Services* 43(4): 665–680; Stuckler D, Steele S, Lurie M & Basu S (2013) Introduction: 'Dying for gold': The effects of mineral mining on HIV, tuberculosis, silicosis and occupational disease in South Africa. *International Journal of Health Services* 43(4): 639–649; Ulicki T (1999) Basotho miners speak: Subcontracting on South African gold mines. Accessed January 2023, https://www.southafricanlabourbulletin.org.za/basotho-miners-speak-subcontracting-on-south-african-gold-mines/92330.

2   Harvey S (2011) Labour brokers and workers' rights: Can they co-exist in South Africa? *South African Law Journal* 128(1). Accessed January 2023 https://hdl.handle.net/10520/EJC53957; Van Eck B (2010) Temporary employment services (labour brokers) in South Africa and Namibia, *Potchefstroom Electronic Law Journal* 13(2): 107–126. Accessed January 2023, https://journals.co.za/doi/abs/10.10520/EJC86769; Brandt F (2022) Asserting autonomy and belonging in precarious times: Working lives of women labour broker workers in Johannesburg, South Africa. *Third World Thematics.* Accessed January 2023, https://doi.org/10.1080/23802014.2022.2070270; Runciman C & Hlungwani K (2021) Organising against precarity: The life of a South African labour broker worker. *Work, Employment and Society* 3693: 557–568. Accessed January 2023, https://journals.sagepub.com/doi/abs/10.1177/09500170211015081

3   Muwaki K (2027) *Forced labour and the South African fruit and wine industries: A scoping report.* Accessed January 2023, https://www.stronger2gether.org/product/scoping-research-report-for-stronger-together-south-africa-forced-labour-and-the-south-african-fruit-and-wine-industries/; Devereux S (2019) Violations of farm workers' labour rights in post-apartheid South Africa. *Development Southern Africa* 37(1): 1–23.

4   An extensive literature which constitutes the social backdrop to domestic servitude has been developed over the years. See, for example, Dilata X (2008) Between sisters: A study of the employment relationship between African domestic workers and African employers in the townships of Soweto. PhD thesis, University of the Witwatersrand; Gaitskell D, Kimble J, Maconachie M & Unterhalter E (1984) Class, race and gender: Domestic workers in South Africa. *Review of African Political Economy* 27(28): 86–108; Ginsburg R (2011) *The hidden landscape of domestic service in Johannesburg.*

Charlottesville: The University of Virginia Press; Galvaan R, Peters L, Smith T, Brittain M, Menegaldo A, et al. (2015). Employers' experiences of having a live-in domestic worker: Insights into the relationship between privilege and occupational justice. *South African Journal of Occupational Therapy* 45(1): 41–47; Magwaza T (2008) Effects of domestic workers act in South Africa: A steep road to recognition. *Agenda* 22(78): 79–92.

5   Frankel, *Between the rainbows and the rain.*
6   On underground conditions, most of which are worse in the case of illegal labour/zama-zamas, see Frankel P (2016) Hell of modern slavery, *Sunday Independent*, 8 May 2016.
7   Surtees R (2008) *Trafficking at sea: The exploitation of south-east Asian fisherman.* International Organization for Migration (IOM) and Nexus Institute; Ratner B, Asgard B & Allison E (2015) Fishing for justice: Human rights development *Global Environment Change* 27: 120–130.
8   Surtees R (2014) *In African waters. The trafficking of Cambodian fishers in South Africa.* International Organization for Migration (IOM) and Nexus Institute.
9   Barrientos SW (2014) 'Labour chains': Analysing the role of labour contractors in global production networks. *The Journal of Development Studies* 49(8): 1058–1071.

CHAPTER 5 COUNTER-TRAFFICKING

1   Clark M (2003) Trafficking in persons: An issue of human security. *Journal of Human Development* 4(2): 247–263; Cho S-Y (2015) Modelling the determinants of human trafficking: An empirical analysis. *Social Inclusion* 3(1): 2–21; Hernandez D & Rudolph A (2015) Modern-day slavery: What drives human trafficking in Europe? *European Journal of Political Economy* 38: 118–139.
2   There are only two studies of anti-trafficking governance – On the role of governance in combating sex trafficking, see Emser, The politics of human trafficking in South Africa; Emser & Francis, Counter-trafficking governance in South Africa. Otherwise, the concept of counter-trafficking coalitions has not been used as a conceptual basis for evaluating counter-trafficking despite a large international literature. See, for example, Lagon M (2015) Traits of transformative anti-trafficking partnerships. *Journal of Human Trafficking*, 1(1): 21–33; Davy D (2013) Understanding the motivations and activities of transnational advocacy networks against child sex trafficking in the Greater Mekong subregion: The value of cosmopolitan globalisation theory. *Cosmopolitan Civil Societies: An Interdisciplinary Journal* 5(1): 39–68; Foot K, Sworn H & Alejano-Steele A (2019) Structures and practices of cross-sector engagement in counter-human trafficking coalitions in the Global South. *Cosmopolitan Civil Societies: An Interdisciplinary Journal* 11(1): 27–47; Heiss A & Kelley J (2017) From the trenches: A global survey of anti-TIP NGOs and their views of U.S. efforts. *Journal of Human Trafficking* 3(3): 231–254.

3   This includes the Slavery Convention (1926), the Forced Labour Convention
     (1930), the Convention relating to the Status of Refugees (1951), the United
     Nations Convention against Corruption (UNCAC of 2005), and CEDAW
     (the Convention on the Elimination of All Forms of Discrimination against
     Women. South Africa has also ratified the United Nations Declaration of
     the Basic Principle of Justice for Victims of Crime and Abuse of Power,
     the Convention on the Rights of Persons with Disabilities (2007) and the
     Domestic Workers Convention of the ILO. In addition, there are a number
     of regional instruments to combat trafficking, including the Banjul Charter
     (the African Charter on Human and People's Rights), the African Charter
     of the Rights and Welfare of the Child (ACRWC), the Ouagadougou Plan
     to Combat Trafficking in Human Beings, Especially Women and Children
     and four SADC Conventions dealing with TIP, Gender and Development,
     Extradition and Mutual Legal Assistance in Criminal Matters. (See the NPF,
     pp. 19–20).
4   For the historic evolution of PACOTIP see Palmary I & De Gruchy T (2019)
     The globalisation of trafficking and its impact on the South African counter-
     trafficking legislation. *Critical Social Policy* 40 (1): 1–19.
5   Kruger B (2016) Towards a sharp prosecution sword to combat human
     trafficking: Comparing the new South African counter-trafficking law with
     international prosecution standards. *The Comparative and International Law
     Journal of Southern Africa* 49(1): 53–84. See also Dafel V (2014) The Prevention
     and Combating of Trafficking in Persons Act 7 of 2013: A critical analysis
     of its potential impact on child trafficking prosecutions in South Africa.
     Master's thesis, University of KwaZulu-Natal.
6   Department of Justice and Constitutional Development (2019) *Prevention
     and combating of trafficking in persons: National Policy Framework*. Accessed
     April 2020, https://www.justice.gov.za/docs/other. -docs/2019-TIP-NPF-
     10April2019.pdf.
7   Bello P & Olutula A (2022) Effective response to human trafficking in South
     Africa: Law as a toothless bulldog. *Sage Open*, January – March, 1–14.
8   Heiss & Kelley, From the trenches.
9   Jac-Kucharski A (2012) The determinants of human trafficking: A US case
     study. *International Migration* 50(6): 150–165.
10   Foot K, Toft A & Cesare N (2015) Developments in anti-trafficking efforts:
     2008–2011. *Journal of Human Trafficking* 1(2): 136–155.
11   Cockayne J (2015) Unshackling development: Why we need a global
     partnership to end modern slavery. New York: United Nations University.
12   Gazley B & Guo C (2015) What do we know about nonprofit collaboration?
     A comprehensive systematic review of the literature. *Academy of
     Management Proceedings*. https://doi.org/10.5465/ambpp.2015.303.
13   There is a large literature that can be used as a reference point for the NPF
     and which forms the intellectual basis of the National Policy Development
     Framework of 2020. See, for example, Ngcaweni B (2019) Ten theses of

effective public policy. Presentation at the China-Africa Institute and Human Sciences Research Council International Conference, Pretoria; Howlett M & Ramesh M (2003) *Studying public policy: Policy cycles and policy subsystems*. Toronto: Oxford University Press.; Grande E (1996) The state and interest groups in a framework of multi-level decision-making: The case of the European Union. *Journal of European Public Policy* 3(3): 313–338.

CHAPTER 6 THE REGIONAL FRAMEWORK

1   A substantial portion of the human trafficking literature on southern Africa consists of official reports by organisations, most notably the SADC (see below). There is, however, a reasonably sized alternative literature among which the annual reports of the US State Department are especially valuable in providing country by country. These have been used extensively in the following chapter. In addition, the regional literature includes many articles dealing with the legal, developmental and security consequences of human trafficking. See, for example, Iroanya R (2018) *Human trafficking and security in southern Africa: the South African and Mozambican experience*. Cham, Switzerland: Springer; Mutasa C (2021) Human trafficking in southern Africa. In AD Hoffman and SO Abidde (Eds.) *Human trafficking in Africa*. Cham, Switzerland: Springer. https://doi.org/10.1007/978-3-030-82163-0_14; Juda-Chembe K (2019) The scourge of human trafficking in the SADC region as hindrance to development: A legal analysis. *Comparative and International Law Journal of Southern Africa* 52(2): 2019. https://hdl.handle.net/10520/EJC-1b5cdd2548; Mugari I & Obioha E (2021) Trends, precipitating factors and control of human trafficking in South Africa and Zimbabwe. *Open Journal for Anthropological Studies* 5(2): 37–48. On forced labour, see Thenga G (2021) Forced labour exploitation: Illegal trading in protected goods in the southern African countries. *Open Journal for Sociological Studies* 5(2): 81–94. The role of organised crime is discussed in Adekoye A (2019) An overview of the effects of organized crime on southern Africa. *Journal of African Foreign Affairs* 6(1): 107–118.

2   Mwambene L (2018) Recent legal responses to child marriage in southern Africa: the case of Zimbabwe, South Africa and Malawi. *African Human Rights Journal* 18(2): 2; Moyo I & Moya GM (2020) Sustaining family ties across the border: Unaccompanied child migration across the Botswana-Zimbabwe and South Africa-Zimbabwe borders. In CN Nshimbi, I Moyo & JP Laine (Eds), *Borders, sociocultural encounters and contestations: Southern African experiences in global view*. London: Routledge.

3   US State Department (2021) *Trafficking in persons report*. Washington: Office to Monitor and Combat Trafficking in Persons. Accessed January 2023, https://www.state.gov/reports/2021-trafficking-in-persons-report/ (The report is hereafter cited as USTIP Report 2021, followed by the reference to the relevant country narrative.); USTIP Report 2021, Mozambique.

4   USTIP Report 2021, Zimbabwe.

5   USTIP Report 2021, Zimbabwe.
6   USTIP Report 2021, Malawi.
7   Otañez M, Sandramu R &, McGill A. (2018) Human trafficking and forced labour in Malawi's tobacco growing sector. *Tobacco Induced Diseases* 16(1): 946–969.
8   USTIP Report 2021, Malawi.
9   Nnabugwu-Otesanya BE (2005) A comparative study of prostitutes in Nigeria and Botswana. Pretoria: University of South Africa, http://hdl.handle.net/10500/1588.
10 USTIP Report 2021, Zimbabwe.
11 On Zimbabwe, see Manumati S (2021) Human trafficking discourse in Zimbabwe. In E Essien (Ed.), *Handbook of research on present and future paradigms in human trafficking*. Hershey: IGI Global.
12 Sigweni SF (2014) Adoption laws and procedures of Botswana: Questioning their effectiveness and compliance with regional and international human rights standards. Master's thesis, University of Cape Town. http://hdl.handle.net/11427/4734.
13 Thenga, Forced labour exploitation.
14 Metsing NE (2020) Evaluating the practice of child labour in Lesotho and identifying strategies to provide for better protection. PhD thesis, University of Pretoria. http://hdl.handle.net/2263/77203.
15 Vambe B & Saroumbe A (2018) Child labour laws in South Africa, Zambia and Zimbabwe: A comparative analysis. *Commonwealth Youth & Development* 16(1). https://hdl.handle.net/10520/EJC-134d5cf90b.
16 Baker C, Lund C, Massah B & Mawerenga J (2021) We are human just like you: Albinism in Malawi – Implications for security. Journal of Humanities 29(1): 57–84.
17 USTIP Report 2021, Botswana.
18 USTIP Report 2021, Eswatini.
19 Vambe & Saroumbe, Child labour laws.
20 USTIP Report 2021, Zambia.
21 USTIP Report 2021, Botswana.
22 USTIP Report 2021, Botswana.
23 USTIP Report 2021, Botswana.
24 USTIP Report 2021, Namibia.
25 USTIP Report 2021, Malawi.
26 USTIP Report 2021, Zimbabwe.
27 See Mushair MR (2020) An evaluation of the laws that govern child online pornography prevention in Zambia. Dissertation for a Bachelor's degree in Mass Communications and Public Relations, Cavendish University, Zambia. Accessed January 2023, http://155.0.3.194:8080/jspui/handle/123456789/586.
28 USTIP Report 2021, Zimbabwe.

29 Pashovskiy I, LaFont S, Chaney R (2021) Sex trafficking and forced sex
    work amongst girls and women in Namibia. In A Elim & J Elim, *Overcoming
    challenges and barriers for women in business and education: Socioeconomic issues
    and strategies for the future.* Hershey: IGI Global.
30 Mabvurira V, Zengeni F & Chigevenga R (2021) Child trafficking and child
    smuggling in Zimbabwe: Legislation and policy gaps. *African Journal of
    Social Work* 12(1): 50–57.
31 Mushohwe B (2018) Child prostitution in Zimbabwe and the tragedy of the
    'victim by choice' tag: An overview. *University of Zimbabwe Law Journal* 1(1):
    11–34.
32 USTIP Report 2021, Mozambique.
33 USTIP Report 2021, Eswatini.
34 USTIP Report 2021, Zambia.
35 Ng'andu P (2019) Challenges of combating Illegal Immigration as cross
    border crime among Southern Africa Development Community (SADC)
    member states: Case study of Zambia. *International Affairs and Global
    Strategy* 74.
36 USTIP Report 2021, Malawi.
37 Frankel P (2013) *Between the rainbows and the rain.*
38 Frankel P (2013) Between the rainbows and the rain.
39 USTIP Report 2021, Malawi.
40 USTIP Report 2021, Zimbabwe.
41 USTIP Report 2021, Zimbabwe.
42 USTIP Report 2021, Zambia.
43 USTIP Report 2021, Zimbabwe.
44 USTIP Report 2021, Mozambique.
45 USTIP Report 2021, Eswataini.
46 USTIP Report 2021, Mozambique.
47 USTIP Report 2021, Botswana.
48 Muti murder is widespread in southern Africa. Among the many studies
    see Bhootra & Weiss, Muti killing: A case report; Bukuluki, Child sacrifice:
    Myth or reality; Cohan, The problem of witchcraft violence in Africa;
    Labuschagne, Features and investigative implications of muti murder in
    South Africa.
49 USTIP Report 2021, Botswana.
50 USTIP Report 2021, Lesotho.
51 USTIP Report 2021, Eswatini.
52 USTIP Report 2021, Namibia.
53 USTIP Report 2021 Zambia.
54 USTIP Report 2021, Zimbabwe. See Zengenene M (2020) Trafficking of
    women and girls in the district of Seke: Lessons from Zimbabwe's Second
    Republic. *Masyarakat, Kebudayaan dan Politik* 33(3): 46–265.
55 USTIP Report 2021, Lesotho.
56 USTIP Report 2021, South Africa.

57   Godwe MM (2019) Utilizing national human rights institutions for the promotion and protection of human rights: A case study of the Malawi Human Rights Commission. *Commonwealth Law Bulletin* 45(3): 556–579.
58   De Souza, MC, Nhtave, DJ & Da Silva Frota F (2020) Specific legislation targeting human trafficking after the approval of Palermo Protocol 2000: Mozambique State Case. *Brazilian Journal of International Law.*
59   De Souza, Nhtave & Da Silva, Specific legislation targeting human trafficking.
60   USTIP Report 2021, Lesotho.
61   Juliet C (2017) Critical analysis of the SADC legal and policy framework for combating corruption in human trafficking. Master's thesis, University of the Western Cape. Also see Bonga WG (2020) Corruption prevalence in SADC regional bloc. *Journal of Research in Humanities and Social Science* 9(1): 8–16; Mugari I & Obioha E (2021) The criminal justice response to human trafficking: Exploring the investigative and prosecutorial hurdles. *ADRRI Journal of Arts and Social Sciences* 18(1)(6): 54–69.
62   Nshimbi & Moyo, Borders, sociocultural encounters and contestations.
63   Chirambwi, K & Nare R (2018) Policing in the borderlands of Zimbabwe. In EO Alemika & M Ruteere (Eds), *Policing reform in Africa: Moving towards a rights-based approach in a climate of terrorism, insurgency and serious violent crime.* Cape Town: African Policing Civilian Oversight Forum (APCOF).
64   USTIP Report 2021, Zimbabwe.
65   Thobejane TD & Ngadhi CM. (2019) The role played by government towards the sex industry: The case of Ngundu, Zimbabwe. Gender and Behaviour 17(1). https://hdl.handle.net/10520/EJC-15d632e440; Mavunga T & Rufaro A (2018). The prohibition of child slavery in South Africa, Uganda and Zimbabwe: Overcoming the challenges of implementation of legislation. *Comparative and International Law Journal of Southern Africa* 51(1): 19–43.
66   USTIP Report 2021, Botswana.
67   USTIP Report 2021, Malawi.
68   USTIP Report 2021, Lesotho.
69   USTIP Report 2021, Lesotho.
70   USTIP Report 2021, Namibia.
71   USTIP Report 2021, Mozambique. See also Nhatave JDG, Arcénio FC & Da Silva Frota FH (2021) Access to justice and development in perspective: An analysis of protection and assistance to victims of trafficking in persons in Mozambique. *Revista Inclusiones* 8: 25–42.
72   Teya W & Kurebwa J (2019) The effectiveness of state and non-state actors in combating human trafficking and ensuring safe migration concerns of Zimbabweans. *Women's International Journal of World Policy and Development Studies* 5(1): 42–52.
73   USTIP Report 2021, Eswatini.
74   USTIP Report 2021, Lesotho.

75   Moyo, L. (2018) Corruption in Zimbabwe: implications for social work
      practice. *Journal of Human Rights and Social Work* 3(2): 55–61.
76   USTIP Report 2021, Lesotho.
77   USTIP Report 2021, Eswatini.
78   USTIP Report 2021, Botswana.
79   USTIP Report 2021, Zimbabwe. See also Munamati, Human trafficking
      discourse.
80   USTIP Report 2021, Nambia.
81   Mushibwe CP, Chambeshi M & Mpolomoka DL (2021) Valuing safehome
      shelters for victims of violence in Lusaka Province, Zambia. *Journal of
      African Interdisciplinary Studies*, 5(9): 41–56.
82   USTIP Report 2021, Lesotho.
83   USTIP Report 2021, Malawi.
84   USTIP Report 2021, Mozambique.
85   Ironya, Conclusion.
86   The SADC has generated numerous studies and protocols related to
      human trafficking. See the SADC Protocol on Gender and Development
      2008. Accessed January 2023, https://www.sadc.int/document/protocol-
      gender-and-development-2008; SADC Secretariat (2009) *10 Year SADC
      strategic plan of action on combating trafficking in persons, especially women and
      children (2009–2019)*. Gaborone: Southern African Development Community
      (SADC) Secretariat; SADC (2010) *Revised edition; Strategic indicative plan
      for the Organ on Politics, Defence and Security Cooperation*. Maputo, SADC;
      SADC (2017) *Revised SADC strategic plan of action on combating trafficking
      in persons, especially women and children (2016–2019)*. Gaborone: SADC
      Secretariat; SADC (2017) *SADC launches trafficking in persons lessons booklet*.
      Accessed January 2023, adc.int/latest-news/sadc-launches-trafficking-
      persons-lessons-booklet; SADC (2017) *Preventing and combating trafficking
      in persons: Lessons from the SADC region*. Gaborone: SADC Secretariat;
      *"SADC/SARPCCO Chiefs of Police Sub-Committee of the Inter-State Defence
      and Security Committee Annual General Meeting held in Lusaka, Zambia*.
      Accessed January 2023, https://www.sadc.int/latest-news/sadcsarpcco-
      chiefs-police-sub-committee-inter-state-defence-and-security-committee;
      UNODC (2018) Trafficking in persons in the SADC region: A statistical
      report (2014–2016). Accessed January 2023, https://www.unodc.org/
      documents/southernafrica/Stories/EN_-_TIP_Statistical_Report.pdf. For
      a general study, see Vhumbunu C (2020) Combating human trafficking in
      the Southern African Development Community: Strategies, challenges, and
      opportunities. *Strategic Review for Southern Africa* 42(2): 179.
87   Mabera F and Naidu S (2020). Entering into the fray? The extremist threat
      in Cabo Delgado; strategic policy choices for South Africa and the SADC
      *Institute for Global Dialogue 137, September 2020: 2–11; Mapfumo L & Danane J
      (2021) Extremisms in Africa*.

CHAPTER 7 CONCLUSION: BEYOND COVID

1　Between 2020 and 2022, extensive literature has developed on the interface between Covid and human trafficking, especially in the public health sector. See, for example, Greenbaum J, Stoklosa H & Murphy L (2020) The public health impact of coronavirus disease on human trafficking. *Public Health* 8. DOI:10.3389/fpubh.2020.561184; Armitage R & Nellums LB (2020) COVID-19: Compounding the health-related harms of human trafficking. *eClinicalMedicine*. DOI: https://doi.org/10.1016/j.eclinm.2020.100409.

2　Nkgadima R, Human trafficking in SA continuing despite coronavirus says Interpol, *Independent Online*, 25 November 2020; Stolz E, Human trafficking is the most pervasive criminal market – Global report, *Mail & Guardian*, 1 October 2021.

3　U.S. Department of State (2022) *Trafficking in persons report*. Washington: Office to Monitor and Combat Trafficking in Persons. Accessed January 2023, https://www.state.gov/reports/2022-trafficking-in-persons-report/ (The report is hereafter cited as USTIP Report 2022, followed by the reference to the relevant country narrative.); USTIP Report 2022, Namibia.

4　Warria A, Roper M, Van der Watt M, Marx & Dixon H, Children are easy targets for exploitation and traffickers during Covid, *Daily Maverick*, 3 June 3rd 2021; Van Zyl C, Gauteng: increase in child trafficking due to Covid-19 pandemic. *The South African* 11 September 2021.

5　*Durban Call to Action on the Elimination of Child Labour (2022)*. 5th Global Conference on the Elimination of Child Labour, Durban 15–20 May.

6　USTIP Report 2022, Malawi and Zimbabwe.

7　USTIP Report 2022, Mozambique.

8　See Ndaba B, No jobs, no pay, no tears; Domestic workers describe the pain of Covid-19 pandemic, Independent Online, 8 March 2021.

9　The United Nations network has produced a number of studies on the relationship between the Covid pandemic and human trafficking. Among these, arguably the best is UNODC (2020) *The effects of the Covid-19 pandemic on trafficking in persons and responses to the challenges: A global study of emerging evidence*. Accessed January 2023, https://reliefweb.int/report/world/effects-covid-19-pandemic-trafficking-persons-and-responses-challenges.

10　USTIP Report 2022, Zambia; Zimbabwe; Malawi.

11　USTIP Report, Botswana; Mozambique.

12　Watchlist. See Appendix 1. IF IT EXISTS

13　USTIP Report 2022, South Africa.

14　USTIP Report 2022, South Africa.

15　USTIP Report 2022, Lesotho.

16　USTIP Report 2022, Botswana.

17　USTIP Report 2022, Mozambique.

18　USTIP Report 2022, Zambia.

19　USTIP Report 2022, Zimbabwe.

20　USTIP Report 2022, Botswana.

21   USTIP Report 2022, Botswana.
22   USTIP Report 2022, South Africa.
23   USTIP Report 2022, South Africa.
24   USTIP Report 2022, Eswatini.
25   USTIP Report 2022, Zambia.
26   USTIP Report 2022, Zimbabwe.
27   USTIP Report 2022, Zimbabwe.
28   USTIP Report 2022, Lesotho.
29   USTIP Report 2022, South Africa.
30   USTIP Report 2022, South Africa.
31   USTIP Report 2022, South Africa.
32   `USTIP Report 2022, Malawi.
33   USTIP Report 2022, Botswana.
34   USTIP Report 2022, Mozambique.
35   USTIP Report 2022, Zambia and Zimbabwe.
36   Impact Report for South Africa.
37   Impact Report for South Africa.
38   Impact Report for South Africa.
39   USTIP Report 2022, Lesotho.
40   USTIP Report 2022, Zimbabwe.
41   USTIP Report 2022, Lesotho.
42   USTIP Report 2022, Eswatini.
43   USTIP Report 2022, South Africa.
44   USTIP Report 2022, Namibia.
45   USTIP Report 2022, South Africa.
46   USTIP Report 2022, Namibia.
47   See, for example, Ramakolo K & Thobane MS (2021) Challenges faced
     during the COVID-19 pandemic in terms of support for victims of
     child trafficking: A case study of Gauteng, South Africa. *Southern African
     Journal of Criminology and Victimology* 34(3): 45–64; Gutura P & Nunlall R
     (2020) Gender-based violence during the COVID-19 pandemic: A critical
     reflection on the global response. *Acta Criminalogica: African Journal of
     Criminology and Victimology* 33(3). Published online 31 December 2020.
     https://hdl.handle.net/10520/ejc-crim-v33-n3-a7; Covid 19 worsening
     gender-based violence, trafficking risk, for women and girls, *UN News;
     Global perspectives on human stories*, 30th November 2020. Accessed January
     2023. https://news.un.org/en/story/2020/11/1078812.
48   On the emotional consequences of women trafficked in the face of Covid,
     see Nordhues HC, Bhagra A, Stroud NN, Vencill JA & Kuhle C (2021)
     COVID-19 gender disparities and mitigation recommendations: A narrative
     review. *Mayo Clinic Proceedings* 96(7): 1907–1920.
49   USTIP Report 2022, Botswana.

Bibliography

Akee R, Basu AK, Bedi A & Chau N (2014) Transnational trafficking, law enforcement, and victim protection: A middleman trafficker's perspective. *Journal of Law and Economics* 57(2): 349–386

Amahazion F (2015) Human Trafficking: The need for human rights and government effectiveness in enforcing anti-trafficking. *Global Crime* 16(3): 167–196

Baarda C (2016) Human trafficking for sexual exploitation from Nigeria to Western Europe: The role of voodoo rituals in the functioning of a criminal network. *European Journal of Criminology* 13(2): 257–273

Ballet J (2016) Recruitment patterns of child trafficking in Madagascar: An analysis based on missing and recovered children. *Journal of Human Trafficking* 2(3): 235-254

Bhootra B & Weiss E (2006) Muti killing: A case report. *Medical Science and Law* 46(3): 255–259

Bledsoe C (1990) No success without struggle: Social mobility and hardship for foster children in Sierra Leone. *MAN*, 25(1): 70–88

Boutellier J. (1991) Prostitution, criminal law, and morality in the Netherlands. *Crime, Law, and Social Change* 15(1): 201-211

Brents BG (2016) Neoliberalism's market morality and heteroflexibility: Protectionist and free market discourses in debates for legal prostitution. *Sexuality Research and Social Policy* 13(1): 402–416

Bruynell M (2012) The dangerous modern day belief in the supernatural: international perceptions of witches and albinos. *Suffolk Transnational Law Review* 35(2): 393–420

Bukuluki P (2014) Child sacrifice: Myth or reality. *International Letters of Social and Humanistic Sciences* 30(1): 1–11

Cantwell N (2017) The sale of children and illegal adoption. Den Haag: Terre des Hommes

Case A, Paxson C & Ableidinger J (2004) Orphans in Africa: Parental death, poverty, and school enrolment. *Demography* 41(3): 483–508

Cho S-Y (2015a) Evaluating policies against human trafficking worldwide: An overview and review of the 3P Index. *Journal of Human Trafficking* 1(1): 86–99

Cho S-Y (2015b) Modelling the determinants of human trafficking: An empirical analysis. *Social Inclusion* 3(1): 2–21

Cho S-Y, Dreher AQ & Neumayer E (2013) Does legalized prostitution increase human trafficking? *World Development* 41(1): 67–82

Clark M (2003) Trafficking in persons: An issue of human security. *Journal of Human Development* 4(2): 247–263

Cockbain E (2018) *Offender and victim networks in human trafficking.* London and New York: Routledge Studies in Crime and Society

Cohan J (2011) The problem of witchcraft in Africa. *Suffolk University Law Review* 44(4): 803–872

Coontz P & Griebel C (2004) International approaches to human trafficking: The call for a gender-sensitive perspective in international law. *Women's Health Journal* 4(1): 47–58

Davidson J (2011). Moving children? Child trafficking, child migration, and child rights. *Critical Social Policy* 31(3): 454–477

Davy D (2013a) Measuring the immeasurable: Understanding the effectiveness of anti-child trafficking transnational advocacy networks, *Cosmopolitan Civil Societies: An Interdisciplinary Journal* 5(2): 84–113

Davy D (2013b) Understanding the motivations and activities of transnational advocacy networks against child sex trafficking in the Greater Mekong subregion: The value of cosmopolitan globalisation theory. *Cosmopolitan Civil Societies: An Interdisciplinary Journal* 5(1): 39–68

Dempsey MM (2017) What counts as trafficking for sexual exploitation? How legal methods can improve empirical research. *Journal of Human Trafficking* 3(1): 61–80

DOS (United States Department of State) (2020) 2020 Country reports on human rights practices; South Africa. Bureau of Democracy, Human Rights and Labor. Accessed January 2023, https://www.state.gov/reports/2020-country-reports-on-human-rights-practices/south-africa/

Farrell A & Cronin S (2015) Policing prostitution in an era of human trafficking enforcement. *Crime, Law, & Social Change* 64(1): 211–228

Farrell A, Owens C & McDevitt J (2014) New laws but few cases: Understanding the challenges to the investigation and prosecution of human trafficking cases. *Crime, Law and Social Change* 61: 139–168

Farrell A & Reichert J (2017) Using U.S. law-enforcement data: Promise and limits in measuring human trafficking. *Journal of Human Trafficking* 3(1): 39–60

Foot K, Sworn H & Alejano-Steele A (2019) Structures and practices of cross-sector engagement in counter-human trafficking coalitions in the Global South. *Cosmopolitan Civil Societies: An Interdisciplinary Journal* 11(1): 27–47

Gallagher A & Holmes P (2008) Developing an effective criminal justice response to human trafficking: Lessons from the front line. *International Criminal Justice Review* 18(3): 318–343

Gazley B & Guo C (2015) What do we know about nonprofit collaboration? A comprehensive systematic review of the literature. *Academy of Management Proceedings.* https://doi.org/10.5465/ambpp.2015.303

Goździak E (2008) On Challenges, dilemmas, and opportunities in studying trafficked children. *Anthropological Quarterly* 81(4): 903–923

Hedlin S (2016) The relationship between prostitution laws and sex trafficking: Theory and evidence on scale, substitution, and replacement effects. *University of Michigan Journal of Law Reform* 50(2): 329–386

Heiss A & Kelley J (2017) From the trenches: A global survey of anti-TIP NGOs and their views of U.S. efforts. *Journal of Human Trafficking* 3(3): 231–254.

Hernandez D & Rudolph, A (2015) Modern-day slavery: What drives human trafficking in Europe? *European Journal of Political Economy* 38: 118–139

Howard N (2011) Is child placement trafficking? Questioning the validity of an accepted discourse. *Anthropology Today* 27(6): 3–7

Huisman W & Kleemans E (2014) The challenges of fighting sex trafficking in the legalized prostitution market of the Netherlands. *Crime, Law and Social Change* 61: 215–228

Ikeora M (2016) The role of African traditional religion and 'juju' in human trafficking: Implications for anti-trafficking. *Journal of International Women's Studies* 17(1): 1–18

ILAB (Bureau of International Labor Affairs) (n.d.) *Child labor report, 2019.* Accessed January 2023, https://www.dol.gov/agencies/ilab/resources/reports/child-labor/south-africa

Jac-Kucharski A (2012) The determinants of human trafficking: A US case study. *International Migration* 50(6): 150–165

Kara S (2017) *Sex trafficking: Inside the business of modern slavery.* New York: Columbia University Press

Kromberg J (2018) *Albinism in Africa.* Massachusetts: Academic Press

Laczko F & Gramegna M (2003). Developing better indicators of human trafficking. *Brown Journal of World Affair;* X(1): 179–194.

Lagon M (2015) Traits of transformative anti-trafficking partnerships. *Journal of Human Trafficking* 2(1): 21–38

Lerum K & Brents B (2016) Sociological perspectives on sex work and human trafficking. *Sociological Perspectives* 59(1): 17–26

Limoncelli S (2009) Human trafficking: Globalization, exploitation, and transnational sociology. *Sociology Compass* 3(1): 72–91

Mbakogu I (2015) Understanding child trafficking from the point of view of trafficked children: The case of rescued children in Nigeria. PhD thesis, McGill University

Miller P (2013) A theoretical perspective on human trafficking and migration-debt contracts. *Journal of Developmental Studies* 49(10): 1332–1343

Moore A & Goldberg E (2015) Victims, perpetrators, and the limits of human rights discourse in post-Palmero fiction about sex trafficking. *The International Journal of Human Rights* 19(1): 16–31

Msuya NH (2017) Tradition and culture in Africa: Practices that facilitate trafficking of women and children. *Dignity: A Journal on Sexual Exploitation and Violence* 2(1) Article 3. Published online. DOI:10.23860/dignity.2017.02.01.03

Outshoorn J (2012) Policy change in prostitution in the Netherlands: From legalization to strict control. *Sexuality Research and Social Policy* 9(1): 233–243

Smit M (2011) Trafficking in human beings for labor exploitation: The case of the Netherlands. *Trends in Organized Crime* 14(1): 184–197

Smith H (2010) Sex trafficking: Trends, challenges, and the limitations of international law. *Human Rights Review* 12(1): 271–286

Spurrier KJ (2015) A multi-perspective report on the status of the knowledge of and response to commercial sexual exploitation of children with a specific focus on child prostitution and child sex tourism: A social work perspective. PhD thesis, University of South Africa

Taylor J (2019) Witchcraft-related abuse and murder of children with albinism in sub-Saharan Africa: A conceptual review 2019. *Child Abuse Review* 28(1): 13–26

UNODC (United Nations Office on Drugs and Crime) (2021) *Global report on trafficking in persons.* New York: UNODC

The United Nations Convention Against Transnational Crime (UNCTAC) (2000) United Nations General Assembly (55/25). Plus -Supplementary -Protocol to Suppress and Punish Trafficking in Persons, especially Women and Children; Protocol against the Smuggling of Migrants by Land, Sea and Air;Against the Illicit Manufacture and Trafficking in Firearms.New York: United Nations.

United Nations Workshop: Corruption and human trafficking: The grease that facilitates the crime. (UN. GIFT B.P.:20). The Vienna Forum to fight Human Trafficking, 13-15 February 2008, Austria Center, Vienna. UNISA. 2007.

United Nations: Issue Paper: The role of corruption in trafficking in persons. Vienna: United Nations. United Nations Office on Drugs and Crime (UNODC). 2012. Global report on trafficking in persons. New York, NY: United Nations.

United Nations. 2000a. Protocol to Prevent, Suppress and Punish Trafficking in Persons, especially women and children, supplementing the United Nations Convention Against Transnational Organized Crime. General Assembly resolution 55/25 of 15 November 2000. Vienna: United Nations. United Nations.

United Nations 2000b. United Nations Convention against Transnational Organized Crime. General Assembly resolution 55/25 of 15 November 2000. Vienna: United Nations. AUT

UN (2020) Covid 19 worsening gender-based-violence, trafficking risk, for women and girls. *UN News*, 30 November 2020. Accessed January 2023, https://news.un.org/en/story/2020/11/1078812

UNODC (2008) Toolkit to combat trafficking in persons: Global programme against trafficking in human beings. New York: United Nations

United States Department of State, Trafficking in Persons Report: Washington – Office to Monitor and Combat Trafficking in Persons, Annual.

United States, Department of Labour - Bureau of Democracy - Reports on Human Rights Practices;Annual.

Wagenaar H (2006) Democracy and prostitution: Deliberating the legalization of brothels in the Netherlands. *Administration and Society* 38(2): 198-35.

Weitzer R (2015) Researching prostitution and sex trafficking comparatively. *Sexuality Research and Social Policy* 12(2): 81-91

Zhang SX (2011) Woman pullers: Pimping and sex trafficking in a Mexican border city. *Crime, Law and Social Change* 56: 509–528

Zhang SX (2016) The ethical minefield in human trafficking research – real and imagined. In D Siegel & R de Wildt (Eds) *Ethical concerns in research on human trafficking*. London: Springer

Zhang SX, Spiller MW, Finch BK & Qin Y (2014) Estimating labour trafficking among unauthorized migrant workers in San Diego. *The Annals of the American Academy of Political and Social Science* 653, May: 65–86

SOUTH AND SOUTHERN AFRICA

Allais C (2013) The profile less considered: The trafficking of men in South Africa. *South African Review of Sociology* 44(1): 40–54

Allais C, Combrinck H, Connors D, Jansen van Rensburg, Tilley M, et al. (2010). *Tsireledzani: Understanding the dimensions of human trafficking in southern Africa*. Ptretoria: Human Sciences Research Council

Bello P & Olutula A (2022) Effective response to human trafficking in South Africa: Law as a toothless bulldog. *Sage Open*, Jan–March, 1–14

Bermudez L (2008) 'No experience necessary': The internal trafficking of persons in South Africa. Pretoria International Organization for Migration (IOM) Regional Office for Southern Africa

Bongareat W (2021) Corruption prevalence in SADC regional bloc. *Journal of Research in Humanities and Social Science*, 9(1): 8–16

Bosch T & McLeod C (2015) The relationship between female domestic workers and their employers in Cape Town, South Africa. *Global Media Journal African Edition* 9(2): 134–150

ECPAT International. (2019). The landscape of sexual exploitation of children in South Africa. Bangkok: ECPAT International

Emser M (2013) The politics of human trafficking in South Africa: A case study of the KwaZulu-Natal intersectoral task Team and South African counter-trafficking governance. PhD thesis, University of KwaZulu-Natal.

Emser M & Francis S (2017) Counter-trafficking governance In South Africa: An analysis of the role of The Kwazulu-Natal human trafficking, prostitution, pornography and brothels task team. *Journal of Contemporary African Studies* 35(2): 190–211.

Emser M & Van der Watt M (2019) '#Stillnotfound: Missing children in South Africa. *Alternation* 26(1): 89–120

Frankel P (2013) Between the rainbows and the rain: Marikana, mining, migration and the crisis of modern South Africa. Johannesburg: ASR Press

Frankel P (2016) *Long walk to nowhere: Human trafficking in post-Mandela South Africa*. London and New York: Routledge

Gaitskell D, Kimble J, Maconachie M & Unterhalter E (1984) Class, race and gender: Domestic workers in South Africa. *Review of African Political Economy* 27(28): 86–108.

Ginsburg R (2011) *The hidden landscape of domestic service in Johannesburg*. Charlottesville, VA: The University of Virginia Press

Gould C (2014) Sex trafficking and prostitution in South Africa. *Annals of the American Academy of Political and Social Science* 653, May: 183–201

Gould C & Fick N (2008) Selling sex in Cape Town: Sex work and human trafficking in a South African city. Pretoria: Institute for Security Studies

Koyana D & Bekker J (2007) The indomitable *Ukuthwala* custom. *De Jure* 40(1): 139–144

Kromberg J (2018) *Albinism in Africa*. Massachusetts: Academic Press

Kruger B (2016) Towards a sharp prosecution sword to combat human trafficking: Comparing the new South African counter-trafficking law with international prosecution standards. *The Comparative and International Law Journal of Southern Africa* 49(1): 53–84

Labuschagne G (2004) Features and investigative implications of muti murder in South Africa. *Journal of Investigative Psychology and Offender Profiling* 1: 191–206.

Leggett T (2002) *Rainbow vice: The drug and sex Industries in the new South Africa.* Cape Town: David Philip

Lutya T (2009) Epi-criminological responses to human trafficking of young women and girls for involuntary prostitution in South Africa. *Journal of Scandinavian Studies in Criminology and Crime* 10(1): 59–78

Makhubela J (2019) Substance abuse and sex work: Protracting the potential of risky sexual behaviors among commercial sex workers in Musina, Limpopo Province of South Africa. *Trames: A Journal of the Humanities and Social Sciences* 23(1): 29

Mugari I & Obioha E (2021) The criminal justice response to human trafficking: Exploring the investigative and prosecutorial hurdles. *ADRRI Journal of Arts and Social Sciences* 18(1(6): 54–69.

Ramotsho K (2018) South Africa must work on collecting accurate statistics on human trafficking. *De Rebus*, 1 October 2018. Accessed January 2023, https://www.derebus.org.za/south-africa-must-work-on-collecting-accurate-statistics-on-human-trafficking/

Naidoo R (1919) Labour broking: The smoke and mirrors Industry. Accessed January 2023, https://www.southafricanlabourbulletin.org.za/labour-broking-the-smoke-and-mirrors-industry/

Mpapa N (2016) Child sex tourism in South Africa: A children's rights perspective. MA thesis, University of the Western Cape

Mwambene L & Kruuse H (2017) The thin edge of the wedge: *Ukuthwala*, alienation and consent. *South African Journal of Human Rights* 33(1): 25–45

O'Connell Davidson J & Sánchez Taylor J (1996) *Child prostitution and sex tourism in South Africa*. Research Paper. Bangkok: ECPAT

Prinsloo J & Ovens M (2015) *Ukuthwala* as an aberrant traditional practice: The State versus Nvumeleni Jezile 2014 WCD. *Acta Criminologica: Southern African Journal of Criminology and Victimology*, Special Edition 4.

Ramakolo K & Thobane MS (2021) Challenges faced during the COVID-19 pandemic in terms of support for victims of child trafficking: A case study of Gauteng, South Africa. *Southern African Journal of Criminology and Victimology* 34(3): 45–64. Accessed January 2023, https://journals.co.za/doi/abs/10.10520/ejc-crim_v34_n3_a4

Reitano T (2017). *Does human trafficking need a new definition?* Accessed January 2023, https://issafrica.org/iss-today/does-human-trafficking-need-a-new-definition

Songololo M (2000a). *The trafficking of children for purposes of sexual exploitation.* Cape Town: Molo Songololo

Songololo M (2000b) The trafficking of women into the South African sex industry. Cape Town: Molo Songololo

Steele S (2013) Human trafficking, labour brokering and mining in southern Africa: Responding to a decentralised and hidden public health disaster. *International Journal of Health Services* 43(4): 665–680

Stuckler D, Steele S, Lurie M & Basu S (2013) Introduction: 'Dying for gold': The effects of mineral mining on HIV, tuberculosis, silicosis and occupational disease in South Africa. *International Journal of Health Services* 43(4): 639–649

Surtees R (2014) *In African waters. The trafficking of Cambodian fishers in South Africa.* International Organization for Migration (IOM) and Nexus Institute

Van der Watt M (2015) Human trafficking in South Africa: An elusive statistical nightmare. *The Conversation*, 16 July.

Van der Watt M (2018) Investigating human trafficking for sexual exploitation: From 'lived experience': Towards a complex system understanding. PhD thesis, University of South Africa

Van der Watt M (2020) Child trafficking and children in South Africa's sex trade: Evidence, undercounting and obfuscations. *Child Abuse Research in South Africa: A South African Journal* (21)1. Published Online: 1 Jun 2020. https://hdl.handle.net/10520/EJC-1d47701005

Van der Watt M & Burger J (2018) The perplexities of human trafficking in South Africa. *ISS Today*. Pretoria Institute for Security Studies, 30 November

Walker R Mahati S & Magaya I (2019) *Child Trafficking in South Africa: Exploring the myths and realities.* Pretoria: Centre for Child Law, University of Pretoria

Watson C (2016) The organised crime of organ trafficking. ML thesis, University of the Free State

Zimmerman F (2003) Cinderella goes to school; the effects of child fostering on school enrollment in South Africa. *The Journal of Human Resources* 38(3): 557–590

Index

HUMAN TRAFFICKING IN SOUTH AFRICA

internet and modern technologies
2 15 36 51 129 151-152
labour trafficking 80-81 86
rehabilitation/reintegration 105 113
140 143
secondary victimisation 164
shelters 54 113 141 157 163-165
socialisation of victims 10
substance abuse 10 12-13 16 18 27 30
36-38 48 52 70 83 90-91 106 114 119
154-155 164-165
training 39-40 167
victim care 140-143

W
West Africa 1 16 64 82 126
World Bank 4 146

Z
Zambia 123 125-131 133 140 143-144 148
153 161 163-164
Zemba 128 167
Zimbabwe 123 125-126 128-131 133 135-
137 139-140 143-144 152 161 163-165